BARINGS LOST

BARINGS LOST

Nick Leeson
and the
Collapse of Barings plc.

Luke Hunt
and
Karen Heinrich

Published by
Butterworth-Heinemann Asia,
an imprint of Reed Academic Publishing Asia,
a division of Reed Elsevier (Singapore) Pte Ltd.
1 Temasek Avenue
#17-01 Millenia Tower
Singapore 039192

ISBN 981-00-6802-6

Typeset by Semantic Graphic Services
Printed in Singapore by KHL Printing Co. Pte. Ltd.

FOR OUR FAMILIES

Luke Hunt is a correspondent in AFX-Asia's Sydney bureau and writes for *The Sunday Age*. He spent six years at Australian Associated Press in Melbourne and Sydney covering finance, politics and general news. He has written for *Asian Business Review* and and holds a Bachelor of Arts degree from Deakin University in Victoria.

Karen Heinrich is a Sydney-based journalist at *The Australian* newspaper, specialising in derivatives, foreign exchange, and fixed interest markets. She previously wrote for Australian Associated Press for three years as a Sydney-based finance and general news reporter, and holds a Bachelor of Arts degree, majoring in journalism, from the University of South Australia.

CONTENTS

FOREWORD

The first stage of the downfall of Barings Brothers, the oldest British merchant banking group, ended with the sentencing of Nick Leeson to six and a half years' imprisonment in a Singapore jail on December 1, 1995.

The swift and efficient conclusion to Leeson's legal battle was in sharp contrast to the messy manner of Leeson's trial-by-media and innuendo that was conducted by newspapers around the world, and by the financial establishment in the United Kingdom.

Leeson was consistently referred to as the 'rogue trader' who singlehandedly broke the bank. The word 'allegedly' was notable in its absence from almost all news coverage of Leeson's story from early on. This abandonment of the presumption of innocence was aided by comments from Eddie George, the governor of the Bank of England, which has responsibility for regulating the UK banking industry. Very shortly after Barings went belly-up, George let it slip to journalists that it seemed a 'rogue trader' had swept through the bank like a malignant, alien virus.

The rogue trader label stuck, and quickly led to an abundant spread of theories as to why, rather than how, Leeson had committed his heinous act of destruction.

The UK tabloids practised their usual brand of thoughtful analysis of the then 28-year-old trader. Among their many creations was Leeson The Class Warrior — a man so brainwashed by the punk rock music of his youth (Leeson was 10 years old when this anarchic form of music peaked in the UK) and so embittered by the early loss of his mother and his tough working-class upbringing, that he had stealthily worked his way to a position where he could hit 'the establishment' where it hurts.

These fantasies may have been out of whack with the rather gentle and responsible young man Leeson apparently had been for most of his life so far, but they fuelled the popular imagination, and sold newspapers. They also helped obscure the possibility that if any class warfare was indeed being waged, the shots were being fired from the other side of the tracks.

Almost as soon as the news broke that Monday morning, a question no-one has yet answered was posed repeatedly by traders of almost any kind of financial tool available. In a nutshell, the question was: 'How could one man be responsible for destroying one of the oldest merchant banks in the world, for losing stg860 million?'.

Easy. The 'rogue trader' did a bit of dodgy book-keeping to cover his tracks on a billion-odd-dollar position in a market moving irresistibly against him.

The Barings bosses in London were a long way away. How could they keep in touch with every tiny detail of activity of their far-flung subsidiaries? Besides, the derivative activities of Baring Securities in Singapore accounted for almost all of the profits made by the entire group in the 1993/94 financial year — the goose that lay the golden egg, on which all their bonuses depended.

And as far as the managers of Baring Securities in Singapore were concerned, how could they have known anything? They had absolute confidence in 'King' Nick Leeson, as some fellow Simex traders called him before his descent from money heaven in February 1995. The idea that Leeson was beyond suspicion is convenient nonsense. Barings managers both in Singapore and London had heard rumours of a big problem with Leeson. These rumours were reported to Peter Baring in London as early as January, when

Leeson started really going off the rails. By the end, Barings' London office had forwarded Lesson funds for margin calls totalling over £800 million. That was twice the capital of Barings, or eight times the 25% limit set by the Bank of England. They suspected nothing?

The simple fact is that none of Leeson's managers did anything to stop him, while auditors assigned to Baring Securities in Singapore were hoodwinked about the nature of Leeson's activities. Most unforgivably of all, Baring Securities gave Leeson authority to perform day-to-day activities on both the trading floor and the settlements side of the business. This straddling of the 'Chinese wall' between the two operations is never supposed to happen and there should never be a reason for it to happen.

By allowing Leeson to settle his own trades and balance his own books, the man had carte blanche to do whatever he liked, yet no-one at Barings had enough of a problem with this to do anything about it. Giving Leeson this dual role should have been perceived as about as acceptable as appointing one political party to the roles of both government and opposition in a democratic country. The need for a division between settlements and trading is really that basic.

Why, then, would the Bank of England be so quick to isolate Leeson as the sole cause of the Barings collapse? It appears that, as senior members of the British financial establishment, Peter Baring and the Baring Brothers hierarchy were known and trusted by George, and that he accepted Barings' interpretation of events at face value.

As in most countries with developed financial sectors, the central bank and the leading domestic banks work closely over a number of issues, and in Britain the clubby nature of their distinctly blue-blooded, blue-chip institutions further increases the familiarity of the leading players.

Eddie George, one could hypothesise, had no particular reason to doubt Baring Brothers' contention that Leeson was a one-man wrecker.

With Baring Brothers presenting such a united front in regard to Leeson's role as the lone assassin, it no doubt made the next challenge easy — to ensure Leeson was sent somewhere where he would get the maximum punishment with the minimum of fuss. Why try him in some high-profile trial in the UK, when they can let the Singaporeans take over? Who knows what may have come out in a UK trial?

The demise of Barings poses a number of questions on a number of fronts. Global derivatives markets are still suffering from the impact, with many leading institutions cutting back derivatives activities while central bankers search for means of reducing the risks involved with derivative trading. In Singapore, Simex may feel it still has work to do to restore its reputation to the heights of 1993, when it was named Euromoney's derivatives exchange of the year.

The global mass media has generally failed to look beyond the headline grabbing elements of the story, but is probably happy enough with its exploitation of the story.

In Britain, the initial wave of interest created by Barings' dramatic collapse and by Leeson's escape from Asia has broken. For most neutrals, the case is now just another example of British shamateurism and incompetence, which many people believe has plumbed new depths in recent years.

Growing instances of political corruption, and the vast profits made by job destroying privatised utilities, are deepening the impression that greed is tarnishing many once positive aspects of British society.

It used to be trade unions and 'social security scroungers' that were regularly accused of epitomising greed in Britain. Barings' insistence that Leeson face trial in Singapore may provide an unexpected opportunity for those who truly have been blinded by greed to be made to stand up and be identified.

Roger James
Knight-Ridder Financial News
London

PREFACE

Confidentiality in the financial world is of paramount importance to traders, bankers and strategists who depend upon the industry for their livelihoods. Many such people were interviewed, including banking and equity analysts from various investment houses, during the course of research for this book, and anonymity was granted where it was sought. The authors would like to point out that Jack David is a fictitious name for a trader who worked alongside Nick Leeson.

For their guidance and assistance, Karen Heinrich and Luke Hunt would like to thank: In Sydney; Christopher Coil, Tony Harper, Les Hosking, Maggie Macrae, Sophie Musgrave, Andrew Powell, Mark Whittaker. In Melbourne; Lisa Healey, Maria Hunt, Tom Hyland, David Perry, Billy Powis (dec). In Singapore; Butterworth-Heinemann commissioning editor Margaret Tresidder and regional director David Catterall, also Tim Magee, Josie Taylor, Judy Tynan, Jim Gelpi, Zulkifflie Ariffin. In London; Roger James, Dominic Kennedy and Edward Pilkington.

Interviews the authors sought with Nick and Lisa Leeson- were, however, declined.

Many of the primary resources for *Barings Lost* were drawn from all forms of media outlets. Given the immense coverage afforded Barings in the wake of the bank's collapse, it is impossible to single out every journalist and publication for mention in the actual text but, where possible, the authors have taken every possible care in recognising the work of others.

The opinions expressed in the body of the work are the authors' own.

Luke Hunt
Karen Heinrich

PROLOGUE

'Care to try it again some day? Man to man. Think you can hack that, sonny? Do you feel shame for what you did? Was it worth it? Are you more of man now, kid? I don't think so, and you might cover it up as best you can, but we both know who won this round, don't we?' from Tom Clancy; *Without Remorse.*

Nick Leeson sits next to his wife shifting uncomfortably in his economy-class seat. The words of Tom Clancy's *Without Remorse* stare accusingly at him from the pages of a novel he had hoped would provide an escape from his real-life hyper-drama. It was an unwanted coincidence.

Everywhere Leeson looked he saw himself. Passengers on the plane were reading newspapers with *him* on the front page. He tried to rationalise what had happened. He would argue that he was simply one innocuous trader who had made a bad mistake. But what he could not have known was how events had overtaken themselves. Nick Leeson was now a commodity and a rare one. He had become and been many things to many people: a star trader, a thief, a liar, a drunken lout, a devoted husband, an honest family man, a working class barrow boy, a Jack the Lad, a bully, a generous boss.

At slightly more than six feet, Leeson found it easy to push his heavy weight around the trading floors of Singapore. His balding head belied his age and boyish looks, and gave him an authority he was not afraid to use. From barely three years earlier, in mid 1993, at just 25 years of age, Leeson had been able to shout down, out-argue and win any point against rivals, colleagues and bosses, and had become something of hero to the folks at home. Success in a foreign land where the rankings are decided purely by how much money you make and not the colour of your school tie was a welcome change for pragmatic East Enders.

Now, at 28, Nick Leeson was a name in every major daily newspaper in the world, regardless of language, politics and geography. Every television and radio station was carrying updates by the hour on the search for this man, blamed for the death of a venerable British institution.

Tom Clancy would have struggled to script a better plot: Is the game over? Can he get away with it? *Maybe*, he thinks, as Royal Brunei flight P1535 comes closer and closer to Frankfurt airport — his gateway to the United Kingdom, and his escape chute from Singapore, the location of his troubles.

It was a long flight from Kota Kinabalu in Borneo to Frankfurt's Am Main Airport. Passengers sat unaware that the world's most wanted man was in their midst. Newspapers bearing pictures of Nick, issued after Interpol swung into action, dotted the aircraft's cabin. Headlines left no doubt why: 'Rogue Trader Flees Singapore After Bringing Down Barings Bank'. The bold fonts on the *International Herald Tribune*, the *Dubai Post*, *Straits Times*, *Business Times*, *Borneo Post*, and *The South China Morning Post* were stark and dogged Leeson every time he looked about. 'They must recognise me', he thinks as he fidgets and attempts to disappear behind a blanket, pulling a pillow closer to his face. His train of thought is interrupted. 'You're being too obvious', his wife, Lisa, whispers. 'Just try to relax.' Still, no-one recognised the couple.

Nick was renowned within his own circles for his coolness under pressure. For his quiet composure and reserved manner. Lisa was different. She had proven herself the outgoing party girl with a lively manner and was known among her friends as a sweet girl with a kind heart. As a student, and later in her days working for stockbroking firms, Lisa had also proven herself to be bright and quickwitted. But since her marriage her personal qualities had been overshadowed by her husband's ability to make money on the trading floors of Asia. The preceding 12 months of their marriage had been difficult. Much of Lisa's time had been spent back in the UK while Nick cut a swathe through the pubs and clubs of Singapore. Lisa knew Nick had had enough and wanted out: the Four Winds removal company in Singapore had been contacted in preparation of a move on several occasions. Lisa was anticipating going home with Nick's annual bonus in excess of stg400,000. But that was behind them now, and the scope of what had happened was beyond anybody's imagination. She now knew her husband had sent Barings Plc broke, and the couple was being systematically hunted down like a pair of foxes.

If Lisa was perhaps a little less kind hearted, she might have found the option of leaving Nick to his own fate a more sensible one. She understood finance speak. She understood what he had done. She understood he faced years in jail, and that their marriage would in effect have to remain in name only.

As much as he tried, relaxation was not an option for Nick Leeson. He had not done that for months, probably years. In Singapore, his peers knew something was wrong. He had been vomiting in the toilets at work with increasing regularity but on these occasions, his nausea was not always related to the amount of booze he had consumed the previous night. He had been forced to reduce his intake of alcohol because of a stress-induced ulcer — although a dozen pints of Heineken a night would not have helped.

The rhythms of capitalism's purest forum, the financial markets, had eaten away at Leeson's integrity, he had cheated and had been caught out. Now all he wanted was to get back to London where he believed he stood a better chance of a fair hearing than in Singapore where his crimes were committed. First he had to negotiate Frankfurt airport where flight P1535 would make its scheduled landing.

Luck was not on his side. As the jet taxied down the tarmac towards the disembarkment terminal, Leeson was not expecting a very friendly welcome. Clutching Lisa's hand, he made his way out of the plane and was met by a group of German border police at the exit gate. It was 6.30 am. He offered no resistance. 'Yes, I'm the man you want', Leeson said, as the police made their approach.

Round number one may have been concluded but the game was far from over. After all, it can take a pack of trained dogs and scores of armed men on horseback to track and kill a simple pair of foxes, and sometimes the fox still outsmarts the hunter.

CHAPTER ONE

BEFORE THE FALL

'Fortitude Under Difficulty'. Baring family motto.

Before the fall, Barings Plc had been the blue-blooded patriarch of English investment institutions, boasting a clientele of the wealthy, the titled and the royal, and with a proud history once firmly entwined with the fortunes of the British empire. Founded in 1762, the investment house had fended off numerous perils to become Britain's oldest established merchant bank and a pillar of the empire's money community. Perhaps only two other investment houses — Cazenove, and long-time rival Rothschilds — could match Barings' credentials in terms of prestige and financial clout in London's central business district.

At Barings headquarters in Bishopsgate, paintings by the Old Masters adorned the walls and antiques furnished the halls where the titled and non-titled alike were immersed in the aura and power of a bank which enjoyed both a rich history and an impressive bottom line. Barings' clientele was its pride — much of Britain's aristocracy, the Royal family and even the Queen were among the bank's depositors and investors, attracted by the prudent management practices and conservative approach that had earned Barings its status, and had enabled the bank to survive more than two centuries of political and economic change. That these years had included wars, scandals and grim periods of economic downturn which had claimed many of Barings' weaker rivals, served further to enhance its reputation.

A history of solid profit-making proved a sound preparation for the so-called 'Big Bang' deregulation of London's financial markets on the 27th of October 1986, which help to revolutionise dealing room activities with the introduction of electronic real-time computer trading. Fast and decisive, the new method of processing vast amounts of cash and commercial paper was launched simultaneously with the eradication of laws that had once protected the local investment community. Stockbroking firms were now allowed to incorporate and invite foreign capital, sparking an expansion race through a flood of takeovers, both friendly and hostile, funded largely by debt.

The Big Bang left Barings bruised and weary, but a survivor once more. Unlike many other merchant banks, Barings had resisted the feverish takeover mentality that prevailed in response to Prime Minister Margaret Thatcher's Big Bang approach. Instead, the Barings board and senior management had shifted the bank's emphasis to domestic corporate advisory work and had devoted offshore capital to Japan and the tiger economies of Asia and Latin America, arenas where North American upstarts like Morgan Stanley and Goldman Sachs were emerging as the dominant powers and taking home enormous profits.

Barings' conservative strategists were convinced that a fertile basis for long-term profits could be established, with minimal expenditure, by relying on traditional banking activities in fast growing but politically stable regions of the world.

Seven years later, 23 international offices had been established and the jewel in the Barings crown had flourished — more than $47.5 billion worth of funds were under management, held in trust for institutions and private citizens around the world. The bank had also created a network of offshore investment houses through wholly-owned subsidiaries and cross-ownerships (including a 40 per cent stake in affluent Wall Street investment firm Dillon Read), had created the largest brokeage operations in the Philippines, and controlled subsidiaries from Australia to Eastern Europe.

In early 1995, Barings' corporate finance team was busy. They were still ebullient after the successful bedding of the $2.0 billion public float of venture capital group, 3i Group Plc. Wellcome Plc had enlisted the team's services to fight-off a hostile buy-out launched by rival drug group Glaxo Plc, and in the background Lloyds Bank was seeking advice on the acquisition of the Cheltenham & Gloucester Building Society.

The previous October the bank had bucked the merchant banking trend of recent times and had posted half year pre-tax profits of stg54.8 million — a 54 per cent jump. This followed a spectacular record result in the 1993 calendar year with the bank delivering a pre-tax stg100.1 million profit. The performance is particularly outstanding considering the significantly more modest results the bank had reported in the preceding years — stg42.4 million in 1990, stg42.5 million in 1991, and a dismal stg21.2 million in 1992, just 12 months before the record result was notched up.

Over the same 52 weeks total assets burgeoned to stg5.94 billion from stg4.92 billion, a rise of slightly more than 20 per cent.

The banking full-year reporting season was now looming, with market analysts forecasting that Barings would easily surpass the stg100 million pre-tax result recorded in 1993, and with it facilitate enough money to fund its ambitious capital expenditure program. New offices were planned for Russia and Turkey, and corporate headhunters were recruiting investment bankers from competing firms to bolster its strategic operations: Barings entered the new year with its future seemingly assured.

Three months later Barings Plc was broke.

Brought to its aristocratic knees by a lone trader operating in a distant outpost of its empire, Barings Bank had become the victim of its own internal politicking, and the inability of its management to cope with an international finance system that had out-paced authorities to the point where one man, Nick Leeson, could inflict previously unimaginable damage to the firm he worked for and the global markets in which he played.

All up, stg2.5 billion held in deposit accounts were frozen, of which stg1.0 billion represented interbank accounts, the remaining stg1.5 billion made up the investments of thousands of bread and butter accounts — private clients and local organisations. Professional investors aside, the fortunes of Queen Elizabeth and Prince Charles were frozen, as was a portion of Hong Kong's foreign reserves, the savings of the Liverpool Philharmonic Orchestra, a trust for thalidomide victims, a stg1.0 million trust for London's inner-city youths, and even struggling charities in Africa. The source of their future funding had also evaporated. More than 4000 people stood to lose their jobs.

While Buckingham Palace made no public comment after the collapse, it has been estimated that Barings held about $100 million worth of protected investments in stocks and bonds on behalf of the Queen, together with a further $5.0 million in cash.

In the seclusion of their London boardroom, directors wept in bewilderment as the magnitude of the disaster homed in on Bishopsgate.

Internationally, real global markets in stocks, bonds, commodities and foreign exchange went into a frenzy, reeling in a marketplace that had evolved beyond the control of the traditional regulatory mechanisms, and beyond the imagination and capability of those in charge.

This was not the first sudden collapse of a major bank. On the 5th of July 1991 regulators seized control of the Bank of Credit and Commerce International (BCCI) after the discovery of massive losses and internal fraud. The trail of corruption and gross malpractice was traced back to the mid 1980s and linked to BCCI staff and reckless speculative trading within the bank's treasury department. United States based Drexel Burnham Lambert Inc filed for bankruptcy protection in February 1990, and North American regulators seized the Bank of New England Corp in January the following year after losses associated with commercial real estate loans reached an estimated $2.3 billion.

What set Barings apart was its history and reputation, its conservative nature, and the dealings of a Singapore trader, Nick Leeson, supposedly in the course of normal business. Within banking circles, few were surprised when the BCCI and Drexel Burnham collapsed — in BCCI's case many were relieved. The bank had forged links with international terrorists and dictators, including Panamanian strongman, Manuel Noriega. BCCI had lost $10 billion through a collusion of practices that had in the decade prior to its collapse shrouded the bank with a dubious reputation, and senior executives were eventually jailed for up to three years for their part.

Drexel Burnham was the employer of renowned junk bond king Michael Milken who rode and ultimately typified the heady 'greed is good' years of the 1980s until he fell foul of United States corporate laws, ultimately pleading guilty to six felony charges. Milken was jailed, fined $650 million, and became a symbol of the fraudulent entrepreneurs that had dominated his era. The American talk show circuit awaited him upon his release from jail.

Some were comparing Barings' plight to that of the once-proud United States brokerage Kidder Peabody & Co, which buckled under one 'dive-bombing' trader, Joseph Jett, who allegedly invented millions of dollars worth of fake profits to bolster his personal bonuses. Jett, once a top ranking government bond trader, cost his firm and its parent $210 million. The gallery of rogue traders also includes James Martignoni, convicted of fraud in November 1993 after losing $70 million for Dutch bank ABN Amro — Martignoni is reputed to have had his daily reports delivered to him at a bar near New York's Grand Central station. No one was overseeing Martignoni as he artificially bolstered the accounts to hide his losses. There were similarities between the problems at Kidder Peabody, ABN Amro and Barings, but the scope and international impact of Barings was unique.

During the last days of February 1995, as Barings edged to the brink through dealings conducted mainly over a period of just several weeks in the distant Singapore office, the finance world was watching with fascination this apparent revisitation of the high-rolling late 1980s. The prevailing mood was in sharp contrast to those heady high-risk, high- profit days which had gone the way of its free market political champions, Ronald Reagan and Margaret Thatcher. Barings' massive exposures had resurrected the scaremongers and revived the misgivings which preceded the spectacular corporate collapses inflicted during the high growth and profit-at-any-cost days of the late 1980s and early 1990s.

Another historical touch, not without its irony, was observed with Dutch insurance and banking giant Internationale Nederlanden Groep NV (ING) leaping into the pool of corporate sharks in search of a cheap acquisition and snapping up the fallen bank for just one British pound.

Barings was founded by protestants of Dutch origin who had cultivated an impressive economic power base through a family dynasty that centuries ago challenged a banking community dominated by established Jewish families. That power base flourished in England and delivered with it political might, prompting writer Alan Hamilton from *The Times* to observe: 'Not since the Middle Ages has one family aspired so successfully to the ranks of British aristocracy'.

The Barings family saga began when Johann Baring moved from Holland to Bremen in northern Germany and then emigrated to England in 1711 where he settled in Exeter, married a local girl and established a modest business as a wool broker.

Johann liked the quiet country-side but his sons soon tired of Devon and moved to London, where the elder son, Francis Baring, expanded the family's merchant businesses and opened the independent and privately controlled bank with his brother John and son-in-law Charles Wall. Their legacy and, in a sense, their attitudes were captured by noted portraitist Sir Thomas Lawrence who painted the ageing trio, with Sir Francis lending a patient ear to Charles and John. Commissioned in 1806, the painting is consistent with folklore that claims that Francis was the driving energy behind Barings early success and was admired as a 'firm man' by his family.

From the outset, Barings Bank was used to finance the family's wool trading activities from an island country considered at that time a middle-ranked extension of Europe. The British empire was in its infancy and it was Amsterdam that was considered the finance capital of the world. But as Britain's dominance of the seas escalated, so did Barings operations, expanding to include shipping and all aspects of international trade. Francis was by far the most ambitious Baring of his generation and was a respected figure in banking circles. The bank and the empire prospered together, and Sir Francis eventually became a director and chairman of the East India Company, was elected to Parliament, and was ultimately created a Baronet under William Pitt in 1793.

The Baring family name spread on the back of British expansionism and colonialism. The bank profited by first filling Britain's war chest to fight the French emperor Napoleon Bonaparte, and then by arranging loans for reparations for the restoration of the Bourbon monarchy after Napoleon was defeated at Waterloo. Waterloo was also the turning point for a long-standing feud between Barings and the more conservative Rothschilds. In 1817, Alexander Baring and his brother-in-law were invited to join in the raising of a 1.0 billion French franc loan, organised by the French financier who had funded Napoleon's Hundred Days,

Gabriel-Julien Ouvrard, who later transferred his allegiance
to Louis XVII. The organisation of the loan totally excluded
Rothschilds who naturally were deeply annoyed and protested this breach of protocol to no avail while Barings
successfully concluded another deal which would earn them
yet another handsome profit.

But the two adversaries had common interests and such
was the combined might of Barings and Rothschild that a
ditty was once penned: 'The shares were a penny! And ever
so many! Were taken by Rothschild and Baring'.

In contrast to their peers at Rothschilds, the bankers at
Barings were not afraid to take risks during the bank's earlier
days. Barings became agents and advisers for both the
United States and Imperial Russia, and issued bonds on
behalf of the Chinese and Japanese governments.

In the heyday of British colonialism, Barings shipped
every major commodity from Malaysian rubber to Australian wool. By 1835, the *Alexander Baring*, flagship of a fleet
that included the *Antoinette*, the *General Palmer* and the
Diana, had been built. At 550 tons she could reach Canton
from London, fully laden, in 103 days. It has been said that
Barings' highly moralistic attitudes were carried onto the
Alexander Baring whose crew were required to swear off
alcohol and pledge not to blaspheme. The naming of the
Alexander Baring was a considered choice. Financial influence had fanned the political influence of the following
generations throughout the English-speaking world, and
Alexander Baring had earlier established himself after moving to the United States, and had married into the country's
developing high society. There in 1803 he negotiated the
purchase of the state of Louisiana from France through a
loan so vast the *New York Times* commented: 'we all tremble
about the magnitude'. He later became the first Lord Ashburton and was appointed Chancellor of the Exchequer.

The Barings prospered in both wealth and social standing.
Five noble titles were bestowed upon the family, more than
on any one family since the Middle Ages — Ashburton,

Cromer, Howick, Northbrook and Revelstoke. In 1818, French statesman the Duc de Richelieu described the Barings as Europe's sixth power, next to France, England, Austria, Russia and Prussia.

The first Earl of Cromer reportedly governed Egypt during his time as Consul-General as if it were a personal fiefdom; his son became Governor of Kenya and later became Lord Howick. The third Earl of Cromer was Britain's ambassador to Washington, and Thomas Baring, the first Lord Northbrook, was Viceroy of India and later First Lord of the Admiralty. Seven Barings have served as directors for the Bank of England. Even today people from all walks of life are happy to claim a Baring in their family lineage as evidence of British pedigree (the Princess of Wales' great-grandfather was a Baring), and being a Baring still guarantees being subjected to the attentions of Britain's insatiable gossip columnists.

'To serve the King with good will', is included among the family mottos. Others to fly beneath the family's crest include 'fortitude under difficulty', and 'by uprightness and labour'. The crest itself is a five-point star perched neatly between two wings.

Few institutions in the banking and finance world can pre-date Barings, but one exception remains Britain's central bank, the Bank of England (BoE). Founded in 1694, the BoE was known by the affectionate title of the Old Lady of Threadneedle Street because of its location in that street of London, and the maternal manner which has characterised its governance of Britain's monetary system.

For over three centuries the BoE has acted as the British government agency influencing interest and exchange rates and regulating the country's banks, including naturally, playing a large role in Barings' financial history. In 1995, Barings had provided the BoE with its third major banking crisis in slightly more than a decade, alongside the BCCI collapse and the failure of Johnson Matthey Bankers in 1984.

Barings may have had a history of survival in the face of
adversity and the BoE an equally solid history of efficient
control of the nation's banking systems, but it was their
combined inability to adjust to a financial new world order
that ultimately led to the bank's demise. Bank directors may
have been forgiven for thinking that history was on their side
and that financial ruin by the hands of their Singapore-based
trader could be averted.

During the Victorian era, South America had held the
same allure as the tiger economies of Asia have had during
last two decades of the twentieth century. Barings had
entered the region in a vigorous fashion, investing in an array
of potentially high growth businesses. But in 1890 Barings
had found itself over-exposed to bad loans in Argentina
where the Buenos Aires Water Supply & Drainage Company
had defaulted. The trouble started after bank rates were
pushed to 5.0 per cent from 3.0 per cent in order to protect
British gold reserves. In Argentina, Barings found itself faced
with liabilities totalling stg21 million — more than twice the
entire contemporary reserves of the BoE.

There was, however, little sympathy for Barings among
Britain's aristocracy. In *The Sixth Great Power*, Barings
biographer Philip Ziegler noted that members of the Baring
family were known for their haughtiness. The canniness,
some might say tight-fistedness, which was the hallmark of
the bank's dealings, had not always endeared the Baring
name to London's high society.

At the time, Queen Victoria wrote in her diary that Lord
Revelstoke had 'rashly and credulously' put all his wealth
into the Latin American country and was cheated by 'Argentine agents who had come to him', and Randolph Churchill,
father of former British prime minister Winston Churchill,
was quoted as saying, 'Fancy the Barings being brought so
low — Lord Revelstoke will not be able to ride the high horse
as much as he used to'.

While Lord Revelstoke was undeniably a seasoned
banker, he was also considered an arrogant and complacent

man, and a gambler. Rothschilds of course delighted in the uncomfortable position of its old rival, and used the crisis as vindication for its own more conservative stance.

As a last resort lender, Threadneedle Street and its governor Lord Lidderdale had provided Barings with a life raft in the wake of the Argentine crisis, and had stitched together a stg17.1 million deal (stg450 million pounds in today's terms), but it was still substantially short of total liabilities.

'I shall be able to tell you on Monday whether we can go on, or whether we have to stop', Lord Revelstoke, head of the Baring family, told his friend Everard Hambro at the time.[1]

A telling point was made in the satirical magazine *Punch*, which on 8 November 1890 published a cartoon depicting a disconcerted old lady as the Mother of Threadneedle Street reaching into a chest of drawers and handing over a cheque to some well-heeled but shamefaced boys. The caption reads: Old Lady of Threadneedle Street. 'You've got yourselves into a nice mess with your precious speculation! Well I'll help you out of it — for this once!!'. *Punch* headlined the cartoon: Same Old Game!'[2]

In the name of mutual interest, old rivalries were set aside — Lord Rothschild presided over the rescue committee, making a personal donation and, through family contacts in Paris, convincing the Bank of France to make a contribution, along with the Bank of England, and a handover of gold was organised from Russia. The rescue package worked. Lord Revelstoke had to sell houses, paintings and other family assets to pay off the bank's debts, but four years later Barings was restored as a European investment power house.

The plaudits flowed freely. *The New York Times* hailed Barings as 'the greatest banking house of all the world' whose 'signature has stood always and everywhere as an absolute guarantee'.

Lord Lidderdale publicly thanked Lord Rothschild for 'willing and cheerful' aid. Lord Revelstoke must have found the comment galling, but the wheels had been placed in motion for a recovery that would see a German diplomat, as early as 1903, reportedly order: 'Anyone who wants to place a loan in London on a grand scale must apply to Barings'.

And Ziegler wrote in *The Sixth Power*: 'Though their judgement had been faulty, their probity was undoubted, and the courage and resolution with which they accepted responsibility for the disaster and set about retrieving it won the admiration of their sourest critics'.

As with most financial disasters, there were incalculable human and personal costs — legend has it that Lord Revelstoke's wife had died of shame.

The 1890 crisis resulted, however, in the bank being restructured — the Barings Brothers partnership was dissolved, and the family could no longer claim outright ownership of the bank that Francis Baring had founded. Baring Brothers & Co was formed to continue the business, and the ownership structure changed again in 1985 with the formation of Barings Plc which acquired the share capital of Baring Brothers & Co and became the parent company of the Barings Group.

Under this umbrella were three principal subsidiaries, each working for the same company and each at odds with the other, in a way not unlike the rivalry that existed between the entire group and Rothschilds. Barings Asset Management Ltd, referred to simply as BAM, held sway over fund and asset management. The second subsidiary was Barings Securities Ltd — the broker — which controlled a host of in-house companies including Barings Securities (Singapore) Pte Ltd. The third, Barings Brothers & Co Ltd, controlled investment banking.

As a UK registered charity, Barings Foundation held the equity in the bank which paid an annual dividend to be distributed among various charities. The family, however, received no voting rights. The voting rights and right of determination of bank policy were held by a succession of bank executives, holding no direct equity and therefore receiving no dividends. Instead, Barings bankers and employees were rewarded with annual bonuses, or profit share payments. In some cases these payments would prove generous to the extreme, although they were technically allocated on a performance basis. Others to claim an interest in the bank included bond holders, perpetual note holders, and preference share holders who acquired a stake after acquiring issued securities that were listed on London exchanges.

The Barings family itself had long since shored up its wealth in real estate and, while it no longer controlled the bank, one legacy of a more illustrious time which remained unshaken was the family's entrenchment within the ranks of the British establishment. The commercial advantage of the family's name ensured that the bank continued to operate under the name Barings. In the 1920s, Cecil Baring told Lord Stamfordham, 'The concern remains, as a whole, a family affair'.[3]

As part of the establishment, the elder Barings were always careful to be heard and seen doing the right thing, while rarely straying from their primary interests as bankers. The First World War provided an illustration of this philosophy. Showing due concern for the troops abroad and the hardships of war at home, Gaspard Farrer, head of Barings at the time, said that if the bank had decided to take the trouble, it could have acted differently but, 'none of us have any desire to make money out of the war'.[4]

In 1913, Barings had reported a gross stg438,000 profit. This fell to stg282,000 the following year, but banking with war-time allies proved profitable. In 1915, gross profit shot to a staggering stg1.189 million, reached stg853,000 the following year and stg683,000 in 1917.

Much of the capital had been generated in Russia where Barings had arranged a shipment of gold as security from

Moscow. The gold was used as collateral for loans raised by
Barings through the Bank of England to help Imperial Russia
in the fight against the Bolsheviks and to maintain the fight
against Germany. Loan followed loan, as did the commissions. The need to sustain Russia's vast armies was great,
and of real military and political importance at home. As
bankers, Barings did a sterling and correct job, which, as the
bottom line reflects, was not without its reward.

Lord Revelstoke was later given the honorary title of
Minister Plenipotentiary and was sent to St Petersburg where
he attempted to establish the real needs and deadlines for
supplies required by the Russians.

The bank's operations were, however, not restricted to
the needs of the British empire. In 1922, the bank raised
stg10 million for the fledgling new state of Czechoslovakia
which was struggling to survive after the collapse of the
Austro-Hungarian empire. By 1959, by which time the
country was communist, it still owed stg240,000, but the new
regime had denied any knowledge of the loan.

Frustrated by Czechoslovakia's continued denials of the
loan's existence, a Barings official went directly to Prague
and demanded the bank's money back. In time, stg60,000
was returned, the remainder was taken in stride and written
off.

Despite its problems, by the end of 1994 Barings was, by
any reading of the profit and loss accounts, well positioned
and had honed its profits. Yet 105 years after Argentina
nearly sent the bank broke, Lord Revelstoke's great-great-
great-grandson, Sir Peter Baring, found himself facing his
own crisis — the probable ruination of the bank, and the end
of the fabled Barings legend, with investors standing to lose
the entire value of their investments.

Despite the enormity of the crisis before them, there were
several reasons for Barings directors to remain optimistic.
Japan's 21 biggest banks had previously disclosed losses
totalling $142 billion and had survived. But the Japanese
have a mindset quite different to that of their financially

weaker British counterparts — one more in keeping with that of a genuine global economic power, struck on a power base of semi-cartels involving private and government owned institutions. Even the nation's Fair Trade Commission was widely regarded as a government servant.

As was the case in most parts of the Western world, the early 1990s were harsh on Japan — the bubble economy had popped and the nation was experiencing a rare period of political instability. But the cartels of government and private enterprise were able to maintain their semi-feudal political system, with the emphasis on raising cash as opposed to formulating social policies. Each helps the other, and the wheels of political success are greased by donations meted out from the boardrooms of corporate Japan.

Strong economic growth had been nurtured for the 45 years of the post-war age, allowing Japanese investment houses to take full advantage of a friendly monetary policy and a conservative government capable of propping up ailing share market investments by diverting $135 billion from pension funds into the Japanese stock market thus inflating the value of their investments and providing some breathing space for their bankers to get their houses in order.

The Japanese attitude was to throw out orthodox practices, avail themselves of all possible assistance, and stand their ground in the face of big losses while extracting full use of private and public sector wealth. As Tokyo correspondent Peter Hartcher puts it, the Japanese are able 'to stop the whole caravan until the broken wagon can be fixed'.[5]

At Barings, bad deals in esoteric derivatives by twenty-something whiz-kid Nick Leeson had snapped the bank's axle beyond repair.

※

The failure to save Barings served as a stark reminder that Britain no longer dominated the world's financial powers, and the inability of the Old Lady of Threadneedle Street to again secure a lifeline for a favourite son facing complete ruin was symptomatic of a rapidly changing world. The fiasco that followed in part reflected this by transcending Britain's eroding class structure and tossing a likely lad from Watford up against the established elite.

Nick and Lisa Leeson had knocked the antics of the Royal family, the privileged and the wealthy off the front page of Britain's tabloids, and the general view on the trading floor and among the expatriates living in Singapore was that if Leeson had been one of *them*, *they* would have covered for him.

Half-way around the world, the problems of Barings were of a different magnitude for a rapidly developed country which could claim to be a financial power house in its own right.

In Singapore, the illustrious history of Barings belonged to the past, and was of little significance to the island republic, which was finally poised to join an elite club where only the world's richest countries are welcome. With an unimpeachable reputation which had made it a role model for fledgling markets, Singapore is a land where playing by the rules is paramount, bribes and corruption are shunned, and white-collar crime is severely punished, regardless of a criminal's economic status or citizenship.

At the centre of the Barings implosion was the Singapore International Monetary Exchange (Simex) where capitalism is practised in its purest form. Since its inception on September 7, 1984, when it began trading in Eurodollar interest rate and US dollar/deutschemark exchange rate futures, Simex's growth has been nothing short of spectacular. Just two futures contracts were initially offered, but by 1995 this had grown to 12 futures and five options contracts. In 1994, a record 24.06 million contracts were traded — a rise of 53 per cent on the 15.7 million turned over in 1993, while daily average turnover exceeded 94,776 contracts, up from 63,090 the year before.[6] The UK-based International

Financing Review had hailed Simex 'International Exchange of the Year' in 1992 and 'Derivatives Exchange of the Year' in 1993.

A derivatives debacle in the financial heart of Singapore would have been unwelcome at any time, but the Barings fiasco came at the worst possible moment for a country ready to claim the reward for years of fiscal restraint and economic rationalism that had dominated its life and culture. In a nation glad to be shedding the unwanted perceptions associated with being a third world nation and an emerging economy, the Barings debacle was a public relations mess.

Singapore's position as a developed nation, and its status in the international community, gave it every right to demand justice on its own terms but, to do that, investigations would have to seen as fair and without bias towards the nation's own.

Singapore was not about to let Nick Leeson get away scot-free.

CHAPTER TWO

THE ZERO-SUM GAME

'It's gone from an advice-giving business to a position-taking business. That's almost a sex change'. Roy Smith, finance expert, New York University, on the explosion of derivatives trade.[1]

London's Big Bang was late, unavoidable, and abruptly shook traditional British banking to its core. The once cosy world of set commissions and regulated profits was consigned to history as British merchant banks were dragged kicking and screaming into the international fold, 11 years behind their Wall Street counterparts.

The United States had set the pace by deregulating brokerage and merchant banking on May Day 1975. Brokerage commissions were freed, became negotiable, and were exposed to the fluctuating fortunes of the free market. Competition for business hotted up and commissions duly plummeted, hauling back profits and forcing North American finance houses to re-focus and develop other forms of financial instruments pitched for growth markets where margins could be improved and bottom lines raised.

America's major players, Salomon Brothers, Morgan Stanley, Goldman Sachs and Merill Lynch drew lines on maps and headed for Europe and eventually Asia, where they expanded their markets naturally, eroding traditional business bases from the likes of Barings in the very regions where the British had once entrenched themselves in regions shaded pink on the global map.

An extensive and finely-targeted range of services was developed and sold by the Americans. They underwrote, issued equity and debt, advised on mergers and takeovers, and did it at the world's cheapest rates. The emerging focus was, however, in the once uncommon derivatives trade, where demand for financial hedging had generated enough wealth to support a secondary market where derivatives were being traded for profit in their own right.

Derivatives were revolutionised and heavily promoted among corporate treasury departments as a safeguard against the volatility of the markets where their capital was raised — in turn an insatiable appetite was developed for the hybrid security.

In financial circles, the term 'derivatives' is used generically for contracts in futures, swaps and options, arguably the oldest form of traded financial instrument. They were initially designed as a hedge, particularly for commodity traders looking for a protection mechanism against future price fluctuations. Rice futures were traded in Japan centuries ago. Traders with wide and varying interests — orange juice, rice, gold, iron ore, stocks, bonds — have a common interest in maintaining long-term price stability and a guaranteed income stream.

Fluctuations in the short term are common but are generally ironed out over longer periods. A futures contract linked to the fortunes of a traded commodity is therefore acquired with a guaranteed payment to be made at a set date to be used as a hedge against volatility in the cash market. All futures contracts must be paid in full under law.

Futures contracts travel the world, paying no heed to international borders and are eventually closed out at clearing houses like the Chicago Mercantile Exchange or the Singapore International Monetary Exchange (Simex), which used its Chicago counterpart as a role model.

The Chicago Mercantile was known originally as the Chicago Butter and Egg Board which changed its name in

1919 and went on to become the second largest commodity exchange in the world. The Chicago Mercantile dealt in pork bellies and live hogs and, through its International Monetary Market, eventually dealt also in currencies and financial instruments such as derivatives.

The mechanics of those operations are essentially divided into two realms, the back and front rooms or offices. Both offices are of equal importance but divide the functions of transaction and settlement. Back office staff are the bean counters, the number crunchers who ensure the figures add up and correlate from the day's trade which is undertaken in the front office. Of the two, the front office is, within the industry, generally considered the more glamorous. Front office is where the deals are cut and the money made or loss, and includes both the frantic and colourful trading floors of the exchange where a dealer's gesture can turn over many million of dollars, and the more sedate office blocks that house traders who conduct their business through computer systems.

The governing laws of supply and demand are constantly influenced by events outside the control of the trader. Political change, wars, natural disasters, and the motives of the traders themselves can manipulate and combine to create havoc on world markets, creating millions of dollars for some and costing millions for others.

Market are driven by sentiment, be it good or bad, particularly since the trade of a derivatives contract has proliferated since the late 1970s. And the scandals they have attracted are not new.

Modern currency futures were first traded in 1972 while trading in interest rate futures followed three years later, but the oldest derivative debacle can be traced back to the 1630s when the Dutch developed an insatiable penchant for tulips. A rare tulip bulb would fetch a fantastic price and since they could be acquired before the bulb had bloomed, tulips came to represent the crudest and perhaps earliest form of a futures investment.

In his 1841 classic, *Extraordinary Popular Delusions and the Madness of Crowds*, Charles Mackay wrote how an English traveller happened upon a conservatory owned by a wealthy Dutchman. The traveller mistook an expensive tulip bulb for an onion and peeled it with his penknife. On spying the traveller, the furious owner of the bulb nabbed the Englishman, who was promptly thrown in gaol until he could find security to cover the 4000 florins that the tulip was worth.

Such was the madness of 'tulipomania' that Mackay wrote of the people's belief: 'The riches of Europe would be concentrated on the shores of Zuyder Zee and poverty banished from the favoured clime of Holland. Nobles, citizens, farmers, mechanics, seamen, footmen, maid-servants and clothes-women all dabbled in tulips'. Tulips were sold on the Exchange of London in 1636 and Mackay noted: 'The operation of the tulip became so extensive and so intricate, that it was found necessary to draw up a code of laws for the guidance of the deal'.

Money poured into Holland. People sold property for cash to convert into flowers. The more prudent realised it could not last forever, and the rich began buying tulips solely for trading purposes and profit, as opposed to planting the bulbs in their gardens.

According to Mackay, the conviction finally spread that someone must lose fearfully in the end and tulip prices never rose again. Tulips once worth up to 6000 florins had their value wiped out overnight, and their unlucky owners were caught with hundreds of thousands of tulip bulbs for which they were lucky to fetch 500 florins each.

'Substantial merchants were reduced to beggary and many a respectable of a noble line saw the fortunes of his house ruined beyond redemption', Mackay wrote.

✄

In the 1970s American dealers initially generated wealth by trading derivatives on behalf of their clients but, as their positions grew, investment houses began establishing their own exposures by trading with their own money in a manner not dissimilar to early tulip traders who sought out the bulb purely for profit.

This was important because it created another income stream for the decades ahead, but also created a tricky situation for traders in determining the respective liabilities for risk between client and trader. It was because of this that an agenda indicating exactly what constituted 'appropriate' and 'prudent' fiscal risk management in contemporary times began to evolve. As with any new concept, cultural differences came to the fore within Wall Street houses as management tinkered with internal controls designed to minimise risks, while at the same time allowing traders to maximise profits. For their British counterparts, it became a conundrum that was never really given a chance to resolve itself fully before the receivers moved on Barings.

In New York and Chicago, the fight for higher margins had proved fierce. No longer were derivatives used solely as a hedge against steep price fluctuations but, as they entered the secondary markets, they also became traded among arbitrageurs who switched in and out of markets and took advantage of the price differentials between them, buying in one market and selling in another.

Twenty years ago derivatives barely existed, and in the late 1970s the term itself was unlikely to rate a mention in any dictionary, even those specialising in finance or economics. Futures were known as a forward market, options were exotic and left to the rare specialist, and swaps were almost unheard of. Then came the explosion. The figures now brandished about are awesome.

In the first three months of 1995, a record 304.5 million futures contracts were traded on exchanges worldwide, and *The Wall Street Journal* had valued the global derivatives market at around $35 trillion. At the Chicago Mercantile, in just one building, $20 trillion, or $200 million million was turned over in 1994 alone. One pit can turn over more money in one day than the total turnover of the real market at the New York Stock Exchange. Corporations buying and selling risk against volatility in the currency and interest rate markets, where for $30,000 a company can cover itself against $1.0 million risk, or can place a million dollar bet. A standard rule of thumb is that a three per cent move in price can double your money, or an average move can force a top up payment of say 3 per cent to maintain the initial deposit. Continued averse moves can wipe you out.

Echoing the scandals and massive losses of centuries ago, the modern-day derivatives trade has had warning bells sounded within its ranks for more than a decade, with international regulatory authorities warning investment houses about the inherent dangers associated with these financial products.

In 1986, Australian-based electronics group AWA Ltd was among the first losers of the modern era with a $35 million loss through bets on the foreign exchange markets. In 1993, it was revealed that interest rate swaps had cost the London councils of Fulham and Hammersmith about $4.2 billion. Those losses were traced back to 1988 when Hammersmith council faced severe spending cuts under the austere conservative administration of the Thatcher government. The council was at that time encouraged by its own advisers to raise capital from alternative sources. To overcome those cuts in funding and to raise additional capital, the council embarked upon a series of interest rate swaps after they discovered it was cheaper to borrow funds from banks than to accept the rates on offer by the government.

During a course of 18 months, 600 trades were placed with a value of stg6.0 billion — which at that time accounted for one per cent of world turnover in the interest rate swap markets. Hammersmith had started out paying just eight per cent on its interest rates but these almost doubled within a year, leaving the council facing 15 per cent interest rate repayments totalling billions of pounds. Desperation soon set

in and drastic measures were called for — the council invited
bank to place bets with them in an attempt to drag back the
losses.

At no stage was the true extent of the hedge known or
kept in check: no computer records were kept, and the
equivalent of betting slips were simply placed in a black box.
Losses soon burgeoned to stg400 million. The players themselves didn't know the extent of their exposure until a council
auditor discovered it, declared it illegal and bundled those
responsible into court. Eventually the House of Lords ruled
the transactions illegal, but local residents were still confronted with a potential bill of stg4000 each.

Also in 1993, the German industrial giant Metalgesellschaft AG, which owns 250 mines, factories and businesses
around the world, bled 2.3 billion deutschmarks in oil
derivatives through its United States subsidiary MG Corp.
Metalgesellschaft was primed for expansion and had just
spent $350 million opening the world's largest zinc mine in
Alaska. The downfall of this industrial giant came with its
push into oil. With the aim of snaring a share of the
lucrative petroleum products market, Metalgesellschaft purchased ageing oil refineries outside of Los Angeles with the
objective of upgrading and bolstering its US oil operations.
The company continued to lose money on the refineries. It
then attempted to secure more customers by offering petrol
wholesalers a 10-year deal, guaranteeing petrol supplies at
1993 prices right through until 2003.

Metalgesellschaft then went about insuring itself against
price movements in a buying spree at the New York Mercantile Exchange, purchasing more than 100 million barrels of
crude oil futures — the equivalent of about 80 days worth of
production in Kuwait — with the plan of rolling them
forward each month for 10 years.

The only problem — one which proved so large it would
bring Metalgesellschaft to its knees — was that this market
strategy was solely dependent on rising oil prices. Instead,
they fell. For Germany's fourteenth largest company, those

losses required a 3.4 billion mark bailout at the expense of shareholders and bankers.

In a similar blunder, Japanese oil refiners Kajima and Showa Shell each lost $1.0 billion speculating in oil and currency futures. Orange County in California, soap powder makers Proctor & Gamble, and Royal Dutch Shell have all watched their profit and loss accounts haemorrhage at the hands of their own decision-making and derivative trading. In the trading area itself, Bankers Trust has been sued by clients over derivative deals that went bad. In New York, one hedge fund went broke by losing $600 million in the form of collateralised mortgage obligations, also known on Wall Street as toxic waste.

By 1994, there were more derivative-related losses than in the previous five years, and in Washington two Bills were presented to Congress demanding that regulators do more than merely mop up the disastrous consequences of these bad deals. But neither the dramatic losses nor the occasional political manoeuvre have had any marked impact on the flourishing derivatives industry, which in some sectors is expanding at an annual rate of 40 per cent. For some banks, derivatives account for more than half their profits, and more and more money is now being concentrated in fewer hands, with about one third of the world's marketable wealth controlled through 200 funds.

Market players have long been aware of the huge risks surrounding the complex financial instruments. Four months before the fall of Barings, Dr Al Wojnilower, economics adviser at CS First Boston, described the derivatives business to the Australian Broadcasting Corporation's current affairs program, *Four Corners*, as alive and well — and frightening.

'I don't think in human history there's been an instance of gambling ever failing to grow or addictions ever failing to capture more addicts, except after what everybody recognises to be a very bad trip', said Dr Wojnilower. 'So it seems to me that this will grow until such time as there is a crisis which is enough to really frighten a lot of people and the politicians for whom they vote'.[2]

The *Four Corners* program was produced in late 1994 and involved a lengthy series of interviews in London and New York with financiers, traders and analysts. The program was screened in Britain and Australia and proved prophetic.

The apprehension surrounding derivatives was such that *Fortune* magazine described them on its front cover as: 'The Risk That Won't Go Away'. Inside, *Fortune* warned: 'Like alligators in a swamp, derivatives lurk in the global economy. Even the CEOs of the companies that use them don't understand them'.

Herein lies one of the keys to unlocking the mystery of Barings' collapse. A common problem in rogue trader cases has been the existence of a financial generation gap. Those in the upper echelons of a company — overwhelmingly middle-aged men, schooled in dated financing techniques — are often not wise to complicated new financial instruments and adopt a resigned attitude toward the hot-shot traders who, unlike themselves, have been reared on a diet of derivatives and arbitrage. Turning a blind eye to the machinations of derivatives trade is made all the easier when the young guns are raking in dream profits and are, by virtue of their hot-shot status, in a position naturally at odds with management.

Inside investment houses, derivatives are sometimes known as the 'zero-sum game', where the essence of the game never changes — for every purchase there is a sale, and for every winner there is a loser. The attitudes of some complacent managers dangerously side-step these critical assumptions.

'Greed can get in people's eyes, so they say: "Here's a whiz-kid who is making a lot of money, so let's just ride the horse",' said Leo Melamed, former chairman of the Chicago Mercantile Exchange and chairman of Sakura Delisher Inc, a Chicago-based futures trading firm. 'But you must never let greed overtake your good sense'.[3]

But not everyone subscribes to *Fortune's* 'swamp' analogy. Jack Sandner, president of the Chicago Mercantile, puts a different slant on the matter. He told the same *Four Corners* program that millions of institutions rely on 'that swamp' to manage risk. 'Because what this is, is insurance — could you imagine if nobody had fire insurance in this country, if nobody had life insurance, if nobody had theft insurance — we would be out of business', Mr Sandner said.

'That swamp is insurance and to call it a swamp rather than a crystal, pristine lake is a complete misdirect to the public. There are thousands of people swimming in this pristine lake and yet somebody drowns — one person drowns — and now we're going to call it a swamp!'[4]

When it was put to him that defenders of derivatives have argued that in a lake it is possible to swim and fish or to even commit suicide, Sandner replied: 'What do you do? Pass a law that says "no suicide here"?'[5]

For most, what is genuinely frightening is the volume and the sheer speed at which derivatives are traded and the transactions closed. Warning of a pending loss can arrive in a matter of minutes or less, and this in itself has promoted the fear that one catastrophic act could spread to the financial system as a whole, precipitating a market crash and, potentially, triggering a general economic malaise similar to the depression that followed the 1927 stock market crash.

In an attempt to contain the fear this possibility generates, major banks employ strategic analysts to simulate a corporate meltdown to determine whether their systems can hold up under stress.

Analysts have argued that the biggest challenges in wrestling with derivatives is trying to determine what the exact risks really are, because those risks can change within minutes. This can result in some traders making mistakes through misreading the market. Other traders can fall victim to a culture of believing that the market can be outsmarted.

Nick Leeson did both.

樂

The global market no longer has any frontiers. Trade occurs 24 hours a day, dictated by people who watch the same news and each other and, like a school of fish, will often charge in the same direction for fear of being left behind and cannibalised by their own kind. The era of fast, split-second trading has spawned real time demands. Dealers trade on information, and profits or losses are scored by decisions based on news delivered as it happens. For news agencies, where the news is traditionally delivered immediately to satisfy the constant demands of radio, television and newspaper deadlines, the evolution of instant publication through a screen-based on-line service was a natural development.

First to meet these new market pressures was international news agency Reuters who revolutionised screen trading with the development of real time news. Telerate, Bloomberg, Knight Ridder, AP-Dow Jones, AFX, and later AFX-Asia, soon followed Reuters and joined the fray, with journalists interpreting and writing the news for their trader clients as it happens.

Behind his or her desk the trader, often referred to as the screen jock, lives in a realm not unlike that of a NASA technician, surrounded by screens that allow trading and close monitoring of market movements, and provide continuous access to both the big and the trivial information of the day. From here the trader facilitates the transaction with client buying and selling contracts and minimising risks.

From his desk on the Simex trading floor, Leeson could punch in a code and access the stock price of even the smallest company in the tiniest country.

The instant a central bank announces a change to monetary policy, a journalist will send a one sentence news flash across the world informing traders of the shift. Two paragraphs follow in what is known as a full-out, and the extent of any subsequent information follows on merit. Company announcements — ranging from gold strikes to sales figures — the fortunes of politicians, disasters, mayhem, profits, losses and analyses are bounced off satellites from news rooms in the remote and major capital cities to the paying subscriber.

For the journalist, filing for the screens is a deceptively simple task that requires a hard nerve. As the first source of public information in a realm where billions of dollars are won or lost on fast and accurate information, the journalist faces the second challenge of being first. At a press conference it is not uncommon to witness half-a-dozen reporters making an early exit, battling through camera crews with mobile phones in the race to be first to file a story.

Their efforts are part of the arguments that surround the inter-dependency of the global economy which are wide and varied but not new. John Maynard Keynes argued that the internationalisation of the global economy was nearly complete in 1914 when a trader in London could order by telephone, while 'sipping his morning tea in bed', almost anything in the entire world, in any quantity, and have it delivered to the front door.

Not even Keynes though, could have foreseen the revolution of the late twentieth century, where split-second trading based on instant decision-making dictates the trends and enhances an atmosphere where events could readily overtake themselves.

In the lead-up to the Gulf War, for example, oil prices rose sharply, hitting the average motorist in the hip pocket, and pulled already floundering share markets back to levels lower than those experienced after global stock markets crashed in October 1987. The War served to highlight the inadequacies of the daily newspaper as a carrier of up-to-the-minute information, contrasted with cable network CNN which was delivering breaking news hourly in suburban homes. The wire services are in similar fashion taking the task to the trader on the floor.

This situation was repeated when Boris Yeltsin ousted Mikhail Gorbechev and became Russian President. Investors held to their screens buying into gold and gold stocks around the world, an investment traditionally sought as a safe haven in times of international uncertainty. But investors were burned as they realised that Yeltsin was not only winning but intended dumping Russia's vast gold reserves onto the global markets in an effort to raise short term capital to help resolve Russia's economic problems. The world gold market was saved from a global glut and depressed prices after Russia decided to maintain reserves and use them instead as collateral to raise loans.

It is this instantaneous access to information that maintains the flow of business in the financial markets, which some call capitalism's 'purest forum'. Each year presents its own problems: in February 1994 it was a strengthening in the world's long recessed economies. Fears that economic growth would lead to a repetition of the excesses of the 1980s and rekindle inflation, pushed bond yields sharply higher. These fears are supposed to pressure world leaders and central banks into raising official interest rates and maintain the cohesion of the bond market.

Traders were more than somewhat annoyed when US president Bill Clinton and his advisers ignored persistent pleas from Wall Street. Politicians were listening to the mortgage belt and the voters, who in the event of an interest rate hike would wind up paying for the bout of 'expandaphobia' — or fear of growth. The bond market went into a prolonged period of volatility causing massive cash losses, particularly to institutions, in any nation with a reasonably sophisticated banking system. This can only be seen as a fairly representative illustration of the herd mentality that often overrides other less frenetic considerations.

Later in 1994 events were gathering pace in Mexico. The circumstances appeared far removed from global bond trading, but the impact on international markets was just as severe and formed an integral part of a three-stage backdrop in which another natural disaster, the Kobe earthquake, would dictate the lives of traders during the first months of 1995.

The third event was the demise of Barings.

Mexico's troubles can be attributed to the North American Free Trade Agreement (NAFTA) and a 15 per cent devaluation of the peso which wiped $US75 billion off Mexican securities held by foreigners. The exodus of capital that followed crippled an already fragile economy on which millions of poverty stricken people were dependent. Share prices tumbled and the value of the peso against the US dollar fell to record lows in the ensuing months, to the point where Washington was forced to intervene after the crisis began eroding confidence on Wall Street and in turn, the global market place.

Eventually a $40 billion international credit package was announced by President Clinton, but the restoration of any faith in Mexico's economy among foreign investors remained a long-term prospect and the crisis was a constant dictator on financial markets when the earthquake struck Kobe in January 1995.

On *Four Corners*, Bank of England executive director Brian Quinn was frank about his worries back in late 1994. Asked whether he feared derivative trading, he said: 'Oh yes, yes I do and it's always the thing you can't see that worries you the most'.

But he added: 'I don't think it worries us unduly. We know what our job is — our job is to stay abreast of these things and to be able to cope with them, or to try to cope with them, so I'm not unduly disturbed by that'.

Among the biggest dangers in dealing with derivatives, as with most other markets, is that an enormous amount of risk is based on only a few underlying assumptions. In some situations those assumptions are so basic that a trader may not even realise that an assumption is being made. If the fundamentals prove to be incorrect, this may prove to be a recipe for disaster.

Asked if he was confident the BoE could cope with a crisis within the system Quinn, who was appointed in April 1988, said: 'That would be really rather a foolish thing to say that I'm confident we can. I'm confident we are trying as hard as we can and I'm confident we are looking in the right areas. But as I say, if you are trying to hit a moving target all the time — and indeed the shape of the target is changing — then it would be a bit presumptuous to say you are absolutely on top of things — I wouldn't say that'.

It was against this backdrop of swamps and pristine lakes that Barings started to dabble in the Far East futures market of Singapore. It began tentatively with the incorporation of Barings Futures (Singapore) Pte Ltd, or as it later became known, simply 'BFS', on September 17, 1986, and with the appointments of Christopher Heath, Paul Hitchcock and Alexander Phillips as the first directors. A little more than a month later the unit applied for, and was later granted, membership of Simex as a corporate non-clearing member.

However, the growth strategy for Singapore was painstakingly slow. It would take nearly another six years before Nick Leeson and Eric Chang would enter the Simex pit and become the first Barings people to trade under the bank's crest.

In the meantime, Singapore developed as a neat cog in Barings' Asian operations which began to emerge under its own steam and under the auspices of Barings' Tokyo business with the appointment of James Bax as a BFS director on the first of June in 1988. In Japan, the bank's agency sales team had spent years building up the company's futures and options, and it was becoming commonplace for clients to place orders in Tokyo that needed execution in Singapore.

The appointment of Bax coincided with the recruitment of Mike Killian and, a short time later, Anthony Dickle. Dickle was hired to firmly establish BFS while Killian had left Chase Manhattan Futures Corporation in Singapore and joined Barings Securities Japan in Tokyo to become Head of Global Equity, Broking and Trading and lead the strategic growth of the agency business. Importantly, Killian was in a position to execute orders at Simex through Chase Manhattan and ensure that the Singapore end of settlements for futures and options trade remained viable and cost effective. At this stage it was difficult to commercially justify installing full time traders at Simex.

CHAPTER THREE

STRIKER

'One person can't lose all that money. They are playing on his background, making him a scapegoat because of his upbringing. There has got to be a conspiracy'. Sarah Leeson, Nick Leeson's sister.[1]

Nicholas William Leeson grew up a mere 24 kilometres from Threadneedle Street and Bishopsgate but, in the scheme of Britain's well-defined class structure, the gap might as well have reached as far as Pluto. Leeson was born into a world of proud working-class people whose identity and values would always provide a cornerstone for his life.

From Marble Arch in Oxford Street, near Hyde Park, the road travels 24 kilometres north to Leeson's home town of Watford, Hertfordshire. Ordinary and nondescript, Watford lacks both the colour of the cockney districts and the smartness of the more stylish suburbs. There are dozens of Watfords in Greater London, each with its own struggling community. Watford's claims to fame — apart from being the birthplace of the now-infamous Nick Leeson — is that it marks the end of the M1 motorway, and that its soccer team was once owned by musician Elton John.

Born on 25 February 1967, Nick Leeson's first years were spent in a small flat in Orbital Crescent, North Watford. The family later moved to a three-bedroom red-brick end terrace house on a council estate at Haines Way, Garston, on the northern edge of Watford. There he grew up with a younger brother Richard and two sisters, Victoria

33

and Sarah, his mother, and his father, a local plasterer.

By all accounts Anne and William Leeson were loving parents. Strugglers with a limited income, they were nevertheless determined to give their children the best they could afford. William was known as Harry to his friends and was an affable man with his family's interest always at heart. He could be spotted around the neighbourhood in his working overalls covered in plaster, or at the local pub, The Hare. He was fair, but wise to the ways of the working class world, and a realist. His job required long working hours and he frequently travelled around the country, often working six or seven days a week to make ends meet. Anne was a nurse and bolstered her family's income working at the Leavesden Mental Hospital.

Nick and his siblings were afforded the best opportunities and education with which the family's budget could cope. He first attended Kingsway Junior School at Garston but, as the family grew, a larger home was needed and they moved. In 1978 Nick was enrolled in Parmiter's state school, a grant-maintained comprehensive which has its origins in Parmiter's Grammar School at Bethnal in East London. The grammar school had long since ceased operation but at Nick's school enrolments were growing. Nick had a chance meeting with the Queen when she officially opened extensions at Parmiter's. Established in 1720, the school's motto was *Nemo Sibi Nasciture*: No Man is Born Unto Himself.[2]

Nick's childhood was nothing out of the ordinary. His world revolved around his cherished position as striker for Parmiter's first football team, a position requiring strong nerve and confidence, given that a team's chances of victory always hinge on the talent of the striker. Nick loved his soccer and was a fiercely loyal Manchester City supporter, with an ability far sharper than that of most soccer-mad kids to accurately recall the obscurest soccer statistics, names and dates. He played for the local Abbots Langley Football Club, and later captained the Old Parmiteran team for two years after leaving school. He also joined Barings' company soccer teams in London and Singapore.

Although Nick was a student who could at times excel, he was in the main seen as reserved and of average abilities and was never considered university material. Parmiter's headmaster, Brian Coulshed, did, however, consider Nick an honest young man who was an asset to the school, qualities demonstrated during his stint as one of the school's prefects.

His marks reflected the opinions of his teachers. Leeson left school at 18 with eight 'ordinary (O) level' and two 'advanced (A) level' certificates. He failed mathematics, a disappointment for Coulshed, who had believed maths was one of Nick's stronger points. He felt the young Leeson had not tried hard enough.

Few were surprised when he decided upon a career in banking. Parmiter's had steered many of its youths into the banking industry, and Nick's decision was in keeping with this tradition: the pride of the school was an Old Boy who had become governor of the Bank of Canada.

Nick Leeson began his search for a job in mid-1985 and secured a position at the establishment bank, Coutts & Co, in its Lombard Street branch. He remained there until 1987, carrying out clerical duties, before transferring to Morgan Stanley as a junior operations clerk in futures and options settlements. It was a lowly position, particularly within the hedonistic investment climate of the late 1980s, but the post taught Nick the ropes of merchant banking, and provided a good education in the nature of derivatives.

It was around this time that Nick's mother died of cancer. This tragedy pulled the family together, and Nick began sharing with his father the responsibility of raising his younger siblings. The added stresses of this responsibility would, however, later cause an erosion of the closeness between Nick and his father.

Leeson was a competent, anonymous back room operator in settlements, with a modest but respectable salary. This salary seemed meagre, however, compared to the numbers rolling around the front offices of banking circles in the twilight years of the 1980s. These were heady times in banking circles, and Nick soon became frustrated and began looking around for better opportunities.

In July 1989 he jumped ship after landing a job in the settlements department of Barings Securities for the salary of stg12,000, working initially on the treasury functions of the company. This was the beginning of the fateful and ultimately catastrophic relationship between Leeson and Barings but, of more immediate importance to Leeson, it was here that he met his future wife, Lisa Jane Sims, who was at the time working for Barings as a stockbrokers' clerk.

Lisa was hired in March 1990. Her background was not unlike Nick's but where Nick was considered difficult to get to know, Lisa was an extrovert, forthright and matter-of-fact. Lisa was at the time living at home with her parents, Alec and Patsy, and divided her time between work, dining out with friends, and aerobics. Born in South London in 1969, Lisa was raised with one sister, Nadene, and a brother, Alex, in a cul-de-sac in a small village in Kent. She was a popular student at the local Swanley Comprehensive and became the envy of her friends who mostly went on to become secretaries or office workers. Lisa gained her A-levels in accountancy and economics, and embarked on a career in banking. Just days after finishing school, she began work as settlements clerk for the Japanese broking firm Nikko Securities.

Like Nick, Lisa started her working life during the rollicking boom times of the late 1980s and, only a year after joining Nikko Securities, was poached by Swiss Bank Corp, where she stayed for three years. But as the cash flows dwindled with harsher economic times, Lisa watched with some trepidation as her employers laid off one colleague after another. She decided to get out quickly. Lisa accepted a back office position at Barings Securities and within weeks found herself bound for the Indonesian capital, Jakarta, as a troubleshooter with a team of five others.

She later said: 'I was just 22 and had always lived at home. But I was really pleased to be working abroad. It was only for a few months, but I wanted to see the world. The work was very tough. Although it sounded glamorous to people back home, it was a real slog'.[3]

She did not know him yet, but Lisa's husband-to-be had been marking out a similar career path for himself. Leeson took his first calculated step up the corporate ladder in 1990 when he accepted an overseas assignment. He no doubt embraced the move as his long-awaited chance to throw off the shackles of his working-class roots and make a name for himself. Since he had left school, Leeson had laboured for what must have seemed like forever in the shadows of his more prominent, high-flying peers. A posting would allow him to bask in the sunshine at last.

His new role within the group heralded a complete change in lifestyle. Leeson began his offshore sortie as a roving troubleshooter, jetting to Indonesia to help set up an office, or to Tokyo as part of a team investigating allegations of internal fraud. But one particular assignment in Jakarta, where he was sent to resolve a disputed settlement in the equities division, proved particularly influential.

Jakarta was Nick's first taste of a balmy climate and an exotic lifestyle, made all the more dramatic by the contrast between the appalling poverty of this overcrowded and alien city, and the newly affluent, profiting from a thriving economy. Barings was among the biggest foreign investment firms in the Indonesian market and, like most other houses, was experiencing problems with the consequences of rapid growth. This had generated an enormous amount of work, and placed extraordinary pressure on the internal systems of the transactions and settlements department.

Leeson headed a four-person team sent to sort out the mess. They stopped first at Barings in Hong Kong, which had responsibility for the Jakarta unit, then flew to Indonesia where Lisa Sims soon joined them. A friendship was struck between Nick and Lisa and it soon became obvious to their colleagues that a romance was blossoming. The two would sit next to each other, laughing and chatting constantly. Lisa had the opportunity to view Nick from a different perspective, one that did not include her usual surroundings of friends and associates, and she liked the ambitious man she saw.

'He took control of us and all the others relied on him because he stayed so cool and calm. Colleagues had always admired him for never showing anxiety over a transaction when it was going wrong — or boasting when it was right. Some people expect traders to be loud and bigheaded but Nick's not', Lisa said.[4]

Street-wise and sharp, Leeson was in many respects unlike his public school educated colleagues who seemed to dominate Britain's investment community. Nick and Lisa's backgrounds may not have been that different from each other, but Lisa knew that as a pair they were very different from many of their colleagues. Outwardly Nick appeared quiet and shy, but the self-confidence that had made him striker for Parmiter's firsts was quietly evident, and Lisa was aware of it, and attracted to it.

To those who knew him, Nick was quiet in the early years of his career. Even friends had described him as hard to get to know. While he may have enjoyed a beer with Dad and the lads at The Hare, at work he was more reserved, the type of person you could get to know only slowly, over the odd coffee or at social functions. Lisa had noted that although Nick was quiet, the aura of being in control was evident.

During an interview with Helena de Bertodano of *The London Sunday Telegraph*, Lisa said: 'When I first met him, I just assumed that he was the one in control. It wasn't like: "Wow, this is the man I am going to marry". But I liked him. He was always kind and we would chat'.

Professionally, Jakarta was a success. Personally, the lifestyle opened up a new world of alternatives to the drabness of London.

'We had some laughs', Lisa told *The Sun*. 'We were a good gang. I'd go out shopping with the lads and I'd meet up with them for nights out at restaurants. It was all very innocent'.[5]

Lisa was later sent to Hong Kong. 'Then we found ourselves talking on the phone all the time. I missed him so much. We made arrangements to meet up in Thailand on our way home to England for Christmas, had dinner and that was the start of it all', Lisa said.[6]

After spending the festive season of 1990 with their respective families, Nick and Lisa returned to Jakarta for two months. 'Then Nick returned to England and we both knew this was the real thing', Lisa said.

Nick proposed shortly after the couple were reunited in England in June 1991. 'I was very proper and said he'd have to ask my Dad', Lisa recalled. 'But I knew it was the right thing to do. You know when it's the right person. We all went to a restaurant and when Nick asked for my hand in marriage, my Dad called the head waiter and said: "Get me some champagne, I think I'm going to have a heart attack. This guy has just asked for my daughter's hand in marriage".'[7]

Lisa did not want to jeopardise her relationship with her fiance through working too closely with him, and on their return to London she transferred to the South East Asian desk where she worked as an assistant to dealers.

Nick's salary was to rise to stg25,000 a year while Lisa's salary reached stg15,000. Together the couple had a relatively comfortable lifestyle, good prospects, and Nick's career was showing promise. Success in Jakarta had prompted a request for him to take a look at the Hong Kong settlements department where similar problems had bedevilled operations. He then joined a Barings business and development group and headed projects and investigations. In September and October of that year, Leeson oversaw parts of an investigation into the suppression of a late margin report, apparently arising from collusion between an employee and a client in connection with a late overdrawn balance and suspected fraud involving proprietary trading. When the client started to suffer large losses, a staff member and the client had apparently connived to bury a report showing late margin calls — a singular object lesson in what could and could not be done, what could be concealed and how. As key staff involved in the affair were sacked, Leeson for a time took charge of the settlements of Japanese options and futures.

Leeson's fast-developing knowledge of the securities and banking industry was not going unnoticed outside the securities unit either. He became more confident when dealing with his superiors, and that self-assuredness prompted Barings executives to take Leeson out of the back room and put him on the trading floors of London. He had been widely hailed as an accounting whiz capable of resolving difficult transactions with a minimum of fuss through a variety of transactions and deals. Where he was once considered shy, a manner accentuated by his boyish looks, he was now becoming noted for keeping a cool head and maintaining a low profile.

Leeson believed he would have no problems in passing any of the required exams, and an application was forwarded to Britain's Securities & Futures Authority (SFA) for a licence, and the relevant questionnaire was completed and returned. Nick had, however, deliberately failed to answer one question which required the applicant to indicate any criminal background or county court judgements for debt. The SFA soon discovered that, according to the Watford Registry of County Court Judgements, Leeson had a judgement registered against him for stg639 for non-payment of a bill in February 1991.[8] Another judgement for stg2426 was made against him in May 1992 on behalf of the National Westminster Bank.[9]

Had Leeson appeared personally before the SFA and provided an adequate explanation, his licence could have been granted, but when queried as to why Leeson had failed to answer the question, Barings declined to respond and several months later the application was withdrawn. This had not, however, precluded Leeson from advancement. It was at about this time that senior executives were taking a closer look at the group's Singapore futures unit.

Between 1987 and 1989, pre-tax profits for the year to September had remained consistently low, with Barings Futures (Singapore) reporting earnings of S$25,000, S$19,000 and S$26,000 over those three respective years.

Transactions and settlements between Tokyo and Singapore had continued to rise steadily and, for the 12 months to September 1991, the unit reported that pre-tax profit had more than doubled to S$61,000. Dickle and Killian recognised that there was now a need to bolster support staff on the ground and to upgrade the bank's trading membership of Simex. At this stage, there was no intention of allowing actual trading to be undertaken by Barings on behalf of Tokyo clients — such trading as was taking place would continue to be executed by Chase Manhattan Futures Corporation. What was required was the appointment of someone to monitor the clearing and settlement of the rising trades that were being undertaken at Simex on Barings' behalf.

After the SFA raised its queries, Leeson approached Anthony Dickle about the possibility of being posted to Barings' Singapore futures operations, and the matter was discussed with Killian. Leeson's experience in Asia was limited, but the climate was appealing and he felt that his chances of promotion in London would improve if he were prepared to specialise and gain further offshore experience.

Mike Killian later returned to Leeson and asked whether he would be interested in running the back office and head the trading floor operations at Simex. Leeson was delighted, and his name was put forward to Barings management committee in London.

Killian thought his young charge would do well in Asia — he had himself gained extensive training there. Leeson's name was accepted by management, and he was told to report to Simon Jones. The appointment was, however, already a cause for concern to James Bax, even though Leeson would not be undertaking any trading activities. Widely and highly regarded in Singapore as a man of integrity, Bax was a stickler for the rule book and was immediately concerned about reporting procedures. He wrote a memorandum to London expressing those concerns when he heard that Leeson would run both front and back offices. But although Bax was unimpressed, concern in any quarters was limited.

Head office was constrained by the rising costs associated with the securities business and Leeson's role at Simex was restricted to overseeing trades as opposed to actually making them happen. Bishopsgate was content that little or no scope for a conflict of interests existed and that Leeson's placement was a reasonable compromise for the time being.

There was one more, happier, task to undertake before the move to Singapore could be finalised. Nick and Lisa were married on 21 March 1992, in the small English village of West Kingsdown in Kent, where Lisa had grown up. Lisa had worn the excitement of the wedding in her normal extroverted way. As usual, Nick was calmer.

On the 21st of March, Nick's mother's birthday, the Leeson's new life together commenced when they exchanged vows at St Edmund the King Church. Lisa wore a traditional white wedding dress with a full veil, while Nick donned top hat and tails. The union was welcomed by all and approved of by Lisa's father, Alec Sims, who said he was proud to welcome the lad from Watford into his family. Alec had done for his family what Harry Leeson had done for his, he loved his children, and had given them the best start in life he could.

The wedding cost about stg20,000 and the newlyweds caught the Orient Express to Venice for their honeymoon, and spent four nights in the Cipriani Hotel.[10]

The newlyweds' arrival in Singapore in late March 1992 was the catalyst for a remarkable change. At the tender age of 25, the suburban Londoner with the modest blue-collar background was transformed into a yuppie Far East trader.

His income had doubled, and the Barings crest on his business cards guaranteed the Leeson's entry to Singapore's most exclusive clubs.

Lisa, however, suffered homesickness from the moment she set foot in Singapore. 'I suppose I had visions of grandeur about living in Singapore. I wasn't going to work because I wasn't granted an employment card. I didn't mind that. I thought it might be nice to stay home and just be a wife', Lisa told *The Sun*. 'In some ways I would rather have stayed home in England and settled down to married life there, but it seemed like we might get a chance to live the good life'.

No such ambivalence affected Nick. This was his chance to shine, and he seized it. His working life to date had been spent entirely in back rooms, an outsider watching the main event from afar. In Singapore, Leeson, clad now in the obligatory designer labels, steered himself with resolution towards centre stage and, after a humble start, his slow but sure metamorphosis from back office clerk to aggressive deal cutter and market maker was under way.

Leeson was technically still in the back office, but this time he was running it while reporting to Simon Jones and the man responsible for futures and options settlements in London, Gordon Bowser. His second duty was to act as floor manager.

In Asia, the Barings shingle was the envy of their rivals to the extent that Barings traders were the brunt of jokes about not having to do the hard work. Barings was known for doing the easy deals simply because people with money had unlimited faith in Barings reputation, established in conjunction with Britain's colonial expansion into Asia.

From the edge of the Middle East to the Pacific Ocean, Barings had charted its growth, and in Singapore it had operated on the island longer than anyone else and in so doing, established an extensive research base on individual countries in the region.

At Barings' head office in Bishopsgate, conversation was mostly in the well modulated tones of the BBC, and non-public school accents were disguised as much as possible. In Singapore there was little heed paid to employees' backgrounds and accents. As one regular visitor to the Singapore branch noted: 'Barings is very English upper crust, self-sufficient and there's not a cockney accent to be heard'. Still, it was a long way from London, and even further from Watford. Those close to Leeson believed he had adopted a less broad accent in his business dealings, but occasionally his drinking betrayed his more familiar speech.

Leeson and his colleagues took full advantage of Barings' name and reputation, particularly with exchange authorities in London, at Simex, and the Bank of England, and together with the Chase Manhattan relationship, Barings enjoyed a good corporate relationship with Wall Street investment firm Spear, Leeds & Kellogg (SLK). At Simex, Barings had arranged infrastructure support and Barings jackets for SLK traders. A similarly close relationship was developed with First Continental Trading Ltd. Cultivating these personal relationships represented another facet of the once-reserved Leeson's growing abilities.

Leeson's duties evolved slowly — his first official appointment was as Derivatives Operations Manager of Barings Securities Singapore. He also mastered some standard accounting manoeuvres which laid the course for his trading activities for nearly the next three years. He was not content with the more menial back office tasks.

In May, Barings had acquired three seats on Simex and Leeson asked James Bax if he could take Singapore's Institute of Banking and Finance, Futures Trading Test which would enable him to 'wear a badge' and ply his futures trading on the Simex floor. Bax was again dubious. He had been hired by Barings after an impressive interview. During it he had said 'Singapore is full of land mines and I know where they are'.[11] It is reasonable to assume that Bax was uncomfortable with Leeson's expanding role, although no doubt even Bax's deepest misgivings could not have foreshadowed the disaster that was to come.

Leeson pressed his case and sat the examinations. Carrying the Barings' name was a significant advantage, and he became the bank's nomination for the paid seats in a growing futures exchange searching for prestige. The right to trade in the Simex pit was subject to the discretionary powers of Simex authorities. Several exams of varying standards could be undertaken and it remains unclear which exams Leeson actually sat, and how well he fared, but sources close to Leeson have suggested that actual permission for him to trade in the pit was never formally obtained. The mere fact that he would represent Barings and its debut at Simex was, however, enough to quell any unlikely concerns the exchange authorities might have held.

It was here that Leeson committed his second dishonest act. Leeson was again required to complete a questionnaire, not dissimilar to the one he had completed for the Securities Futures Authority in London. Again, Leeson failed to disclose the county court judgements, and it is more than reasonable that Simex could expect that any such matters would be brought to their attention by Leeson's superiors in London.

Had the unpaid fines become known, Leeson would not have been allowed to sit the exams, but sit and pass he did on 26 June 1992 and shortly afterwards Killian recommended that Leeson — whose experience had been mainly limited to being a settlements clerk — be promoted to Assistant Director and General Manager, Barings Futures (Singapore).

Leeson was in the ascendant, and was now an official trader in the front office, buying and selling futures contracts linked to the performance of Japanese stocks on the Nikkei 225 index. The contracts were to be acquired in Osaka, and sold in Singapore. His profits were derived from the minor price differentials between the two markets through switching books.

To the casual outsider, Osaka and Singapore may not appear to be the obvious choice of venues for investment houses looking for profits from exotic financial instruments.

But like gold prices in London and Zurich, futures generally move in the same direction in Osaka and Singapore and both cities are attractive destinations for foreign capital. Osaka is Japan's second largest commercial capital and a major centre for big companies dealing in derivatives, while Singapore with its light tax regime, political stability and obvious wealth made it an equally desirable destination for traders.

Leeson was ordered to maintain buying in one market (Japan) and selling in another (Singapore) when profitable, and strictly only on behalf of clients. 'Make them money and retrieve a commission', was the creed. Buying in one market and selling in the other would simplify trading activities, while allowing Leeson to cash in with minimised risk. It was a prudent philosophy because dealing in both markets would substantially increase Barings' exposure to big market fluctuations. Initially the gains to be made may appear small, but they have the potential to add up to a lot of money when dealings are conducted on a large scale.

Barings Singapore futures operations comprised mainly three types of futures contracts, each traded on two exchanges — the Nikkei 225 as traded on Simex and the Osaka Securities Exchange, the 10-year Japanese Government Bond (JGB) contract as traded on Simex and the Tokyo Stock Exchange (TSE), and the three-month Euroyen contract as traded on Simex and the Tokyo International Financial Futures Exchange (TIFFE).

Between these pairs there were essential differences in the way they were traded. At Simex, the contracts were auctioned in an open pit by traders through an outcry system of shouting and hand signals that borders on an arcane form of sign language. There are also differences from market to market in the price limits between which the contracts could move, and different margin call requirements.

The Nikkei 225 futures contract, JGB, and Euroyen are traded on four-month cycle — March, June, September and December. In the case of the Nikkei 225, which formed the bulk of Nick Leeson's work, the contract is turned over until its last trade one business day before the second last Friday of the contract month.

Together with Eric Chang, Leeson entered the frenetic outcries of the Simex pit on the first of July as a registered Barings seat holder. It was a modest start, though Leeson's knowledge extended beyond the rules of Simex. He had already acquired more than a few accounting tricks through his investigative work with Barings, and knew how to apply them to the trading floor.

From a reconstruction of subsequent events, it is difficult to draw a conclusion other than that Leeson was establishing the required logistics that would enable him to trade outside his authorised activities virtually from his first moments on the floor. A mere two days after his trading debut, Leeson opened account number 88888 as an error account, and the following week computer technician Edmund Wong was instructed to reprogram Leeson's computer software to exclude the account from most reports sent to London.[12]

Although Leeson was not regarded as superstitious, he could take comfort in the beliefs of others. According to Chinese mythology, eight is a lucky number. In Cantonese the number eight sounds similar to the word for prosperity and is therefore considered good luck.

Error accounts in themselves are not unusual. They enable back office staff to hold tricky transactions and allow for glitches and market fluctuations which can be squared and sorted out at a later date this also includes mismatched trades where a trader may have brought as opposed to selling (or vice versa). However, Leeson's situation was quite different. He controlled both the trade and the settlement, and this enabled him to dictate reported profits, and to easily disguise the true state of Barings' finances.

Judging by the size of Barings' first foray into Singapore futures, it could be argued with some merit that Leeson had not set out deliberately to falsify accounts and create fictitious profits. Rather, error account 88888 had provided a useful safety margin where profits could be stashed and brought out when business was weak to create a better overall position. Alternatively, losses could be hidden in the account until a turnaround in market fortunes allowed the deficit to be brought out and declared. This meant that sharp fluctuations on the profit and loss accounts could be averted, and the perception of solid stable growth could be maintained.

While these error accounts may not comprise an altogether honest practice, it is a practice widely adopted by traders, and is the sort of subject management turns a blind eye to. No-one talks about error accounts. As one observer puts it: 'Error accounts are a bit like masturbation. Everybody does it but no-one admits to it'.

Regardless of Leeson's real intentions, Bishopsgate had committed its second blunder by not removing Leeson from the back room settlements. Justification for maintaining the status quo were that the risks involved with Leeson's appointment were considered so low that orthodox practices could be safely side-stepped. This weak reasoning was proffered after the collapse, and gives an accurate, if alarming, portrayal of Barings' lax risk management culture. Leeson's being given permission to both trade and settle contracts would probably never have been allowed in an American investment firm. It has also been argued that Barings' willingness to tolerate this unusual situation was motivated by the potential to save on staff overheads, but this is not an argument given much weight in the industry.

Allowing one person to control both the back room and the trading floor flies in the face of all established principles of financial risk management — it is precisely the separation of the two operations that allows for the maintenance of internal checks and balances. Divorcing these functions allows for the independent monitoring and assessment of the transaction and the settlement, and provides for full disclosure to head office of all trades made. Giving Leeson the control and supervision of both transactions and settlements was a significant and ultimately fatal departure from accepted practice. Leeson's free rein had raised more than a few eyebrows.

More important than the potential for fiddling the figures, creation and control of the error account meant Leeson was now placed to conduct trades using Barings' capital and adopting his own risk positions. This was in line with the developing principles of the securities division, but against the grain of the merchant banking arm and the conflict was one cause for a restructuring of the entire group.

Such confusion was evident in Leeson's reporting to Simex. When registering these trades with the Simex computer, he initially labelled them as house trades, but from 17 July they were listed as client trades. By the end of that month error account 88888 contained a loss of S$300,000. The confusion resurfaced a month later when Leeson was required to inform Simex of the owner of the account. He listed it as Barings Securities London — Error Account. This was later amended with the reference to 'Error Account' dropped.

By the end of December 1992, Barings ranked 26th among all clearing members in terms of volume traded through Simex. Leeson's ability on the floor was gaining credibility, although secretly his error account was already providing its first headache. After booking up early small losses in July, Leeson's loss-making position had swollen to S$10.7 million by September before he whittled them back to zero over the ensuing months. By December, however, his error account held losses containing S$4.9 million.[13] It was the first signal that Leeson was prepared to compromise his own integrity. The reported paper performance to London remained solid and was enough to land Nick his largest-ever pay cheque — topped up by an annual bonus of stg35,746.

In comparison with other traders, Leeson was at this point just another face at Simex making a comparatively reasonable living. He remained a long way behind the star traders who raked in six-figure bonuses and could dictate trade on reputation alone.

However, devices for hiding red ink were already proving personally lucrative.

CHAPTER FOUR

INSIDE BARINGS
HOUSE OF CARDS

'Derivatives need to be well controlled and understood but we believe we do that well here'. Barings Plc chairman Sir Peter Baring.

'Someone, somewhere has certainly failed to carry out even the most elementary types of appropriate supervision in ensuring the demarcation between the different jobs that people should be doing. This whole question of the difference between the back office and the front office may seem arcane but it s terribly important'. Britain's Securities and Futures Authority chief Christopher Sharples.[1]

The demise of Barings began with a crack in the upper echelons of management, splintering throughout the core of the group, dislocating operations to a point where hundreds of years of combined banking experience with the Bank of England proved incapable of averting an otherwise avoidable collapse.

Both institutions had, over the years, learnt to combat internal problems with a relative conservatism that stands in stark contrast to practices of their latter day peers, particularly when comparisons are drawn with their Wall Street counterparts. At its headquarters in Threadneedle Street, the BoE is a well-guarded building covering three acres of land in the heart of the usually grey City. At its entrance, gatekeepers clad in red waistcoats, pink tails and top hats stand at the ready, while a sombre head gatekeeper — distinguished by his red velvet robe and a black tricorn hat — greets each of the central bank directors upon their arrival.

Such is the seclusion of Britain's central bank that it has been compared to a monastery — its windows face inwards overlooking the courtyard, and rarely have the lives of its staff been subject to public scrutiny. In isolation, generations of faceless bankers evolved the traditions and economic principles designed to serve an international power.

By clinging to those mores of merchant banking, Barings had, under the auspices of the BoE, survived the Big Bang and the resultant turmoil which had steered most western countries into recession during the early 1990s. While this safe approach had worked, it would ironically be the same approach that would bring about bank's implosion at the hands of a sole derivatives dealer. The rapid pace of change, the ever-present rivals, and fresh demands within the banking industry had tipped the entire sector on its head, and had cultivated a new breed of money merchants who were the antithesis of contemporary management in both thought and practice.

Nevertheless, the top management at Barings had extensive experience. Chairman Sir Peter Baring became a director in 1967, was group finance director between 1986 and 1992, and became chairman in 1992. Sir Peter was more than ably supported by deputy chairman, Andrew Tuckey, who had joined the bank in 1968 in corporate finance after commanding a wide range of responsibilities in corporate finance and international capital markets. He was groomed to replace Sir Peter at the top by the end of 1995.

Not all of Britain's banking community was quite so staid. The banking culture remained dominated by a mix of personalities in the early 1990s that formed a basis for sometimes difficult and volatile relationships.

At Barings, quibbling and in-fighting between the broking and merchant banking arms had become common while, outside, politicking and the drive for consolidation of power were the dominating traits among the regulatory authorities, led by a self confident Chancellor of the Exchequer, Kenneth Clarke, a puritanical BoE Governor, Eddie George, and his more pragmatic deputy, Rupert Pennant-Rea.

The role of the BoE had altered significantly since the 1970s, as one crisis followed another, forcing change along lines similar to those already established in the United States. Calls had been made for tighter supervisory arrangements throughout the ensuing decades, a quest seized on eagerly by the opportunistic Eddie George when he assumed the role of governor.

Efforts to bolster scrutiny within the industry was, however, often met with resistance from the British banks themselves who had never warmed to the intrusive manner adopted by the more aggressive Americans — and the Office of Comptroller of the Currency — who had served as a role model for their UK equivalents. In the US, rigid risk management practices were seen as necessary for deregulation in order to ensure that honest profits were obtained within a freer framework.

Rumblings increased over what constituted 'appropriate' rigour, and became a sore point between the banks, the Chancellor of the Exchequer, and the BoE, on whose shoulders responsibility for the banking system rested.

Formally, the BoE only received real supervisory clout under the 1979 Banking Act which enabled it to revoke banking licences. That move was by-product of the secondary banking crisis in the mid 1970s, and was a forerunner to the 1987 Banking Act which again increased the central bank's power, this time after it rescued Johnson Matthey Bankers in 1984. A special investigation unit was formed in response to the collapse of the Bank of Credit and Commerce International (BCCI) but, overall, BoE resources were wanting, compared to their well resourced counterparts in the United States.

The way the BoE exercised its supervisory powers seemed to only ever receive an impetus after each crisis, giving the impression that it was constantly trying to catch up in a game it was slowly losing. The figures supported the critics. When Barings' fate was being determined, the BoE had 322 supervisors covering 518 banks. The largest banks had just one supervisor allocated full-time to oversee its activities. In Barings' case, visits were not considered warranted, and the BoE relied on informal gatherings and Barings auditors, Coopers & Lybrand, to provide the financial reports it required to stay abreast of developments at Bishopsgate.

At best, reporting procedures between the BoE and Barings' merchant banking division were weak, and with the securities division it was virtually non-existent, the BoE relying on the personal relationships that existed between management and officials at Threadneedle Street and Bishopsgate to remain informed.

While tradition remained a powerful force, Barings was shrewd enough to realise that change was in the winds and it established its securities business through the acquisition of a stockbroking unit from Henderson Crosthwaite in 1984. Purchased for stg6.0 million, it was later incorporated as Barings Securities Ltd through the Cayman Islands, with head office and all activities associated with that role remaining in London.

Under Henderson Crosthwaite, the broking arm had established strong links in Asia through its chief, Christopher Heath, who would relocate with the acquisition and become chairman of Barings Securities. Gaining the services of Heath was considered as much a coup for Barings as was acquiring the new unit. The archetypal superbroker of the late 1980s, Heath was aggressive and immediately plotted an expansion strategy that delivered the services of Barings Securities throughout Asia. With that came a dramatic rise in personnel and new blood.

Heath's energy in using his Japanese resources in promoting Barings made him an industry legend and ensured that the culture within the stockbroking group would be to a large extent moulded by his own personality. With boundless energy, the rounded and bespectacled Heath would bounce around the Tokyo office delivering the thumbs up sign as new orders rang in over the telephones.

The life of traders at Barings Far East operations was frenetic, monopolised by clients and the pursuit of profits. In their spare time, staff entertained clients in restaurants or on the golf course, and were given generous expense accounts capable of providing a heady lifestyle. The wealth was obvious, and the move into Asia was smart. Other broking houses and banks which formed strategic alliances after the Big Bang had suffered from focussing on the mature, established markets of Europe and the United States. Asia was proving to be an ever growing boom market, with Tokyo at its centre.

Heath has been credited with having attracted many of the personalities in Barings securities. These were not the traditionally stuffy banking types who spent six months to a year in each department, winning promotion slowly and through hard won experience. Rather, these were the twenty-something individuals with chutzpah to burn. A generation who released stress by sky-diving over weekends and battling it out in office water-pistol fights while turning over millions in a day for a cut.

While high jinks were common, the focus was always on the client, and this was emphasised by a sign which hung in the Tokyo office reminding staff: 'The client is the most important person ever in this office. The client does not depend on us; we depend on the client. The client is not the nuisance of our work; he is the mainframe of it. We are not doing him a favour by having him; he is doing us a favour by giving us the opportunity to have him. The client is not someone to argue or match wits with. Nobody ever wins an argument with the client. The client is the person who brings us the bonus and it is our job to give him anything and everything he wants'.

The last directive included such perks as trips to the snow fields and apparently, on one occasion, clients could enjoy playing a round with golfing great, Nick Faldo, who was brought in for a round at the local course. More importantly, the lengths to which staff at Barings securities would go to please clients in Asia highlighted the emphasis the bank placed on the customer, as opposed to proprietary trading, which later to become a source of much anxiety.

Barings became a major force in the Japanese warrant market which led directly to higher profits and, to the chagrin of the banking side, generous remunerations were awarded to directors and staff. This was made possible by Heath's aggressiveness. He poached an entire trading team from Robert Fleming & Co. But this rate of growth had impacted in two key areas.

First, the pace of expansion in the emerging Asian markets had strained the unit's capital base, requiring it to raise funding through short-term loans. Secondly, the expansion trail had outpaced existing infrastructure to the point where the need to overhaul existing means of communications and install effective internal controls was urgent, but was ignored. A third and equally important point were the petty jealousies that emerged in the banking division when senior executives learned of the over-the-top salaries being paid to staff in broking. The structure of the deal struck when Barings entered the securities market proved critical to both its initial success and its eventual collapse. The new unit was allowed complete autonomy, and the interests of staff were linked directly to profits with 50 per cent of pretax earnings to be distributed among them. And as for the newcomer Heath, he was being paid in excess of stg2.0 million a year, while his entire package, inclusive of bonuses, was rumoured to be near stg5.0 million.

The short-term loans were of serious concern to the securities division's parent. Baring Brothers & Co wanted to consolidate the loans within its own accounts because it feared that bankers to Barings Securities could withdraw the short-term loans designed to fund long-term working capital, and that this had the potential for Barings' rivals to undermine its longer term strategies.

Differing interests and concerns created a potent mix of problems that began to fester, typifying the cultural legacy of bankers versus traders. The cultural gap was exacerbated by the housing of banking and securities divisions in separate London office blocks. Staff from either side rarely mixed, and there was little or no appreciation for people outside their respective units. Only group deputy chairman Andrew Tuckey served on the boards of both units, and any notion of injecting fresh blood at a senior level within the parent body was stifled by a Barings tradition of rarely hiring people outside the bank at director level. The dialogue that did exist was dependent upon Tuckey's relationship with Heath.

The securities unit, naturally, did not have an established culture within its corporate ranks. This created its own separate set of internal problems. There was no formal management structure and no internal audit functions and, although a management committee had been formed, controls within the securities unit were also considered weak by merchant banking standards with most key decisions being made by Heath, and/or his deputy, Andrew Bayliss.

While the board of Barings was concerned about the differences between the banking and securities operations, the directors were also disturbed by the rivalry emerging between the front room traders and back office staff within the securities unit itself. The distaste between the people employed in each section was becoming quite blatant, and this had developed into a procedural matter after Coopers & Lybrand detected problems within reporting lines to the Britain's Securities & Futures Authority. In 1992, enough doubts existed to suggest that controls within Barings Securities required a significant lift.

Rivalry and cynicism were problems globally, but nowhere more so than in London, where the coordination and well-being of group operations was determined. It was amid this air of suspicion that James Bax sent a letter from Singapore to Andrew Fraser, the Head of Equity Broking and

Trading. Dated May 25, it expressed his fears about the powers Nick Leeson had been endowed with, covering transactions and settlements.

'My concern is that once again we are in danger of setting up a structure which will subsequently prove disastrous and which will succeed in losing either a lot of money, or client goodwill, or both', Bax wrote.

'In my view it is critical that we should keep clear reporting lines and if this office is involved in Simex at all then Nick should report to Simon and then be ultimately responsible for the operations side'.[2]

The concerns expressed in the letter were typical of those held in some quarters, and serve to illuminate a two-fold problem: firstly that Bax's warning was ignored highlighted the indifference of management to foreign posts dealing in securities, and in particular somewhere like Singapore, where the pace of growth for Barings had remained slow when compared with elsewhere in Asia. Secondly, the attitude showed the lack of a much deserved confidence in Bax, who was held in high esteem by Singapore's money men.

It was also conservative and complacent thinking that prevented Barings' board from intervening with the securities side until profits had started to sour. By the end of the eighties the recession was starting to bite, and in the early 1990s Japan's bubble economy ran out of steam. Group earnings had been dwindling from 1989, but after striking a retained profit of just stg19.1 million in 1991, it was becoming obvious that the comparable figure for 1992 could be a loss. At Barings Securities the cost base had continued to expand, while the unit compiled one sizeable loss after another. The overall group was heading for an annual retained profit of just stg1.8 million, with the summer months of 1992 proving to be the most torrid.

At the time of the bank's collapse, Peter Norris was Tuckey's right-hand man and the implementer of Tuckey's strategies. Widely regarded as being a talented number cruncher, he joined Barings in 1976 and held several senior appointments within the bank, including a senior post in Asia. He had been asked by Sir Peter and Tuckey to independently review the securities operation, to prepare a strategy which included the possibility of closing loss-making businesses, and to formalise a long-term plan for senior management in New York, Tokyo, Hong Kong and Singapore. Norris relished the task but soon became disheartened by what he found. He could see no coherent structure and recognised that the division had become 'a deeply troubled and divided group'.[3]

His dismay was compounded by talk of proprietary trading. This was often discussed around Heath, but was a term that did not fit in well with the Norris agenda. Essentially, proprietary trading allows the house to take on the responsibility of its own risk position as opposed to a client's risk position. Adopting risk positions with the bank's capital is not a friendly concept to merchant bankers. They make their money out of having their *clients* adopting risk positions and receiving brokerage commisions on transactions.

The term 'proprietary trading' is itself open to various definitions used to describe over-the-counter business in exchange traded derivatives, switching, and volatility books undertaken in London, Hong Kong, Tokyo and Singapore. More generally, the term referred to large risk-taking positions which the board viewed as capricious and was firmly against.

It is difficult to ascertain the exact major risk positions taken by Barings under Heath in proprietary trading — if indeed there were any. Certainly, Nick Leeson had already adopted an unauthorised, albeit relatively small, position in error account 88888, but the lines that separate what was officially sanctioned and what was accepted practice are blurred and, in some respects, further served by the relaxed relationship between traders and authorities at the Bank of England which allowed Barings to exceed limits placed on capital transfers. Among the dealers on the floor at Simex it was assumed that Barings traders had regularly adopted

positions on behalf of the bank, and the subject was sometimes broached during the daily post-mortems conducted in
the bars along Singapore's bustling Boat Quay.

However, the attitudes to proprietary trading that had
evolved in Barings Securities' short history were similar to
those of its highly successful rivals on Wall Street, where the
business climate demanded that investment houses adopt big
positions of their own undertaking in the chase for big
rewards. The only way Barings would be able to compete on
the same scale as their trans-Atlantic rivals was to develop a
tight risk-managed securities team with access to large-scale
funding.

In light of this, the Norris recommendations that Barings
Securities be kept, but that it start again from scratch,
abandon concepts of large-scale proprietary trading, and
introduce a new management structure, was bound to conflict with the entrenched ideal held by Heath and Bayliss.
This may have been a logical position to take, but the
decision to slash costs by one-fifth and staff by not much less,
sent each member of staff into a self-preservation panic.
Around stg20 million was to be saved, and the prospect of
offshore postings was reduced with the planned hiving-off of
the Australian operations and, with the exception of London
and Paris, all European offices were to be closed. The overall
group would inject stg45 million into the securities unit as
the new investment bank was forged over the ensuing three
years. From the board's perspective, the change made sense.
From the shop floor, it created new factions and dangerously
shifting alliances of which Nick Leeson was acutely aware.

In reference to differences between the securities and the
rest of the group, Norris later commented: 'The ethos was,
really, that the last thing you need in a stockbroking outfit is
management in a formal bureaucratic sense'.[4]

Norris was unrelenting, and the change began at the top.
Sir Peter appointed Norris chief operating officer of Barings
Securities in September 1992 with Heath as chairman,
although he lost the post of chief executive officer. Within six

months a formal management structure with designated responsibilities was put in place. New people with like-minded principles were brought in, and thoughts of major proprietary trading were dismissed.

Ron Baker had actually joined Barings several months earlier, in April 1992. With six years' experience at Bankers Trust and the establishment of what became the Debt Financial Products Group on his curriculum vitae, he decided to write up a business plan incorporating the instigation of a debt trading operation within a small British merchant bank. Michael Baring was then running Treasury and Trading at his namesake bank, and had acquired more than 20 years of merchant banking experience. He liked Baker's plan enough to go against company policy to recruit Baker and poach three other senior specialists from Barings rival, Bankers Trust.

By Baker's own admission, his appointment as a director and the placement of equity derivatives within his sphere meant that he had taken on more than he was capable of maintaining.[5] Baker had a cavalier attitude and his ability to motivate people was seen as crucial to the division's performance, but his own knowledge of derivatives was somewhat wanting and he was forced to rely on second-hand information to stay on top of developments. He did, however, believe that at all times prior to the collapse he was fully and reliably informed.

Another decision was taken to place proprietary equity derivative trading business under Baker. It was considered a relatively small part of the operations and not of the scale that had raised fears in Norris. Nevertheless, it did not fit comfortably within the main broking division, and seemed to be more at ease with the Debt Financial Products Group, for which Baker had been charged with responsibility, and where he had dealt with derivatives on a proprietary basis.

It was at this point that Baker first heard of 'Leeson's business', an obscure 'switching book' involving trading activity between Barings Futures Singapore and Barings Securities

Japan. Switching was a common term within Barings, outside the bank it is more commonly known as arbitraging.

There was certainly nothing untoward about such a book, and Baker had larger problems looming. By December 1992, Sir Peter and Tuckey were deliberating on the prospect of taking the restructuring one leap forward, and combining all the investment banking businesses into a core unit operating out of one centralised building. Tuckey later used a metaphor to explain his concerns to investigators, saying the difference was in the time scale: where brokers saw everything in terms of today and tomorrow, in corporate finance, the banker was more interested in what the client would be doing 12 months later.

For this reason it was decided that a group restructure would be undertaken over a lengthy period, possibly several years and while such a mindset may have sat comfortably within Barings banking culture, the timing was out of step with contemporary management thinking. Essentially, Sir Peter and Tuckey wanted to form a new umbrella group, initially called the Investment Banking Group, but which later became known as Barings Investment Bank, within which were four core groups: Equity Broking, Banking, Trading, and Corporate Finance and Emerging Markets Corporate Finance.

To support and blend the operations, a matrix management system was to be introduced, with the idea of installing the quality controls already in existence in the banking division into the securities operations.

Sociologists use the term 'culture clash' in describing the meeting of two alien worlds; in investment circles the concept of merging the staid and conservative banking division with the fast profit-generating securities arena is metaphorically not dissimilar. Al Dunlap had earned an international reputation as a highly successful, hard-nosed American businessman; his efforts in restructuring and resuscitating ailing businesses had earned him nicknames like 'Chainsaw' and 'Rambo In Pinstripes'.

Dunlap's philosophies are simple. He holds a firm belief that restructuring is a requirement in turning a business around, but warns that it must be done fast. 'If you can't do it in the first year, you'll never do it. This is the great enigma. It seems to paralyse people', Dunlap said.[6]

It would take another six months for the Barings board to ratify and approve the group restructuring, but the shift in emphasis had already sparked deep misgivings and had led to Heath exiting the securities unit in March. With him went Bayliss and the entire derivatives team that had been cultivated over the preceding years in London. Heath had overseen the derivatives operation in Asia and recognised the problems much earlier. But he was not happy with the way his conservative bosses were steering the bank. He wanted capital, and wanted Barings to expand. Size and access to capital are two very big advantages, and he had argued hard for more resources to expand the Asian trading arm and continued to advocate in favour of proprietary trading. If a firm wants to trade on its own behalf and not just for its clients, it must be able to weather the occasional hard knock — and that requires cash.

However, falling profits had eroded confidence in Heath's ability to lead the securities division, and some claimed that his previous success had gone to his head and that his interest had been diverted into prestige cars and race horses. During the previous years, he had pushed for a massive capital injection to allow the securities division to expand, and became incensed when, in 1991, Barings spent stg70 million for a 40 per cent stake in the Wall Street investment firm Dillion, Read & Co. He believed a gentlemen's agreement had existed that would allow the securities to unit to take in outside capital. The board was not at all enthusiastic about this concept, and snubbed attempts by Heath to prioritise a capital raising on the group's agenda.

At Barings, the already fractured morale was being widened by the split between Heath and his supporters, and the traditional bankers, most of whom had little or no insight into the nature of derivatives or any other forms of securities. Sir Peter and his deputy, Andrew Tuckey, had ignited the row by appointing the likeminded Norris. Tuckey is understood to have told Heath that 'in no way would the bank use its balance sheets and the bank's capital to finance risk management'. Barings' board members were obviously keen to maintain in-coming profits from futures, but others believed that futures should not be a part of the firm's long-term strategy.

Senior managers at Barings weren't the only ones who were content to remain ignorant. At a meeting between BoE supervisors and Barings executives, on February 4, 1993, the supervisors admitted they did not 'really understand'[7] Barings Securities' business. Threadneedle Street was worried about rapid decline in profits from the securities unit, its very existence, and the effect that would have on the merchant banking division. The BoE also expressed concern that its jurisdictions, and those of Britain's Securities and Futures Authority, did not cover Barings Securities' offshore operations. However, it was concluded: 'It appears that the Bank was reassured . . . and now has a far better understanding of our business, our recent past and our future plans'.[8]

Shortly afterwards, another round of staff cuts was implemented and the now-ostracised Heath found himself in the firing line. On March 14, he was called before Sir Peter and Tuckey was told a new management team was required. He was shown a press release announcing his resignation. Heath, Bayliss and several other senior allies were shown the door.

The resignations elevated people like James Bax, Simon Jones, Ron Baker and Nick Leeson, and upgraded the roles of Norris and Diarmid Kelly, the Deputy Head of Equity Broking and Trading. Their importance escalated, and so did the reliance upon Baker to obtain clear and accurate information. But the restructuring remained painstakingly slow. In December 1993, Tuckey issued a memorandum stating: 'I am convinced that, by combining our merchant banking and securities business . . . we shall be in a position to make the most of all the talents employed in the two businesses and of the opportunities which are now in front of us'.[9] Public knowledge of the restructuring was another 12 months away but in fact it would never witness completion.

Various people, including Simex chairwoman Elizabeth Sam, would later argue with benefit of hindsight that the seeds which led to the Barings collapse had been sown during the embryonic days of the restructure when the bank embraced the matrix system of management. It was implemented during the second half of 1993, although by this stage the logistics required for Leeson to carry out his trading activities had been largely in place. Nevertheless, the matrix system was important because it inextricably linked profits with performance and entrenched a mindset that would allow Leeson to continue to expand his private portfolio of futures contracts, while successfully avoiding scrutiny from his blissfully ignorant superiors.

Business management consultants have recommended the installation of the matrix management system to companies through an array of industries, as diverse as publishing, engineering, and investment banking. It takes into account the demands of an increasingly specialised world and in a company situation, it allows people to work for various departments while enabling the joint completion of individual projects. Strategically the system has two sets of executives, one dictating the day to day operations of products and services, the second handling the longer term objectives.

Typically, companies have introduced the matrix system after growing from small business ventures into medium sized firms. Such firms often experience difficulties in coping with the complications arising from diversifying operations.

Barings may have been an old and revered name in merchant banking, but it was relatively new to broking securities, and the matrix approach appealed as the most appropriate way of merging two entities under one cultural umbrella.

A matrix system can create complex relationships between management and highly skilled, highly paid staff where it is sometimes difficult to hold staff accountable and to assign blame or credit where due. There are varied forms of matrix, but the problem of accountability can be made easier by linking the fortunes of a product, and the responsible people, with performance and profit. A company's needs are usually judged on five criteria: diversity, specialisation, competitive conditions, technology, and size, with the objective being to gain optimum performance from resources and to achieve desired tasks within the constraints of an organisation. Academics and management theorists list 11 possible reasons for failure within a matrix management system. They are broad ranging and include the obvious such as failing to appoint the right person, and failure to appropriate adequate recognition to the right people for success. More pertinently, theorists argue that the matrix system will fail when management fails to define working relationships within departments, and fails to develop a system that will give prompt information to all involved.

The latter became a source of grievance for Sir William Ryrie, a Barings executive director who joined the bank in April 1994 after vacating his position as head of the World Bank's International Finance Corporation. He was never comfortable with the idea of people reporting to more than one boss, and argued that reporting lines were too complex. His view clashed with that of Sir Peter and Norris, who regarded the new reporting procedures as quite clear.

At Barings, under the new matrix system, each line, such as derivatives, within the organisation was labelled a 'global product' and was described as a column in the management structure, while each of the bank's offices and regional centres were considered floors within the group. In the larger scheme of Barings' operations, this meant that a person who was in charge of a business unit dealt with the chief in charge of the location where the business operated, and with the manager of the product itself, wherever that person was located. Each role was supposed to be of equal importance, and the essential idea was to enhance the ability of key personnel responsible for each line and the associated profit performance.

In international operations under matrix, overseas based managers report to both regional and head offices, and in so doing responsibility for profits is placed on a product by product basis while ensuring that local management play a key role in the maintenance of infrastructure such as administration, controls, settlement, and accounting.

Nick Leeson's situation entailed dealing with Bax in Singapore and Baker in London. Both his superiors were thousands of kilometres apart, but of supposed equal importance to Leeson's trading activities. In theory, the matrix system would ensure that Leeson and his profit and losses were kept in check by London, while Bax could oversee the finer details of his operations in Singapore, and make certain that all his obligations were met. But the decision by Bishopsgate to grant Leeson control of both front and back offices fundamentally flawed the matrix approach by eroding Simon Jones and James Bax's power, enabling Leeson to stash away losses in his error account and beguile his superiors in London. Bax and Jones lacked a full understanding of derivatives, neither were seasoned in this market and, in hindsight, both were uninterested in the machinations of Simex unless it affected the bottom line.

As Leeson's position and standing evolved, neither Bax nor Jones considered Leeson and his operations as part of their responsibility, and it became easier to shift accountability to London. Instead, in respect of front office operations Leeson was answerable directly to Ron Baker in London who headed the Financial Products Group, and in others to Mary Waltz who joined Barings in 1992 with Baker and who was now Global Head of Equity Financial Products. It is possible that Bax may have preferred Leeson to report to Jones on back office matters but under the new structure, the settlements department, seven times zones away in London, assumed that task. There were also kudos for the aggressive types like Baker in taking on Leeson because his success was starting to show and rub off. In another situation, it might even have been thought commendable that Bax and Jones had preferred not to overlord trades they did not understand.

Clarifying exactly who answered to whom at Barings after matrix was installed can be complex, however, this is simplified by the matrix system of allocating responsibility to key personnel and Barings' faith in Ron Baker's personal charm. Overriding all was Baker's developing relationship with Leeson. Fellow traders on the floor at Simex had noted that the pair, whose personalities were not dissimilar, were becoming close. Both were known to be game, at times their unshakeable belief in themselves being confused for arrogance, and there was always the common drive to bolstering the bottom line. Success breeds its own, and from Singapore, word was coming back that everyone thought Leeson was doing well in a new and relatively unknown field. This had not escaped Baker's attention.

The characters of those around Leeson, combined with the matrix style of management, was important, and resulted in a line of reporting that depended upon a number of critical links. Leeson reported to Baker. Baker reported to Norris. Norris reported to the board, and the board reported to the Bank of England. And all had formed cosy informal relationships where the other's word was enough to satisfy the odd query.

Specifically, it is the link between Norris and the board, and in turn the BoE, that would prime Barings for disaster. The success of Barings Securities rested on the shoulders of Norris. He had inherited the unit after it had piled up losses in the vicinity of stg11 million. He had decided not to offload the business but to start again from scratch and initially, to Norris at least, this appeared an easier task than was at first advocated. Following losses such as the division had already sustained, matters within the securities division could hardly get any worse.

Financially, the restructuring had several effects. Near the latter part of 1993 it was granted solo consolidation, and revised treasury limits were approved. The consolidation allowed the group to report as a single unit, and in doing so treasury limits were reduced to stg364 million from stg394 million. This meant that exposures by Barings units had been maintained at 25 per cent of the overall capital base.

Ensuring that the new unified group met internal and external rigours was the revamped Internal Audit Department, a department which had originated in the merchant banking arm in the mid 1980s. No such department had existed for the securities side until late 1992, and the entire concept was quite alien.

In conjunction with the BoE and the Securities and Futures Authority, these three groups formalised the parameters within which Leeson could operate.

Present at the meeting between Barings executives and BoE supervisors in February 1993 was Christopher Thompson. Shortly afterwards, Thompson was made a senior manager in the BoE's merchant bank supervision department, where he was supported by banking analyst John Mackintosh. Both were personable men who, like Quinn and Sir Peter, relied more on the prevailing culture than formalised structures to undertake their tasks, and between them a direct link was forged between Leeson in Singapore and the BoE, creating an environment in which the normal lines of reporting could be bypassed and informal concessions granted.

Of this group, some were a part of Britain's aristocratic establishment, while others had cut it in British banking circles as outsiders. All had been educated at the best colleges, and had accumulated years of well honed experience. None of them had much in common with Nick Leeson — who had proved himself a competent clerk and adept at understanding the fundamentals of the securities business.

The Barings Plc board comprised Sir Peter and Tuckey, Michael Miles, John Bolsover, John Dare, Sir William Ryrie. The board of the securities division prior to restructuring had included Bax and Tuckey. An Australian, Baker was not part of the old school club, though he was widely regarded as a high flier with a solid track record in banking.

Of those controlling the ultimate levers — Sir Peter, Tuckey, George and Quinn — all were in their late forties and fifties and reigned over a derivatives business where a 30-year-old trader with a few successful years under his belt was considered a veteran.

In the aftermath of the Barings debacle, London's *Sunday Times* paraphrased Oscar Wilde when describing Eddie George as a man who 'knows the price of everything and the meaning of nothing'. It was perhaps unfair, but in one sense apt: although well credentialled, George was not the traditional type of banker, nor was he part of the establishment. He was born the son of a post office clerk in 1938 and won a scholarship to Dulwich College, played rugby, read economics at Sir Peter's alma mater, Cambridge, and eventually made a name for himself in the money markets. He was hired by the BoE in 1962 and in those early years worked primarily in East European affairs before being seconded to the Bank of International Settlements and the International Monetary Fund. More importantly, he later forged a close relationship with the then Chancellor of the Exchequer, Nigel Lawson, and in doing so acquired a solid ally for his future rise.

Religious, genial and skilful, George was known effectively as the BoE's chief executive officer for his reputation as a market player and manipulator.

George was appointed governor by Prime Minister John Major when Robin Leigh-Pemberton stood down in 1993 during the soul-searching following the collapse of the BCCI.

The BCCI was by this stage being jokingly referred to as the Bank of Crooks and Cocaine, and it became apparent that mistakes had been made and overlooked.

There is no doubting George's love of the institution in which he had spent the bulk of his working life. This love had taken the form of George's push for an independent bank that would rid the BoE of meddling politicians and allow the governor to overlord Britain's monetary system. Lawson had placed the push firmly on the political agenda and it had fallen to BoE heads to carry this through. Critics have argued, however, that his dedication to increasing the BoE's power base had gone too far, and that this had pitted George against the Chancellor of the Exchequer, Kenneth Clarke.

There had been several points where George and Clarke had clashed over the direction of Britain's monetary policy and its banking system, and George's zeal in pushing the BoE line was, by the time the Barings crisis erupted, already threatening to undermine his own credibility.

The collapse of the pound and its humiliating exit from the European exchange rate mechanism (ERM), combined with serious flaws in regulating the BCCI, compounded matters. It was often a cause for laughter that George had opposed every interest rate cut since 1962. This later proved characteristic of the careers both men. In mid-1995, official British statistics showed a slowing in economic growth which would normally point to an easing in interest rates.

However, George had opposed a rate cut during a meeting with Clarke, and the minutes of their discussions were later released. This was nothing new. Clarke believed interest rate policies should be based on month-by-month evidence, while George advocated a longer term approach, but when a central bank governor who is pushing for higher rates is openly opposed by the chancellor, the result should be a run on the pound. This did not happen, though, and the prevailing view was: 'George's views do not carry the credibility in the market that was commanded by many of his predecessors'.[10]

More importantly, it was this combination of George's desire for BoE independence, and his belief in pure market dynamics as opposed to the hitherto unquestioned worth of simply being a 'gentleman of the Bank of England', that constituted a wild card in whether, for example, a British bank could be rescued in a real crisis.

Barings was about to find out.

BARING GROUP STRUCTURE 31st DECEMBER 1992
(adopted from the BOE Report)

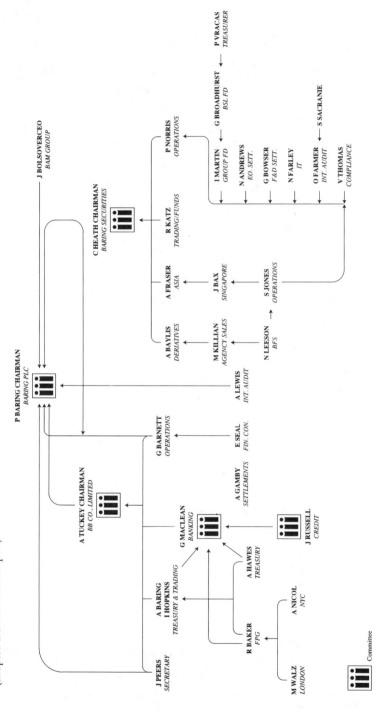

BARING GROUP STRUCTURE 31st DECEMBER 1993
(adopted from the BOE Report)

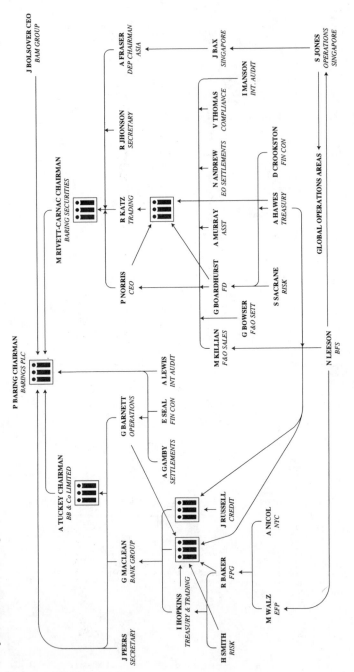

Committee

BARING GROUP STRUCTURE 24th FEBRUARY 1995
(adopted from the BOE Report)

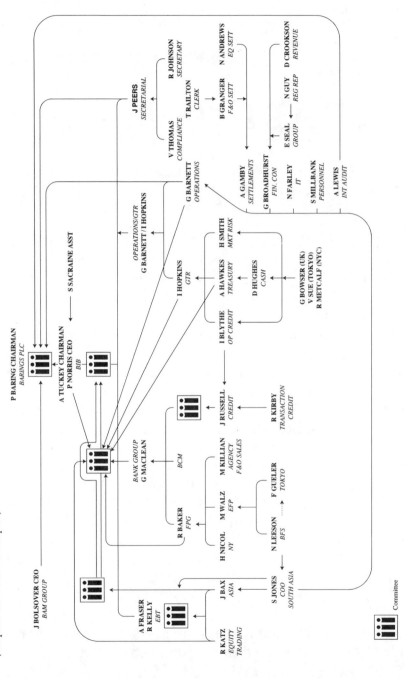

CHAPTER FIVE

HARRY'S BAR

'You sure knew when Nick was having a bad day — he could be very obnoxious. He wasn't a bully but there was certainly an amount of arrogance about him as the East End boy who had done good'. Simex trader.

The entrance to Simex is not grand. A modest gold shingle cast in grey stone and an obscure small elevator guide the trader through a narrow corridor to a tiny lobby and a reception desk which would not look out of place in a suburban doctor's surgery.

The inauspicious surroundings are in stark contrast to what takes place in the pit behind the well-guarded glass doors, where fortunes can be made and lost with the blink of an eye. Hardened attitudes and steeled nerves prevail as the deal is cut. Traders are frantic as they cut deals on behalf of clients, broking houses, banks, and between themselves. Numbers and codes career across a digital screen across the back wall of Simex, relaying the performance of various types of securities to the crowded trading floor below. Dealers cling to their telephones, one eye on the market, another on a rival, one ear for the client, and one for the pit.

Simex had a slow start. The current pit inside Number 1 Raffles Place was opened in October 1989 by Finance Minister, Dr Richard Hu, who watched volumes escalate and the value of derivatives to Singapore's economy blossom as foreign capital departed the bleak markets of Europe and the United States and arrived in the island en masse.

With it came the lifestyle.

Sipping boutique beer in one of Singapore's expensive nightspots in 1995, visitors could be forgiven for thinking they had been caught in a time warp and transported back to the 1980s. Although in most of the recession-hit developed world, the abrasive young urban professionals who characterised the 1980s had become deeply unfashionable, but in the ensuing years Asia's financial centres welcomed them with open arms and Singapore was no exception.

At its worst, the 1980s was typified as an era when wearing the wrong labels was social suicide, when yuppies with 20:20 vision made fake spectacles a fashion item, and a time when wearing pirated knock-off luxury items was better than wearing a good but non 'status' brand.

In Singapore, the best and worst of this conspicuous consumerism continued into the nineties, and in comparison with the western world the city was at an economic peak. Salaries still read like telephone numbers, yuppie traders flashed real Rolexes and drove 'Beamers' and Saabs. Loud braces and designer suits, cellular phones and expense accounts were all standard status symbols, and successful deals were celebrated with French champagne in elite restaurants, and paid for with gold corporate credit cards.

This rarefied atmosphere was promoted both on and off the trading floor. Excess and risk were words firmly entrenched in the trader's vernacular, and risk management was not a much practised concept.

By January 1993, Leeson had fashioned for himself a lifestyle which working class boys from Watford could normally only dream about. He could work hard and play hard, and do it in an exotic location. Be his own man. Be his own boss. And make lots of money doing it.

Such power and prestige ensured that Nick Leeson was well looked after by head office. The expatriate package would include provisions for a house, car, and club membership. Membership at a local country club could cost up to S$250,000, and an apartment for expat accommodation was worth around S$5,000 a month.

To actually buy a car in Singapore it is necessary to first obtain a licence, which essentially grants a person the right to own a car, and is offered through a tender process. Aimed at limiting the number of cars in the congested city-state, tender prices for a licence are linked to the state of the economy, and become a sign of economic strength or weakness. During peaks of the economic cycle a licence alone could be sold for S$80,000, the price of the car being additional to this. Leeson chose a Rover.

Even on a basic annual wage of S$50,000, an expat trader could earn a further S$200,000 through a bonus system, while the corporate cost of establishing an expat employee in Singapore could top S$500,000.

The social life of an expat was of as much importance to business as it was for the personal lives of the many who flocked to the male-dominated societies of the Far East. Doing deals in Chinese nightclubs was an accepted part of business, and meant that head offices in London, New York, Sydney, Tokyo and Frankfurt were obliged to meet the costs of occasionally questionable 'business' expenses.

While the expat clubs were full of Brits, Australians, Europeans, Canadians and Americans who mixed freely, the notable exceptions were the Chinese and, to some extent, the English who worked for Barings. In the main, these people preferred the company of their own.

Like thousands of others, Leeson was an 'angmo', a left-over nickname from the merchant sailing hey-days of Singapore when visiting caucasians were called 'angmo', meaning 'redhead'. The term can be derogatory like the Hong Kong term 'gweiloh', meaning 'white devil', and can be dependent on intent and context. The most derogatory term in the region is the acronym 'FILTH' for 'Failed In London, Try Honkers'.

Leeson was no snob, but he remained oblivious to the locals and was not much more aware of the in-house politics unfolding back at Bishopsgate — where ultimate responsibility for his dealings lay — and Heath's eventual departure from the bank. Satisfied with his results, executives were too preoccupied with the restructuring to be concerned with outposts like Singapore.

Leeson began the year with a cumulative loss of S$4.9 million hidden away in error account 88888 — this was not a good start, though the loss was trimmed somewhat back to S$4.7 million by the end of the month. Over the next six months Leeson gradually reduced losses to just S$100,000 by the end of July.[1]

Leeson's business activities were still modest, with little or no need for limits. Leeson was indirectly establishing how Barings, a relative newcomer to Simex, would conduct its business. Apart from hiding only relatively small losses and his personal exploits there was little happening on the floor that could have sounded a warning of the hazards ahead. A minor exception to this was that in early 1993, Leeson began executing orders on behalf of proprietary traders in Barings Securities Japan.

The task was assigned to Leeson as part of a cost-cutting strategy. Profits earned by Barings traders in Japan, who conducted agency business for clients such as institutions, were being hurt. Japanese clients were establishing their own logistics and execution capabilities and, in doing so, Barings' role had been diminished. To offset this, Barings traders were ignoring cautions and warnings from the banking side, and were increasing activity in proprietary trading. Initially, traders in Japan would buy baskets of shares consisting of all component stocks listed under the Nikkei 225. Simultaneously, purchases were made in Nikkei futures. These cash baskets and futures were first bought and sold as a package with real stocks acquired through the Tokyo Stock Exchange, and the futures through the Osaka Securities Exchange.

The shift in executing the orders to Simex was then made in early 1993. Simex deals were simply cheaper: deposits on margin calls at Simex were 15 per cent of the face value of a contract, compared to 30 per cent of the face value required by the Osaka Securities Exchange.[2]

For every contract Leeson acquired, a mandatory payment had to be made to the clearing house to cover adverse movements in prices on the futures market. It is a form of protection money, collateral against losses, and responsibility for its provision lies solely with the trader. Failure to meet the payments can result in a clearing house closing out a trader's position, with the trader wearing any losses.

During those first six months of modest dealings, Nick and Lisa Leeson settled into a comfortable life. Jack David (*not his real name*) and Judy Tynan and their spouses were among the first to meet and socialise with the Leesons, and the closeness of their relationships would fluctuate somewhat over the following years. There were shared holidays, cocktail parties and dinners. There were also friends like Mike Sale, and Daniel Argyropoulous, a trader with First Continental Trading (Singapore) Pte Ltd.

Work was the common bond. After a day's trading, the men would usually meet at Harry's Quayside Bar. It had become a regular haunt and a Friday night ritual for yuppie dealers and the investment community. It was an expensive watering hole frequented by a steady stream of Sarong Party Girls, commonly referred to as SPGs. The bar's close proximity to Singapore's central business district made it an ideal venue for strung-out professionals to relax in. Nick Leeson was not noted as a womaniser, though he fitted the overworked expatriate description well. Many of the women who knew Nick thought of him as oafish and sometimes tiresome. His behaviour could be boorish, particularly when he was drinking heavily, and girlfriends close to Lisa were at times concerned about Nick's treatment of his wife.

Harry's was typical of the ritzy pubs sprinkled throughout South East Asia, reflecting both the wealth and the financial prudence of Singapore. That prudence was about to pay off.

Even as Barings was collapsing, international credit agency Standard & Poor's had placed the island state on credit watch for a possible upgrade. If successful, Singapore's debt rating would rise from AA-plus to AAA and enable the nation to join the elite club of sovereign borrowers. Fewer than a dozen countries enjoy the agency's top rating which effectively allows nations to borrow long-term funds at the world's cheapest rates.

Sovereign borrowers include Britain, the Netherlands, Germany, France and the United States. In the Asia-Pacific region only Japan holds the top rating. Australia once held the elusive AAA grade but had been downgraded several years earlier to AA after high debt levels were amassed to meet government spending commitments.

Between 1988 and 1994 Singapore had boasted an average annual growth rate of 8.4 per cent, and had achieved the highest standard of living in Asia outside Japan. Surpluses of between 6.0 per cent and 11 per cent of Gross Domestic Product (GDP) had lead to a steady accumulation of government assets, although the full extent of those assets remain a closely guarded secret. Current account surpluses had boosted foreign exchange reserves to an all time high of $58 billion. Any nation with a savings rate of 48.9 per cent of GDP is entitled to regard itself as rich, and Singapore did.

The government wanted the top-notch rating desperately. Old hands in the government and bureaucracy had spent years steering the country from the third world doldrums, through an era of rapid development towards first world status. To be on par with and treated with the same respect as a western nation was no longer an elusive dream.

Harry's Bar was the antithesis of Singapore's by-gone days when merchant sailors dominated the foreigners who haunted the brothels and late night strip clubs along Bugis Street. Cheap booze and cheap sex set in a tropical climate amid an exotic culture represented for many the allure of the Far East in those days when Singapore was establishing itself

as a strategic centrepoint for international trade and a
lucrative colonial outpost for London. The traditional culture of Singapore had as much in common with Bishopsgate,
as did the Leesons with the Queen Mum. Old hands are
always wary of young traders out to make their mark in an
intoxicating atmosphere known to nourish egos.

With its teal blue and white terraced facade, Harry's is
decorated with elegant cane furniture and ceiling fans. A
bottle of Moet et Chandon Vintage costs S$150, an Austra-
lian Rosemount Estate Cabernet Sauvignon will fetch S$50
and Sauvignon-Blanc Montana from New Zealand is worth
S$46 a bottle. Patrons spill out of the bar and across the wide
pavement onto a canopied al fresco area with chairs and
tables on the waterfront. Inside, jazz musicians jam while the
SPGs flirt with businessman.

Nick could be found perched at the top end of the bar on
most nights, at times drinking with such friends as Jack
David and Daniel Argyropoulous. Leeson was a beer drinker
by preference, and had made Heineken his brand in Singapore. But as he got to know the city, he developed a taste for
the seedier places.

David noticed these tendencies and where he would
prefer to have a few beers after work before calling it a night,
Nick would follow this by heading off for Top 10, Caesars,
Genevieves, or 392. He loved a beer and a chat and
gravitated towards men who shared his main interests: beer
and football. 'He would go out drinking every night with the
people who worked for him', David said. 'A love of soccer
and the ability to drink all night were prerequisites to being
Nick's mate. He was a real Jack the Lad who would drink
anything that was put in front of him. And the more he
drank, the thicker his [Watford] accent became'.

Asked if Nick discussed topics such as politics, David
said: 'He wasn't that deep. Nick is a very simple guy. He just
liked sitting at the pub. His friends are very basic, blue-collar
people. He wasn't flashy but at times he was certainly very
aware that "money people" looked up to him'.

Leeson's generosity ensured he suffered no shortage of drinking partners. Jim Gelpi, a former part owner of Harry's Bar, remembers Nick as a man who became a 'mover and shaker' and agreed with David's sentiments, saying Leeson had remained 'basically a normal guy'.

'One thing I do remember about him was that he would always hand his Barings corporate gold American Express card over the bar at the beginning of the night, everyone would put their drinks on his tab, and at the end of the evening he'd pay with cash,' he said.

Gelpi, an American, has lived in South East Asia on and off for 20 years, working initially as a civilian for telephone company ITT during the Vietnam War, followed by a variety of other positions. He is protective of most of the traders — invariably young, single men — who would retreat to Harry's to unwind and dissect the day's trading activities. He said it is a fallacy that every trader in Singapore drives a Porsche, as is often thought. 'These guys are generally not obnoxious people; they are pretty down to earth. All they need is a bad day to knock them down a couple of pegs', he said.

Mary Bell, a Singapore family therapist who works mostly with expatriates, agreed: 'They really are just kids . . . When they are all together at Harry's Pub, it seems like they are a universe to themselves'.[3]

Gelpi recalled that he had once warned Leeson that everyone was putting their drinks on his tab, abusing his inordinate generosity. 'He said that was fine, that I shouldn't worry', Gelpi said. The perception of Leeson as a market mover was gaining momentum by the middle of 1993 — an image underpinned by Leeson's ability to spend. It was also at this stage that Leeson began another lie. He needed an effective cover to justify the rising trades that were being undertaken not at a client's behest but his own. Leeson began telling people at work and at social functions that he had stolen a big customer from a rival investment house during a business lunch at Raffles. 'He always said that the customer wouldn't speak to anyone but him — it was a great cover-up,' David said.

The talk became a convenience, and was not openly bragged about but slowly cultivated. As Leeson's experience as a trader was in its formative stages, so was the development of his personality. In many innocent ways, Leeson was a paradox. He was careful, for example, about concealing his Watford accent, but this facade slipped with the confidence he gained from his drinking and, while he was beginning to dictate the market, he was not considered by Gelpi to be a natural leader.

'With some of the groups of traders that come in here, you can easily tell who the leader is. But with his group, I couldn't tell. Leeson wouldn't sit in the middle or anything like that, but he always paid for his group's drinks. If there were five of them, they'd easily go through S$200 in two hours ... They were probably going over every little trade that they did during the day. Leeson was a mover and a shaker so the guys stuck close to him', Gelpi said.

It was on the frantic trading floor of Simex that Leeson became known as a market maker, an enviable title reserved for the best in his field. The top guns set prices and others followed, and in so doing the market makers dictated profits and losses.

A former colleague said: 'Leeson was one of the first three market makers in Singapore. He was very good at what he did as far as the back office was concerned'.

Fellow traders were not his only admirers.

'Nick was a kind of boy wonder as far as [Simex] was concerned', David said. This was more a reference to Leeson's growing ability to move markets and take on big orders. As long as margin call payments were being met, there was no desire by Simex to query the astounding growth rates coming from Barings' corner of the pit. This argument would later receive some support from Singapore investigators who found that Simex 'may not have been sufficiently sensitive to the risks associated with the very large volume of business transacted by BFS'.[4]

'Singapore bought a lot of prospects for a lot of people. It is a place which is thirsty for excellence and having the best of the west, so they hold out open arms to anyone with expertise, and Nick certainly had a level of expertise', David explained.

By all accounts, Nick Leeson enjoyed his lifestyle in Singapore and in the early stages so did Lisa, before her homesickness became more pronounced. It was a lot of fun. 'He liked it here', David said. 'Nick once said Barings had been keen to send him to Hong Kong but that he'd refused because he was happy in Singapore'.

Expats on the right package can live very comfortably. 'It's a great life. When I die, I'd like be reincarnated as an expat's wife', David said.

The Leesons' first apartment was off Sixth Avenue and considered quite ordinary. Friends estimated they paid about S$3,500 a month, a modest sum by Singapore standards. There they would often have dinner parties and serve solid English dishes such as shepherd's pie, or bangers and mash.

Typically, the couple would rise at 6:00 am and while Nick worked, Lisa would potter around their flat and spend the remainder of her day meeting friends. She worked occasionally in a local kindergarten and, because Lisa was a former Barings employee, she would sometimes help out with clerical duties on a voluntary basis. [There has been, however, no imputation linking these occasional tasks with her husband's trading activities.]

On Saturdays, Nick would play soccer for Barings or one of the local teams, usually the Admiralty Club. While he may

have been the striker at Parmiter's, and cut a fine figure in
the pit, Nick usually found himself outplayed by the more
agile Singaporeans. A fellow sportsman noted that Leeson
would arrive at training sessions in a taxi — a stark contrast
to his teammates, who preferred to make an entrance in their
latest Porsche or BMW. The Rover was more trouble than it
was worth, and it was eventually sold. Leeson also played the
odd game of golf, but without demonstrating very much skill
— the week before the collapse, he played one of his best
rounds ever, shooting 145 [!].

Singapore is an easy place to live. The streets are manicured
and clean, and set among endless lush tropical gardens. The
sultry climate forces the inhabitants to operate at a slower
pace. There are no obvious signs of poverty, street crime is
unheard of, and the western drug culture has had little
impact. Chewing gum is forbidden, and graffiti is punishable
by the cane, but it is possible to walk down virtually any
street without fear. Unlike other Asian countries, the water
can be drunk straight from the tap and supermarkets stock
fresh supplies of meat, fruit, dairy produce and vegetables,
much of it flown in from Australia. These commodities can
be expensive, but were easily affordable to the Leesons.
Lounging around the Leesons' flat, you could really be
anywhere in the western world. Anywhere suburban with
middle-class affluence and a conservative feel. The Leesons
had access to *Baring Up*, a small company boat, though
David notes that Leeson was not the type to sail out into
Singapore Harbour. Occasionally a client might use it, but
Nick was a beer and football man. There were, however, trips
to Thailand, neighbouring Malaysia, and islands in Indonesia, and if the homesickness became too much to bear, it was
always possible, and affordable, to head back to London.

Lisa could shop in the world's most exclusive stores along
Orchard Road and stroll through endless arcades, while Nick

began work at about 8:00 am and was often gone by 2:15 pm. He would then split his time between the back offices on the 24th floor — a number shunned by the Chinese for its unluckiness — and the trading offices on the 14th floor in Ocean Towers.

After the collapse and while Barings' assets were disposed of, the Leesons' public relations machine would move into overdrive, with Lisa attempting to convince the world the couple had led a 'normal lifestyle' in Singapore.

In one interview she told *The London Sunday Telegraph*: 'All this stuff about yachts and champagne and wild tequila parties is fantasy. I don't even like tequila'. However, David and others scoff at such suggestions. There was growing concern that the Leesons' marriage may have been in trouble, speculation prompted in part by Nick's drinking. But David echoed the feelings of many. He noted: 'Lisa was no wallflower. She was a great girl who loved a party. She nearly got me into a fight once at The Hard Rock Cafe after she had agreed to dance with some sailors. When they wouldn't stop hanging around us and I told them to get lost, there was a bit of push and shove'.

Another friend tells of a night out with the Leesons during which Lisa sang karaoke upstairs while Nick watched in horror as his wife's woeful rendition was televised in the downstairs part of the pub, where he was sitting with friends.

'I'll never forget the look on Nick's face while he was watching Lisa singing while she was blind drunk', she said.

Indeed, Leeson's friends in Singapore remember wild parties and decadent times when they reminisce about The Leeson Years. 'One night Nick was dancing on a table at The Hard Rock Cafe, wobbling back and forward, when he fell off and landed on his head', David said, recalling the incident as a metaphor for Leeson's ability to bounce back after a fall at Simex. 'We were all standing around, thinking that he'd broken his neck, when he got back up and ordered another beer'.

Leeson's name for partying after work was as legendary as his reputation on the trading floor. But his preferences for all-night drinking binges resulted in Nick and David drifting apart. David is not British, does not like soccer and preferred restaurants to drinking holes. When he started there were few expats working the Simex floor and the pair took to each other simply because they were caucasians working the same pit in an Asian environment. As Simex and Barings grew, and the Leesons met more people, the number of opportunities for Leeson to go out drinking with like-minded souls also increased, and he and David began going their separate ways.

'Nick wanted to hang out with British people — his own kind — and drink every night', David said. 'Nick was definitely a man's man. He liked to hang out with the guys. But I wouldn't consider him a womaniser by any stretch of the imagination'.

'Often Nick would be out drinking until 5.00 am or 6.00 am. I can't remember how many times I saw Lisa meet Nick outside the front of the exchange building early in the morning with a fresh shirt and tie after he'd been out drinking all night. They were probably the same mornings I'd hear Nick throwing his guts up in the toilets at Simex'.

However, one incident did upset David and, with hindsight, should have served as an indication of things to come. As Leeson's confidence developed, David was increasingly put off by his behaviour. Leeson often would not answer people in the pit. He was not afraid to use his six-foot frame to intimidate traders with slighter builds.

'You sure knew when Nick was having a bad day — he could be very obnoxious', David said. 'He wasn't a bully but there was certainly an amount of arrogance about him as the East End boy who had done good'.

In trading, the client is all important, and at times other traders can be both rivals and customers. When David attempted to do a deal with Leeson as a customer, Leeson virtually ignored him, and shut him out of the market. This reaction raised enough concern to warrant David warning

Leeson's superiors that there was an attitude problem. It was also one of the first signs that Leeson's concentration at work was geared more towards proprietary trading and his developing unauthorised positions, than towards carrying out the tasks to which he was assigned.

'Some liked him and some didn't. A lot of people had little respect for him', David said. 'Nick had an obvious irreverence for the customer. He ran two traders out of town — they can't make a living anymore'.

The Leesons enjoyed the high life that had evaded them at home, but homesickness was becoming a problem for Lisa, and Nick had begun displaying the occasional sign that had his more observant friends and colleagues wondering just how well he was adjusting to life in Singapore.

Zulkifflie Ariffin is one of the longest serving bartenders at Harry's. He watched as Leeson frequented the bar about three times a week for drinking sessions with colleagues which usually lasted up to four hours. 'He'd normally hang out at the head of the bar, near the cashier', Ariffin said. 'He was just a normal customer'.

But Ariffin recalls that Leeson had his moments of oddness, some might say eccentricity: 'One particularly hot night, Leeson left Harry's at about midnight and then returned at about 1:30 am dressed in a European overcoat and a scarf. I remember thinking that that was pretty weird'.

Strutting down the stony path of a tropical quay rugged up for a British winter is certain to raise a few eyebrows, but another matter that raised the occasional eyebrow was the 'discovery' that Nick Leeson was married. The impression to the contrary probably arose in consequence of his apparently limitless capacity for a boys' night out, but many simply assumed that he was single. Except to a few, Lisa's name was rarely mentioned, and she rarely accompanied Nick on his nights out. A number of sources said Lisa was often left home alone. Gelpi said he never once saw Leeson with his wife. 'I didn't even know that he was married', he said. 'Most of the traders don't bring their wives or girlfriends here. They all act like single guys'.

David was blunt: 'He liked Lisa to be his wife, to have his dinner on the table when he wanted it, and to only speak when spoken to. He said that she had to understand that he had to [go out drinking to] entertain clients as part of his job'.

Nick's fellow traders were not the only ones to fall foul of Leeson's obnoxious behaviour. In October 1993, the Singapore Cricket Club banned him for a year following an ugly incident for which he later apologised. Leeson and his friends had again been drinking heavily and decided to play some snooker at the club. Leeson became upset when staff at the club failed to recognise him and asked him to produce his membership card. He became abusive and when a member of the billiards committee confronted the three, he was called a 'f**king black bastard'.[5] The racial slurs continued into the evening until he departed. He was followed and a scuffle broke out. Punches were thrown.[6]

'Leeson and his mates were very rowdy, very unruly, they were shouting, laughing, using vulgarities and making racial remarks', the member said. 'I did not expect such behaviour from a guy like Leeson. I would have expected better from him. Being a member of the cricket club as well, it was really not right'.[7]

Nick Leeson may have shocked and offended people in Singapore but, as far as the Barings bosses in London were concerned, he was beyond reproach. Bank executives were delighted with the profits from Singapore. In 1993, Barings Futures accounted for 20 per cent of the bank's overall profit. Sir Peter offered: 'Derivatives need to be well controlled and understood, but we believe we do that well here'.

Around this time, talk began to intensify that Leeson with his rising trades had booked himself a big client. In fact, for the traders who regularly talked and socialised together, the mysterious investor became known as the Big Client. As far as London was concerned, Leeson was a young man on the rise in Singapore, a developing place with limited influence and altogether a relatively small Barings outpost. But gradually Leeson's contributions to the bank's bottom line rose, and with it his power, and the remaining control over the Singapore operations which were exercised by Tokyo, where orders were taken, began shifting subtly to London.

As the restructuring continued after Heath's resignation, it was decided to increase Ron Baker's responsibilities, and he was eventually made head of the Financial Products Group (FPG). In the last quarter of calendar 1993, Baker made several trips to Tokyo, Osaka and Hong Kong to gain an understanding of the businesses he was going to run. He had been told that Leeson's operations were essentially an execution service for orders undertaken in Japan for Barings clients, along with some proprietary trading. Baker was pleased. He had heard of Leeson's abilities, and was slowly discovering the significant contribution to profits arising from the fledgling Simex/OSE arbitraging business. It was thought that derivatives had suffered from a 'lack of leadership', and Baker was to provide this.

On the second of November, Peter Norris issued a letter formalising the newly created positions under the matrix system. Simon Jones became a director of operations for southern and western Asia with 'specific responsibilities for operations in offices in Singapore, Kuala Lumpur, Bangkok and Jakarta'.[8] As regional managing director, James Bax assumed responsibility for operations within Asia. Under this format, Leeson reported to Ron Baker as part of FPG.

At a personal level, Jack David said Baker 'kind of took Nick on because everyone thought he was going so well'.

'Barings Singapore was confronting a big dilemma in house. Ron Baker came up from Bankers Trust and changed it all and canned some people in Tokyo on the sales side,' David said.

Towards the second half of 1993, Sir Peter and his deputy were satisfied with the adjustments made with the group restructuring to date. When the chairman stopped by

Threadneedle Street for a cup of tea and a chat with the BoE's executive director of supervision, Brian Quinn, it was technically an official meeting between two bankers on the state of the industry and the state of Barings and its finances, but was essentially really an informal talk over a cuppa between two colleagues from the same old boys' network.

Sir Peter was in a bouyant mood and, content with the bank's prospects, he told Quinn that the bank was making solid profits and that the crisis within the securities division had been resolved. With the benefit of hindsight, his conclusion appears simplistic. Notes recording the meeting would indicate Sir Peter's sentiment that 'recovery in profitability had been amazing, leaving Barings to conclude it was actually not terribly difficult to make money in the securities business'.[9]

It had indeed been a good year for Barings, and the bank appeared to be reclaiming the ground once lost to the Americans. Barings retained profits after tax had surged to stg54.299 million for the 12 months to 31 December, compared with just stg1.867 million in the previous corresponding period. More telling were the bonuses. In that year American investment houses, like most others, had performed so poorly that they were forced to slash their bonus payments by about 30 per cent. At Barings, profit sharing more than trebled. Bonus payments rose to stg5.0 million from stg1.53 million. Nick Leeson picked up a handy stg130,000 — on Ron Baker's recommendation.

Had Sir Peter, Quinn, or Baker gained access to the 88888 error account, they would have been stunned.

By the end of December, losses stood at S$57.7 million. [10]

CHAPTER SIX

NOT REAL MONEY

'Stupid as it may sound, none of this is really real money. It's not as if you have cash sitting in front of you'. Nick Leeson.[1]

Nick Leeson began 1994 as one of a small number of brash leading traders of Singapore. Four months later he would emerge from the pit as the cock-sure maestro of Simex, self-confident to the point where he had his e-mail password changed to Superman.[2]

For bond traders, the early months of that year had been abysmal. The previous years had been a period of consolidation after recession and had been, as politicians referred to it, an era of sustainable growth where inflation and interest rates were kept in check. Inflation's savage ability to erode real wages and undermine the value of currencies has proved a constant presence in international financial markets.

Politicians entered the new year optimistically. The economy was going full circle, and rising growth prospects held the promise of reduced unemployment. In response, the markets began factoring in an interest rate rise on expectations that central banks would mount a pre-emptive strike on inflation before it could emerge. But politicians and banks alike hesitated, for fear that an interest rate rise would stymie the tentative economic recovery. Official short-term interest rate rises had been rare since 1989, and the resolve to deal with the negative fall-out of such a move was relatively untested. Bond traders had pushed yields higher but had been caught out and the market went into a state of flux. The US Federal Reserve eventually acted on February 4, raising interest rates by a quarter of a percentage point. Central banks elsewhere followed suit but this was not enough to quell the inflationary fears that had gripped the markets. The state of flux became a state of chaos, and eventually bond markets in the US, Europe and Asia spread the turmoil into stock and foreign exchange markets. Politicians reluctantly succumbed to market forces, and interest rates were pushed higher.

In early March, long-term bond yields in Australia had struck an eight-month high, and in Japan bond prices had also collapsed and pushed yields to a six-month peak. On Wall Street, the bond market was described as 'a blood bath'; another economist had dubbed the situation 'a world-wide margin' call and there was speculation that hedge funds were manipulating the market after arbitrageurs began shifting massive positions in and out of futures and across real markets. This prompted a joint investigation by the Federal Reserve and the Bank of England. Many believed bonds had been oversold but, after finding their nerve, politicians and bankers were confronting inflationary prospects head-on. This was highlighted by Federal Reserve chairman Dr Alan Greenspan, who declined to rule out further interest rate rises, sparking another round of selling, with plummeting prices triggering program selling.

Program selling can create its own headaches. Used extensively in the US, it is essentially a computer-controlled selling mechanism widely used by huge investment funds holding portfolios of stocks and bonds. When an index breaches a technical barrier, computer-activated selling takes over and automatically begins dumping specified amounts of securities onto the market, a move which can exacerbate falls and sometimes defy logic.

One volatile wave followed another to the point where the Federal Reserve mounted an extraordinary intervention and began buying bonds in an attempt to cap rising long-term interest rates in the marketplace. By April, the Federal Reserve had lifted official interest rates twice more, and central banks around the world had more or less followed.

Finally, market fears surrounding inflation subsided, and traders were left to count their costs from a battered market.

Everybody lost money — banks, institutions, hedge funds, brokers, companies, small investors and big investors alike, fund managers — everybody in every country with a dollar linked to a financial market lost money. Everyone except Nick Leeson.

Publicly, Leeson was claiming victory over the market forces which had eradicated some colleagues and left the remainder to lick their wounds and consolidate before tackling another day. The reality was starkly different. By the end of January, losses stashed away in error account 88888 had more than doubled from the previous month to S$131.5 million, and then ballooned to S$166.7 million in February as the full impact of the bond market turbulence began to strike.

Like everybody else, Leeson had worked furiously during this time and had managed to whittle back his losses to S$107.1 million by March.[3] This was an extraordinary embarrassment. The damage was done but Leeson held out, confident in his own ability and a well developed reputation that he would be able to turn the situation around.

By May, the full extent of the crisis in the bond market and overlap effects in stocks and futures were reflected in error account 88888. It held cumulative losses of S$217.3 million.[4] Leeson was also able to impress his bosses by claiming that exposures to the bond market had been limited though his own prudence.

During this tumultuous time, the frequency of traders' visits to Harry's Bar no doubt increased. Traders would gather and compare notes of the nightmare losses they had suffered. These scenes were repeated later as they wandered over to fashionable nightclubs such as Studebaker's, Fabrices, and Zukes. An alternative was No. 5, a stucco-walled pub off Orchard Road in the older part of the city where the fledgling arts community thrives. There, they would drink and hear whispers that Leeson had, incredibly, defied the markets, turning a loss-making situation into profits. His reputation scored him a spot on the pages of the Asian edition of *Futures and Options World* — within his industry, Leeson was emerging as a bona fide international top gun.

Jack David may have been annoyed by Leeson's disdain for the client, but he was mesmerised by his performance. While others, including himself, were hurting, Leeson would stroll into work undaunted by the greatest market crisis since the stock market crash of 1987. David watched as Leeson built a largely autonomous empire. American traders referred to Nick as 'the nuts man', meaning he was the best.

'Every other firm on the floor lost money', said David. 'The scope of what happened is immense; just a masterpiece. He would just put trades in different places. I don't know how he lived with himself every day. Nick got them [Barings executives in London] so confused that they didn't want to hear about it'.

As Leeson's paper profits rose, so did his stature and power. The more money he made, the more difficult it became for Bishopsgate to justify removing him from either settlement or transactions. With improved profits from Singapore, and Leeson apparently competently in charge, Bishopsgate was content, and with unhindered access to account 88888, Leeson was content also. Few, if any, in Bishopsgate had any real understanding of derivatives or risk management, and there can be little doubting that Leeson's presence in Singapore ensured many of his superiors a good night's sleep.

Evidence later given to the BoE inquiry into the collapse of the bank confirmed that Leeson, in light of his perceived high levels of profitability, was afforded much leeway by Barings' upper echelons. 'Leeson was his [Ron Baker's] star trader; he did not want him roughed up', said Ian Hopkins, Barings Head of Group Treasury and Risk. Head of Global Equity Broking and Trading Andrew Fraser added: 'Insofar as one had a feeling about him [it was]: For God's sake, don't interfere'.[5]

Ron Baker knew Leeson had been treated with kid gloves. 'I thought Nick was a lone star and did his own thing at the time', Baker said[6]. He added that he had received orders from James Bax that if there were issues to be taken up with Leeson, Bax would handle it himself. The head of proprietary equity and derivatives trading for Barings in Japan, Fernando Gueler, said: 'Because he was so trusted, he was regarded as almost a miracle worker. He had a lot of free rein to do what he had to do'.[7]

Confusion over who handled Leeson was compounded by the restructuring that was taking place back at home, which allowed Leeson to milk the bedlam surrounding his superiors, and enabled him to bluff his way through, without directly answering to anyone.

Ron Baker's description of the period highlighted this: 'There was a lot of ambiguity about where Nick sat during 1994 . . . De facto without knowing it, I inherited the income stream and the trading strategy that Nick was pursuing from 1 January 1994 . . . I did not feel that Nick reported to me or that I had any real organisational control over him until the second half of 1994'.[8]

With her stockbroking background, Lisa Leeson must have been aware to some extent of the prevailing situation in the bond markets, though it is doubtful whether she could have had any idea of the true extent of her husband's portfolio. She was in England when the bonus from the previous year arrived, and immediately set out on an investment splurge. A flat was acquired in Blackheath and a second purchase followed as part of a plan to rent one and pay the mortgage off on the other. Nick asked her to pay stg25,000 for a membership and share of a golf club near where the couple had married, and Lisa obliged. She believed Nick had earned the right to indulge himself a little.

Holidays followed in Hong Kong, Thailand, Malaysia and Vietnam, and Nick often spoke to friends about his first major investments at home. Trips to Singapore were organised for members of their families, and the bonus was soon followed by a rise in basic annual salary from stg28,000 to stg50,000. Nick Leeson's monthly rental allowance also rose, to stg2000 from stg500.

The increased salary and rental subsidy meant Nick and Lisa could move to a more upmarket flat. The couple rented a condominium at Anguella View costing S$4000 a month. Lisa has said that she and Nick enjoyed a 'lovely' but not overly extravagant lifestyle in Singapore. Their idea of real indulgence was being able to pay for one of their brothers or sisters to visit them in Singapore, Lisa said.

The Leeson's fifth floor apartment was in the neighbourhood of plush Orchard Road, and the couple hired a part-time maid. Nearby apartment blocks include Anguella Park, Anguella Mansion, Skyline Anguella and the more salubrious Anguella Heights. Set on neatly manicured grounds, the Leeson's three-bedroom Anguella View apartment was modern but not ostentatious, and came furnished with bamboo furniture.

The block itself had mainly Japanese occupants. Neighbour Christine Sampang told the Associated Press the Leesons were a nice young couple: 'There seemed nothing unusual about them'. On the back lawns of the apartment complex was a swimming pool and an ever-present security guard who kept an eye on who came or left, not a very taxing task in Singapore with its extremely low crime rates.

There had been offers for Nick to accept new postings in Barings' offices in Hong Kong and in Brazil. Both were turned down. In reality, it would have been impossible for the Leesons to move until the slate of the hidden error account was wiped clean, and sufficient documentation created to satisfy any inconvenient queries which might arise after they left.

Barings was not the only bank duped into being impressed by Leeson's abilities. According to a report in *Time* magazine, another firm had considered poaching him in late

1994, but had been talked out of the move by a corporate headhunter. The sticking point was neither Leeson's background nor his performance. The headhunter just 'didn't trust him'. His report apparently described Leeson as 'very bright but it might be quickness without an underlying depth ... After you have Leeson for six months he might hold you up for a bigger package'.[9]

Jack David confirmed that Leeson had bragged about other companies attempting to lure him away from Barings. 'He spoke of other firms trying to poach him, that he'd been offered this or that', David said. 'He was very confident. I wouldn't be at all surprised if people were approaching him'.

At Bishopsgate, the management overhaul was finally settling into place by mid-1994. In August, Ian Hopkins became head of a new department dealing with group treasury and risk. Tony Hawes headed treasury, market risk was under the control of Helen Smith, and operational credit was attended to by Iain Blyth. Responsibility for transaction credit remained with the Bank Group and Blyth also reported to Barings director Johnnie Russell, who was also the director of credit exposure management of the new Barings Investment Bank (BIB). Risk controllers in Tokyo, Hong Kong and New York continued to answer to Hopkins.

Broadhurst, the previous Group Finance Director of Barings Securities Ltd, became responsible for finance and accounting within BIB. His new role encompassed Group reporting, regulatory reporting, and revenue reporting.

Tony Gamby took control of futures, options and equities settlements, having previously held the title of Settlements Director of BIB. Gamby had three settlements units in London reporting directly to him. However, the Bank of England's eventual inquiry into the collapse of the bank encountered 'some confusion over [Brenda] Granger's [Manager of Futures and Options Settlements, BIB] reporting lines in the derivatives settlements area'.[10] Bill Hawes told investigators that although there had been an organisational chart showing Granger reporting to him, 'I would say that

Brenda Granger reported more to Tony Gamby than myself, directly'.[11]

Nick Farley, the previous Head of Information Technology of Barings Securities Ltd, became the new head of a combined IT department. Farley told the BoE inquiry that he reported to Norris prior to the formation of BIB and to Barnett after the restructure, although he pointed out: 'I was not closely supervised by Geoffrey Barnett . . . [he] was more involved with the London operation and tended to spend less time focussing on operations overseas'.[12]

Ron Baker was responsible to Maclean after having previously reported to Hopkins while Ash Lewis, Head of Internal Audit, Barings Plc, and Assistant Director of Barings Brothers & Co (BB&Co), was appointed BIB Group Internal Auditor.

At the time of the collapse, Nick Leeson reported as part of FPG to Ron Baker. He spoke regularly with Walz and Gueler to discuss his day-to-day trading activities, and reported on operational matters related to Barings Futures Singapore to Bax and Jones.

However, when interviewed later by the Bank of England's investigative team, both Bax and Jones said they had not considered themselves operationally responsible for Leeson.[13]

For his part, Bax was never entirely happy with the situation which allowed Leeson to police his own work. But Bax was in a difficult situation, as Leeson had long had a free rein in his dealings. Bax was a nominal director, as was Leeson, of Barings Futures, making him also responsible under Singapore laws for the group's operations. Singapore law also requires directors to live locally.

Directly above Baker was George Maclean, Peter Norris, Andrew Tuckey and, ultimately, Sir Peter Baring.

As Baker gradually assumed control for the derivatives side, it was decided that he should take a tour of the operations in Singapore, Tokyo and Hong Kong. It was Baker's first trip to Singapore and his second meeting with

Nick Leeson. After a day with him in the Simex pit, and another day going through presentations of Leeson's activities, Baker concluded that it would be difficult for anyone to judge how the operations were being conducted or to evaluate the information flow. He was prepared to rely on those at the shop-floor level for advice. Leeson's hand at turning a profit was enough justification to maintain the status quo, and his cosy position in Singapore meant his local power base was strong and in need of no alteration.

Placating his staff was easy. Leeson dominated them. Barings' bonus system was linked to individual achievements rather than the collective performance of a business unit, and Leeson was a generous boss who believed in looking after his colleagues. He was able to rely heavily on compliant and generously-compensated backroom staff who unwittingly helped him cover his tracks simply by not interfering. For the 1993 financial year, the 18 or so traders and backroom staff who worked under Leeson controlled operations were awarded with bonuses equivalent to 13 months' salary, according to the Bank of England inquiry.

Others thought this might have been even higher. According to Jack David: 'His staff received bonuses equal to anything from 48 to 60 months' pay. Nick had complete loyalty from the people who worked under him. They were good friends to him'.

To everybody except Leeson, who knew the truth, Singapore was a success story with a reputation rising constantly. Those working for Barings in the Ocean Towers building in Singapore's central business district benefited richly. Leeson was their hero and together they were the market maker. In September 1994, Barings Securities Singapore was awarded the title 'Number One Volume House' by Simex management at an annual dinner. It was the tenth anniversary of Simex's creation, and Leeson was out that night for another party and another opportunity to show off, although this time it was an official affair. Singapore's long serving prime minister Lee Kuan Yew was present, and the occasion had a serious air. David recalled: 'After the Simex 10th anniversary dinner, Nick spent S$12,000 on Krug champagne at Studebaker's for friends, colleagues and customers'. Leeson had reached the pinnacle of his career. He was the Number One trader in the Simex pit.

His generosity that night was certainly extravagant but not unusual to those close to him. He drank with his staff after working hours, socialised with them on weekends, and is believed to have sent a fax soon after his disappearance from Singapore apologising that he could not celebrate his 28th birthday with them. But by that stage, a lynch party and then a wake were the only items on the social agenda.

Barings executives in London had ignored Bax's warning letter of two years earlier, but there remained the question of whether high profits, in the order of stg20 million in the previous year, indicated any breach of law or excessive risk-taking. Barings executives began a review of the situation.

A full audit of Barings Futures operations in Singapore was undertaken over July and August of 1994. The first was done internally by the bank's internal audit team under Ash Lewis and Ian Manson, the second was an external audit whereby the bank's auditors, Coopers & Lybrand, scrutinised activities in Singapore through the course of normal annual audits.

During the planning stage for the internal audit, which covered the South East Asian activities of the securities division, there were claims that London had run into a brick wall when trying to establish an open line of communication with Singapore. Simon Jones was considered 'a very parochial individual' who had not favoured a working relationship between London and Singapore, preferring his patch to be left alone. This sentiment had developed fiercely as profits climbed and bolstered the in-house political clout that Singapore carried.

There were other side-issues. Jones was offside with Group Finance Director Geoffrey Broadhurst, and Broadhurst wanted Jones sacked. Discussions over Jones's removal were held with Bax, and while the audit team knew about the situation, it was told that any conflict between Broadhurst and Jones should not influence their findings. Meanwhile, Ash Lewis believed Leeson was probably doing back-office work but claimed she had no idea that he was actually responsible for it.

This was the first internal audit of the securities unit. The Barings' banking unit had an established internal audit department in the early 1980s with a comprehensive staff of 12. In was different story in securities, where lax attitudes towards risk management had delayed the formation of an internal audit unit until the end of 1992. Just three people were sent to probe the operations of Barings Futures in Singapore.

On their arrival, discussions were held with Leeson and Jones. Jones had proved himself reasonable and 'not quite the awkward customer' the audit team had expected. Meanwhile, Leeson made himself available to James Baker for interviews focussing mainly on profits.

Baker was responsible for the bulk of the Singapore audit, though his task included a series of interviews with staffers elsewhere in the group. Baker initially found that there were concerns about Leeson's combined agency and trading role, and that this might contravene local rules. It was also expressed that Leeson wielded 'too much power and influence'.[14] Baker also noted: 'We had to consider the segregation of duties there, look for ourselves and draw our own conclusions. I was left in no doubt that that was an issue'.[15]

Tony Hawes had cited futures as a major concern, and argued that Leeson was too dominant, pointing out that there was no deputy to challenge him. Underpinning his list of grievances was the vast amounts of money involved in a very fast and complicated market. Hawes had reached his own conclusions that Jones had basically left Leeson to his own devices and, while there had been no evidence to suggest that Leeson abused his position, there might have been the potential for doing so.

Without appreciating its magnitude, Hawes had nevertheless successfully identified the problem. He realised that Leeson's controlling both front and back offices had the potential for disaster, and noted this breach of standard procedure.

Unreconciled accounts surfaced en masse. When a margin call payment was made through the bank's clearing house, Citibank, there was not always sufficient funds in Singapore to make up the difference, so London received the request and duly made top-up payments, often at short notice, and debited from various client accounts. Leeson deliberately did not say whether these payments were on behalf of the actual client or for house trading, the extent of which Leeson continued to report as minimal. The size of the hidden portfolio compared with the overall worth of the bank remained of a scale which allowed Leeson to sufficiently fudge the paper work.

A draft recommendation was put by James Baker to Leeson that a weekly reconciliation procedure, indicating exactly to whom all margin payments were made, and what accounts they were being paid on behalf of, be introduced as soon as possible. This would enable London to keep a closer eye on margin payments. Obviously, there was a tremendous risk that this would expose error account 88888 and the systematic fraud which was occurring. Leeson was obstinate. He vehemently argued that implementing such a control was unnecessary and was 'unduly burdensome'.

Baker took a second shot and suggested that a reconciliation procedure could be done monthly, but Leeson was not to be budged. More arguments followed, with Baker enlisting support from Geoffrey Broadhurst who had joined the team in Singapore towards the end of its audit in August. Leeson's power was now so well entrenched that he could dismiss the very reasonable recommendation of an auditor and the Group Finance Director with unnerving ease, and the subject was finally dropped.

This marked the passing of perhaps the last opportunity to impose some sort of compliance requirements on Leeson, and with it, the last opportunity to avert the bank's eventual collapse.

All-important profits continued to cloud good judgement. There was a real fear that if Leeson was upset too much, he might succumb to an alternative offer and be poached by a rival firm. In an ironic twist, it was found that if such a scenario eventuated, the loss of Leeson would 'greatly speed' an erosion of Barings' supposed profitability.

As with most reports, the internal auditors stated the obvious. In Barings' case, the obvious concerns about Leeson's extraordinary power had by now been occurring for slightly more than two years. The auditors had noted that in normal circumstances it was not desirable for the roles of trading manager and settlements to be combined. They were also sympathetic to the lack of resources in Singapore, saying they recognised that Leeson must continue to take an active role in both front and back offices. Nevertheless, their recommendations were clear:

- Leeson should not retain responsibility for back office operations;
- Leeson should not be able to sign cheques or hold control over journals;
- Leeson should not be able to sign off Simex deposits or bank reconciliations.[16]

Nick Leeson had a major problem. He was to continue doing what everyone thought he was good at — being the star trader on the floor of Simex — but he had been denied access to what he was really good at — toying with error account 88888.

While Baker was tidying up his findings, Coopers & Lybrand were undertaking their usual first-hand look at the operations in August 1994. As professional number crunchers, the auditors were not interested in profit for profit's sake, nor in the personalities who delivered them. Unusually high profits that occur seemingly out of place are supposed to be enough to raise their suspicion. Unrealised profits were continuing to grow in Singapore, reaching $30 million for the first seven months, compared to a stg54.8 million pre-tax half year profit for the entire group. With adjustments for currency differences, Singapore was responsible for nearly 30 per cent of Barings' pre-tax profits.

Such an achievement from one unit in the Barings group — which lists 62 principal operating companies in its annual report — should have caused any accountant to demur in signing off the bank's 1994 accounts. But sign off they did, for some quite interesting reasons of their own.

Pre-dating the 1994 audit was a succession of audits reinforcing the opinion that controls within Barings were adequate. These were carried out by Deloitte & Touche who had resigned as Barings' Singapore auditors in July 1994 and had been replaced by Coopers & Lybrand Singapore. Coopers & Lybrand in London had handled Barings accounts for many year and regarded the bank as a safe ship. They had previously concluded that controls within Barings were good, and that 'good computer and application controls exist'.[17]

In 1993, it was concluded there was a 'good attitude towards control and in general the control environment can be relied upon'. It was further stated: 'The environment appears to have strengthened in the year and operational controls operated more effectively as a result'.[18] In 1992 it was concluded that: 'There is a good attitude towards control and in general the control environment can be relied upon'.[19]

And this was compiled in a management letter written in 1992 when splits between the securities and merchant banking division were surfacing. In respect of derivative settlement: 'The areas of internal control weakness which we believe require immediate attention are detailed below'. These included that the derivatives controller 'has not acted in a review capacity due to high staff turnover, and lack of resources on the desk'. And: 'Since most of the derivatives business originates in the Far East the Derivatives Controller, who is London based, has found it difficult to exercise the degree of global control'.[20]

After the internal report, Leeson and Jones had no option but to agree to immediately implement the recommendations made by Baker's team. They made a commitment with 'immediate effect'[21] that Leeson's responsibility for back office operations would cease. The accounts department would now handle bank reconciliations, a finance manager would sign off journals and open new accounts, and Jones would ensure that adequate supervision of the settlements department was maintained.

Leeson could not afford to be dictated to by the findings and had no intention of doing so. It was a reversion to 'situation normal' after the auditors left and after their findings were circulated amongst senior management, and in this he was unwittingly aided by Jones's own lax attitudes. Jones had lacked any sense of urgency in adopting the changes. This was not out of the ordinary for he had rarely shown much interest in the derivatives side and, in a manner not unlike that shared by Ron Baker, Peter Norris, the board and senior management of Barings, he had little understanding of the product and the dangers associated with it. While Broadhurst wanted Jones sacked, others in the audit team had also 'stated they had little faith in Mr Jones's management ability'.[22]

Clearly no trace of error account 88888 had been uncovered by either party, despite some evidence of its existence being on file in London. When Leeson had instructed Wong

to remove the account from reports to London, it was
removed from the trade file, which discloses daily activity,
the price file which contained closing settlement prices, and
the London gross which provided details of positions. However, some details of the account were included in the margin
file. This contained details of margins by accounts and their
currencies. Being within the margin file report, information
on account 88888 was sent to London daily, but there was
insufficient information to guarantee that the account would
be recognised by the master file in the First Futures computer system at Barings Securities. This meant that information was not downloaded and entered into the First Futures
ledger, but was instead held in a suspense file and escaped
detection.

But in November, further warnings were sounded with
those responsible for overseeing reporting duties to the
Bank of England lamented that it was becoming increasingly difficult to obtain hard information about controls
on transactions. Head of treasury and risk, Ian Hopkins,
wrote two memos to Peter Norris complaining that 'it
is becoming much clearer that our systems and control
culture are distinctly flaky'[23], and that there were 'some
startling weaknesses in the control of our core equity
product'.[24] He also wrote that Barings had a well established practice of defeating controls when accounting in
many currencies.

Although these highly critical memoranda were not directly relevant to Leeson's dealings, they did offer an insight
into the concerns of some operating within the group. This
also means that calculating the risk capital at Barings could
prove difficult. The latter was important, given that the
culture it created lent itself to Barings transferring vast sums
of money abroad with the express permission of Threadneedle Street.

Throughout 1993 and 1994, Leeson's ability to meet
margin call payments and Bishopsgate's ability to meet his
demands remained dependent on the personal relationship

with Christopher Thompson and his analysts at Thread-needle Street.

✄

Nick Leeson may never have played it as a child, but he might have found amusing a children's game called 52-pick-up. It's simple. Child A picks up a deck of cards and asks Child B whether B is interested in a game of 52-pick-up. Thinking a new game of cards is on the horizon, B agrees, at which point A, holding the deck of cards, tosses them in the air then orders B to clean up the mess.

For more than three years, an overhaul at Barings had been underway. It was a long time for any organisation to be in a state of flux and, by September 1994, the cards were starting to fall.

✄

No internal limits of any consequence had been set on exposures. They had at one time reached 73 per cent of the bank's consolidated capital base on the Osaka exchange, and at another, 40 per cent against Simex, in breach of the 25 per cent limit imposed by the BoE. Money was routinely passed from Barings' treasury department to the securities unit, and in turn was used to fund exposures generated by margin payments by the futures unit in Singapore. While the bulk of the funds were used by Leeson to meet margin requirements for trades out of error account 88888, members of the senior executive believed they were short-term advances to Barings' clients who, through the vague checks and balances system, would have met normal lending criteria.

'Many times when we had reported in the Japanese exchanges, we had gone above 25 per cent; so there was no embarrassment about that. They [the BoE] were aware', Maclean said.[25]

The reorganisation of Barings had made it difficult for the BoE to keep tabs on the transfer of capital to offshore

exchanges and units. Thompson was at the meeting with
Barings officials in February 1993 when confusion over
the restructuring was expressed. The culture of the old
boys' network and the understandable problems faced by
a bank going through massive change was enough to
effect the granting of an informal concession by Thompson
which allowed Barings to continually exceed the 25 per cent
limit.

Thompson had been assisted by John Mackintosh, an
analyst responsible for Barings between March 1993 and
April 1994, and then by Howard Walwyn. The granting of
the concession was never documented, and it was not known
exactly when it took effect. However, Thompson and
Walwyn both thought it had been granted during in 1993.

With the benefit of hindsight, the Chancellor of the
Exchequer, Kenneth Clarke, later called this a 'grave mistake'. The rate and mix of capital transfers also made it
difficult to know how much money was going where, to
whom, when, and how often. These questions were only
answered after the fact, when limits had already been
exceeded.

For two years, Barings had consistently gone beyond 25
per cent. Between January and June 1993, 25 per cent of
Baring's consolidated base stood at stg70.8 million. Its
maximum exposure had reached stg89.6 million with the
Osaka Stock Exchange. Between October and December
1994, the 25 per cent limit was worth stg117.4 million, while
maximum reported exposures reached stg131.0 million in
Osaka and 118.7 million on Simex.[26]

Maclean had noted that limits were again being
breached in early September and he telephoned Thompson
at Threadneedle Street asking for clarification on where the
BoE stood on exposures to Japanese exchanges. Thompson
had advised several months earlier that his policy unit was
examining such exposures and that he would be writing to
Barings at a later date informing them of its views. This
had not happened. According to Maclean, Thompson was

relaxed about the situation because it was understood that funding requirements were for individual members of the various exchanges.

'I reminded him that although that was indeed our view it would be impossible for us to prove it in a legal sense. He was happy with us having reported the situation and that we should continue to exceed 25 per cent of our capital base from time to time', Maclean said.[27]

Shortly before Hopkins warned of a 'distinctly flaky' control culture in October, Barings requested an increase in treasury concession limits to stg843 million, but this was rejected by the BoE and the limit remained at stg364 million. Confusion lingered, however, over where Barings stood in regards to capital transfers. The onus remained on individual judgement, and the honesty of traders in the pit.

⚔

In October, Barings defied the recent poor performance of its rivals and officially booked a stg54.8 million interim pre-tax profit, and all other concerns were pushed aside. The board, directors, investors and staff were delighted. Senior employees were now anticipating a full year profit in excess of stg100 million, and that carried the promise of generous bonuses being dished out. 'I think we chose the right things to do and avoided the wrong things', Sir Peter said in announcing the profit.

The half-year results were substantially helped by a strong performance within the corporate finance division with income from fees and commissions rising by 47 per cent to stg238.8 million. The bank also claimed it had benefited from a decision to limit its exposure to the bond market during the turbulent period of early 1994.

In reality, their exposure to the bond market was a factor contributing heavily to what came next. By the later part of 1994, the strains of Leeson's risk-taking were beginning to emerge in his personality, and he began acting in a manner considered by his friends to be out of character, even compared to his usual drunken exploits.

On the night of the Simex anniversary dinner Leeson, with his staff in tow, went on a drinking binge after the dinner. In one pub, Leeson dropped his pants in front of a group of young women, then offered them his cellular phone and dared them to call the police. They did, landing Leeson a night in jail, a $140 fine, and a sex offence on his record. His arrogance prevailed and Leeson started telling people that the charges were essentially irrelevant and that he'd have few problems overcoming the latest hassle. Some of his friends were of the opinion that this sort of humour was wearing a bit thin.

Such was his profile among traders that the *International Financing Review* got wind of the story, and Barings executives apparently used 'friendly persuasion' to keep the story out of the newspaper's gossip column. For executives it was an embarrassment. Leeson apparently thought differently.

Lisa never realised the stress her husband was under. She spent a lot of their last year in Singapore back in the United Kingdom. There had been two deaths in her family and commitments had prevented her from spending time with Nick. Instead, she admired her husband for being 'a cool character' and rarely asked what type of day he had had.

'Just once he said to me: "If I'm short with you, don't worry. It's just that I'm under pressure." But he never was short with me. It was more the other way around. I would nag, telling him to get his feet off the sofa, that sort of thing,' she said. 'If you ask anyone, they will tell you Nick is a cool character. His mood never changes. Not like me. If something goes wrong with me, you'll know. I'm screaming and shouting. Nick's never ruffled.'[28].

With Lisa absent, Nick blitzed the local pubs and clubs as if he were once again a single man about town. His behaviour did not pass unnoticed. 'His behaviour was more like that of a bachelor', said one friend. Others noted that when it came to a party, Barings in Asia was 'more like Animal House than a trading house'.[29]

Nick and Lisa had been in Singapore for nearly two years when they decided it was time to get out, although Lisa had spent the bulk of the previous 12 months at home in England. They both wanted children, and planned to start a family the following year. However, Nick was stuck. He and Lisa wanted a big bonus to help consolidate themselves financially, but to do this Nick needed to turn in an equally big profit while at the same time making enough to remove all losses and any trace of error account 88888. They decided to stay in Singapore until March, meet Lisa's holidaying parents in Australia, and then travel back to Britain with them. But before they could do this, Leeson had to prove himself a modern day alchemist.

While his more recent activities had raised several eyebrows, it was a single decision made towards the end of 1994 that would ultimately precipitate the collapse of the bank. Leeson began to engage in a procedure known as straddling.

The straddle is complicated and usually belongs only to the risky realm of the speculative trader. Essentially, the trader starts playing both markets by simultaneously purchasing contracts in one month and selling them in another to take advantage of anticipated price fluctuations.

Leeson sold an equal number of put and call options. The seller of a call is speculating that the market will fall, the seller of a put believes it will rise. Selling both in a market that neither substantially rises nor falls over a period of time can bring great riches.

In Leeson's situation, he bet that the Nikkei index would neither substantially rise nor fall but would remain between 18,500 and 19,500 points. By the end of the calendar year more than 40,000 contracts had been accumulated. The straddling position was in direct breach of his brief from London which dictated buying contracts in Osaka and only selling them in Singapore when profitable. Sir Peter, Andrew Tuckey, Peter Norris and Ron Baker — the chain of

command — had failed to compel Simon Jones and Nick
Leeson to put in practice their own internal audit recommendations. Leeson was still running the back office and
was able carry his new strategy with relative ease. His
popularity with staff in the back room also meant the
straddle would never be seriously questioned.

By straddling his position through real accounts held in
Japan and fictitious accounts in Singapore, Leeson was able
to hold a short position in Osaka and a long position at
home. In other words, by controlling the accounts in Singapore, he was able to have all the contracts acquired in Osaka
pre-sold to false clients in Singapore.

Leeson had previously been active in straddles on only a
limited scale. Jack David remembered: 'Options are a self-
fulfilling prophecy. You have a strong hand and a weak hand.
He sold straddles at all sorts of prices and bought them back
dirt cheap.' But this time was different. Leeson was prepared
to engage a position big enough to clean out more than
S$400 million worth of losses in error account 88888. Again,
the position was being made in the name of Leeson's
fictitious Big Client.

'It was common knowledge on the floor that Nick had a
very big customer and he sold straddles and strangles', Jack
David said. 'To be honest with you, I don't know how he lost
money unless he had a bona fide customer.'

The expectation of a big windfall was in place when
Leeson was called to a seminar weekend held in New York
for the 150-plus members of Ron Baker's Financial Products
Group from around the globe. It was December 1994 and
Leeson attended the conference en route to a holiday in
Ireland with Lisa.

It was not just on the trading floor that Leeson's attitude
to money was viewed as contemptuous. At about 3 am on the
Sunday morning, Leeson and a group of like-minded souls
from the seminar stumbled into a bar in downtown New
York which served cocktails in foot-long novelty-shaped
glasses.

As the night degenerated, Leeson and another of his party bet a stranger $300 each that he would be unable to scull a vodka martini in one gulp. While the person was contemplating whether to exercise his option, Leeson promptly fell asleep with his head on the bar, only to be awoken by cheers minutes later and told that he owed the stranger $600.

Leeson then good-naturedly whipped out his bulging wallet and placed six one-hundred dollar bills on the bar. While perusing the contents of his wallet and nursing a hangover the next morning over breakfast, Leeson was heard to mutter: 'God, I must have had a good time last night'.[30]

The $600 Leeson lost in New York was comparatively a drop in the Hudson River. By the end of 1994, Leeson's Singapore operations had technically recorded a stg28.5 million in earnings, accounting for more than 75 per cent of Barings group profits. But in reality, error account 88888's losses totalled stg208 million — this compared with Barings group profit before tax and bonuses of stg205 million.

About stg102 million had been allocated for bonuses, and Leeson was due to get stg450,000. Lisa was over the moon: 'It was more me [who wanted the bonus] but, you can imagine, who would turn down something like that?' Lisa once told reporters. 'It would be like a lottery win and set you up for the rest of your life.'

Andrew Tuckey was anticipating the largest bonus at stg1.65 million, Sir Peter and Peter Norris would each get stg1.0 million, and Barings securities chief Peter Norris was looking forward to receiving stg880,000. Of remaining staff, 26 directors of Barings bank and 32 employees of the securities division were to receive between stg250,000 and stg499,999, four bank directors and one securities person would get between stg500,000 and stg749,000.

Of the 4000 people employed by Barings, at 27 years of age Leeson sat comfortably among the star performers, as rated by the bonus system encompassing the entire group.

It was shortly after this payout that a huge hole emerged in the accounts, to become known as the Spear, Leeds &

Kellogg (SLK) receivable. It was initially discovered by the external auditors for Coopers & Lybrand in Singapore. The discovery of a missing S$115 million was made during an audit of Barings Futures Singapore financial statements for the year ending December 31. The auditors had noted an unreconciled difference between a Barings ledger for a Simex settlement, and the balance shown for the same account as shown by Simex.

The discrepancy was brought to the attention of Geoffrey Broadhurst, who spoke to a number of people in the securities division and noted that it was apparent that 'the explanation that had been offered to the external auditors in Singapore did not make any sense whatsoever to those in London.'[31].

CHAPTER SEVEN

KOBE

'[Nick] didn't lose his cool over the Japanese earthquake which had a huge effect on trading'.: Lisa Leeson.[1]

When a massive earthquake rocked western Japan at dawn on January 17, Nick Leeson was fast asleep 5000 km away in Singapore. Blissfully unaware of the devastating consequences the earthquake would later bear upon his own life, he didn't stir.

The Great Hanshin Earthquake began with a lateral shift in a fault line 20 km below the southern end of Awaji Island at 5.46 am. From its epicentre, the shift resulted in a rupture that rocked the earth's surface around the Kansai region, inhabited by 2.5 million people. The shaking escalated into a violent ground-breaking calamity, the first earthquake in modern Japanese history to strike an urban district, and the biggest since the Great Kanto Earthquake of 1923 which left 140,000 dead.

Osaka, Kyoto and, in particular, Kobe, bore the brunt of the earthquake, with thousands buried alive in homes that were turned into rubble within minutes. Those who survived faced out-of-control fires and the hundreds of aftershocks that further crippled Kobe and its outlying suburbs. Six hundred and sixteen aftershocks were reported by 8:00 pm alone on the first day and there were fears that more were to come, with seismologists predicting tremors in the vicinity of 6.0 on the Richter Scale.

Initially, five bridge sections collapsed between Shin-Osaka and Nishi-Akashi. One large chunk teetered for 15 minutes before it came crashing down. Bullet train services between Nagoya and Hiroshima were halted, and telephone services, gas and water supplies were cut.

At the Port of Kobe, a major commercial centre for container shipping, most of the 239 berths, including 21 container berths were rendered useless. Elevated highways, bridges and train tracks buckled and smashed. Transit sheds, cranes and cargo handling equipment were ruined. Blackouts struck 900,000 homes. Buildings as high as eight stories toppled, a seven-storey hospital collapsed, and timber-made houses snapped and burned.

The ease with which the earthquake tipped over whole sections of elevated expressways, taking with them many cars carrying the cities' earliest commuters, must have been the realisation of the worst nightmares of the engineers who had prided themselves on their supposedly quake-proof structures. A half-kilometre piece of the Hanshin Freeway tumbled over in a single slab. Transport and communications were paralysed and for the citizens of Kansai, life had been either taken or suspended.

By day's end, more than 5000 people were dead. Tens of thousands more were injured and another 275,000 people were left homeless as rescuers were left to fight fires and continue combing what was left of the region in the hope of finding survivors. Ultimately more than 6000 deaths would be recorded. Officials began to count the costs of rebuilding. Slightly more than 11,000 homes and buildings were damaged or destroyed, and 100 hectares were razed by fires. Basic items — blankets, food and water — were in short supply.

Japanese Prime Minister Tomiichi Murayama assured a hastily-arranged press conference that emergency relief supplies would be sent to the area, and that the government would spare no efforts to put out the fires and to ensure that services would be rebuilt as soon as possible. He immediately made arrangements to visit Kobe, where the devastation was reminiscent of the World War II carpet bombings.[2]

Japan's history of earthquakes is well documented, and is a constant in its people's lives. While no amount of preparation can fully prepare anyone for the sheer terror and panic that follows, the standard of the response and preparedness of Japan's emergency services were found sadly wanting. The world's shock at the extent of the devastation, and sadness at the mounting death toll was evidenced in front page headlines, and offers of aid and support poured in. Foreign embassies both in and outside of Japan were deluged with calls from relatives and friends desperate for news of loved ones. About 44,380 foreign nationals from 97 countries were living in Kobe at the time.

The effects of the tragedy were also felt on the global financial markets.

Scientifically, the Great Hanshin earthquake measured 7.2 on the Richter scale. The consequences would, however, eventually jolt Barings with a ferocity which, if the financial world measured its disasters with a similar yardstick, would have rocketed the reading beyond measurement.

For Leeson, it was a rude awakening. The earthquake had effectively robbed him of the linchpin in his grand plan — stability in the Nikkei 225 index.

In reaction to the overall devastation to the Japanese economy, local share prices eventually went into a steep decline. It was, however, by no means inevitable that the market would weaken, let alone that it would plunge as deeply into negative territory as it did.

As the catastrophic effects of the earthquake unravelled Leeson's precarious position, and the bank subsided into collapse, analysts were quick to blame the massive losses suffered by the bank's securities unit entirely on the earthquake, arguing that an act of God had been the final straw for Leeson's finely-balanced straddling position. Nature herself had played a hand in this financial calamity. But while hindsight has its supporters, the overview at the time was quite different, and opinion was wide-ranging.

At the time, the thinking of analysts, brokers, chartists, and directors was dominated by thoughts that such large-scale havoc and the extensive rebuilding required must prompt the injection of massive amounts of capital — this would provide a boon to any number of listed companies (reflected in their profit and loss accounts) with interests in the re-building of the Kansai region and in turn trigger a sharp rise in the overall bourse.

The need for such an injection gained credence when Prime Minister Murayama visited Kobe two days after the quake. He was visibly stunned. He walked the streets and viewed the region from a helicopter: 'Although I received reports from officials, the destruction was beyond my imagination', Murayama said. 'I'd like to extend my condolences to all the victims. We'll do all we can to help the affected'.[3]

Meanwhile, as people started to pick up the remnants of their lives, the chaos kicked in again. Thirty spot fires broke out on the day of Murayama's tour. In Choo Ward on the man-made Port Island a 5000 square metre plant occupied by the Mitsubishi Warehouse & Transportation Co burst into flames.

Strong winds fanned the indiscriminate blazes, testing despairing firefighters who also had to contend with water shortages across the region. The Self-Defence Force still had not arrived and neighbours were forced to rescue each other, dragging the dead from the debris, and supporting each other as best they could.

Signs of imminent chaos on the Nikkei 225 index were much slower to emerge, although the confusion was evident with some European analysts in Tokyo predicting immediate losses of up to 1000 points, or six per cent. This was in direct contrast to the forecasts of others. For the first six days after the quake struck, Leeson's straddling position appeared surprisingly safe, with the Nikkei comfortably holding itself around the crucial 19,500 mark.

But even as the last fires were being extinguished, the aftermath of the earthquake was far from over, with its full effects yet to be felt in numerous areas. Many ramifications of the earthquake were yet to play themselves out, splintering perceptions about Japan's fragile economic recovery as people starting to add up the costs. Barings was left at its most vulnerable. A sharp movement either way in the Nikkei 225 would unravel Leeson's strategy, and movement either way was entirely possible, with businesses across western Japan grinding to a halt as power lines collapsed, railways and highways became unpassable, and the Port of Kobe became inoperable.

Some of the most serious structural damage was incurred by Kobe's rail network which services the city's 1.4 million people. Trains were overturned, tracks twisted and the railway stations were levelled.

Heavyweight companies such as computer giant Fujitsu Ltd, Mitsubishi Electric Corp, Kobe Steel Ltd and Daihatsu Motor Co Ltd ceased production at plants across Japan.

When the Japanese currency market opened for trade only a matter of hours after the earthquake struck, the yen fell sharply against the greenback and other major currencies. Tokyo's share prices also began to slip as nervous investors panicked that the earthquake would shatter Japan's already tenuous economic upturn. Japan had benefited in recent months from the US dollar's exposure to the Mexican peso crisis, with fund managers switching from the greenback to the yen. They were now looking at ditching the Japanese currency in search of a safer haven.

The Osaka Securities Exchange suspended stock and bond transactions for the day, although futures and options trading were allowed in the afternoon. The Kansai Agricultural Commodities Exchange, where grain and sugar are traded, the Osaka Textile Exchange, the Kobe Rubber Exchange, and the Kobe Raw Silk Exchange were also shut down.

Branch offices of most major banks and automatic teller networks were also shut and people were denied access to their cash.

Initial estimates put the damage at more than $10 billion, some suggested $20 billion, and the money men were casting a keen but distant eye over the region.

Investors on Japan's stock market initially held their nerve, preferring to wait for a clearer picture to emerge before responding to the quake. The market had already been beset with the economic gloom that had suppressed share prices and had cornered the Nikkei around the 19,000 mark. It was a long way short of the record highs achieved during the 1980s.

For three days after the devastation at Kobe, the Nikkei teetered, losing ground at a slow rate but at a pace that under normal conditions would be considered neither surprising nor out of the ordinary. As it passed through the 19,360 mark the Nikkei matched the weighted average strike price of the straddle, and represented a profit of about 3.1 billion yen or stg20 million.[4]

One day after the quake, Japan's key index dropped 89.85 points to 19,241.32. A day later the Nikkei slipped a further 18.01 points to 19,233.31 with companies that had a heavy exposure to the quake-related ramifications, like Kobe Steel, leading the falls. Investors battered the steel group further when the company announced that production at its two blast furnaces in Kobe had been halted. But by Thursday night, the trickle of selling had turned into a steady stream and the index sank 147.57 points to 19,075.74, with the market barometer breaking the 19,000 technical resistance barrier during the day for the first time in five weeks. A dip below the 19,000 support level stood to trigger a fresh wave of selling.

Mindful of the massive insurance claims soon to be presented, investors battered insurance shares. Tokyo Marine & Fire Insurance shed more than five per cent while Sumitomo Marine & Fire lost almost six per cent on the back of expected profit downgrades by investment houses and the companies themselves.

Railroad shares also fell as reports of devastation to the rail system in the business centre of Osaka and Kobe mounted. Hanshin Electric Railway, the major railroad linking Osaka and Kobe, plunged to a two-year low. Worst affected were Hankyu Corp, which operates a railway whose station collapsed in Itami, Kinki Nippon Railway, which operates largely in western Japan, and Sagami Railway.

Brokerage shares weakened as the forced closure of Osaka financial markets kept trading to a minimum and ate away at profits. Japan's largest broker, Nomura Securities led declines. Daiwa Securities and Nikko Securities shadowed Nomura's move into negative territory.

The vice president of Nomura Investment Management Co, Nobumitsu Kagami, commented that the Tokyo stock market had never before suffered so many simultaneous negative influences at once. His comments were indicative of the deep apprehension gripping Tokyo. One local economist was quoted as saying: 'There is no locomotive in the economy and there is no good news on the way that we can see'.

If a massive earthquake were not enough to rattle the Japanese economy, a domestic political crisis because of resistance to the bail-out of two failed credit unions associated with EIE International only served to add to concerns that a recovery might have stalled. Internationally, the Mexican peso crisis was still proving to be a general market millstone and would no longer provide an adequate stimulus for the besieged yen.

The more optimistic analysts believed though, that government spending to repair Kobe could eventually stimulate the economy by introducing fresh foreign investments with the potential to boost the yen. Such observers believed that the rebuilding of Kobe would pressure Japan's public resources and refocus its private ones, diverting the nation's cash deployment inwards just as it was beginning to look outward after three years of restructuring the collective balance sheet. Kobe's history prior to the earthquake lent itself to this pocket of positive sentiment as much as anything else. The city's reputation was built on astuteness and aggressiveness, and within the cluster of Japanese cities it was known proudly as Kobe Inc.

In 1994, Japan's growth rate was a bare 0.7 per cent and the reconstruction of the corridor linking Kobe with Osaka was considered big enough to add another half of a percentage point to 1995 growth rates and boost forecast GDP growth to around two per cent.[5]

It was on this hope that Leeson elected not to reduce his exposure to Japanese financial markets and maintained his straddle.

To some extent this reasoning was being proved correct, with investors buying into specific stocks which stood to benefit from future construction contracts. Industries such as steel, automobile and stevedoring, and building companies became popular. Construction topped the list of favourites, with Obayashi Construction Co, based in Osaka, the most active share on the Japanese exchanges. Glass and cement stocks made solid gains as a sector. Entrepreneurs were already talking up the future. Town planners envisaged a new disaster-proof city laid out with wide roads and spacious public parks. It was not too long before new high rise apartments were planned for the city's residents.

But on Thursday the 19th of January, the first signs began to emerge that investors were not convinced that the rebuilding after the earthquake was strong enough to offset general pessimism and support a sustained rally on Japan's share market.

The devastation at Kobe was extraordinary by any measure of human misery. All efforts by the Japanese government, volunteers, and emergency service groups were strained in the extreme by the sheer magnitude of the catastrophe. Though there are no parallels between such devastation and the performance of financial markets, the degree to which investors were rattled cannot be underestimated, particularly foreign institutions who pay more attention to the bottom line than sentiment and took the early lead among the bearish market players.

These investors came to the fore as the first signs of a large scale sell-off in Japanese stocks presented itself on the last trading day of that week, Friday January 20. The Nikkei slumped 235.3 points, or 1.2 per cent, to 18,840.22.

Leeson's position still looked safe. He was, however, forced to begin rethinking his strategy and widen the parameters to account for an act of God. Leeson may have prayed for divine intervention but the omens were not good. That same day he rapidly built up a long position of 10,814 March 1995 contracts in the vain hope of a recovery in March futures. The market index for those contracts had fallen 400 points in the previous two days.[5]

Another probable explanation for his move was that Leeson believed he was good enough to single-handedly prop up the Japanese stock market in an attempt to protect the equivalent long position arising from the written option straddles and cash-up on the new futures position. He would later be bitterly disappointed.

CHAPTER EIGHT

PLEASE PAY

'We are all Leesons in varying degrees. In his case, he just built up numbers that couldn't be counted anymore'. An anonymous trader.

The turning point in Leeson's year-long strategy arrived on Monday, January 23, when the Nikkei followed the previous Friday's lead, and went into a belated nose-dive in direct response to the Kobe disaster, now six days old.

Leeson's position initially appeared relatively safe, with the Nikkei hovering between 18,500 and 19,500, but investors were by now fully informed of the damage inflicted by the quake, and their nerves were frazzled. They besieged the Nikkei 225, dragging the index below the critical 18,000 barrier for the first time since June 6, 1994, abetted by foreign investors who were ditching Japanese stocks en masse.

Leeson must have been greatly encouraged when he returned to work after the weekend to see the market up 30 points from the opening bell. It would climb a further 30 points before falling sharply.

The index tumbled 1054.73 points to 17,785.49, substantially eroding the value of Leeson's futures position, to close 1175 points weaker on the day. Leeson closed his position during that rocky session and lost Y5.37 billion or stg34 million in the process. Over this short period his portfolio had incurred a loss of Y10.91 billion, or stg69 million. Barings' exposure was serious, and dangerous.

Realising that the straddle was going to land Barings with a heavy loss, Leeson made a second calculated gamble that had the potential to either recoup the losses and bring him and the bank incredible riches, or take his recklessness to a calamitous pinnacle.

He had two choices. With the Nikkei heading in the wrong direction and increasing Barings' exposure, the first and prudent course should have been to reduce the bank's risk by continuing to purchase Osaka written contracts and on-selling them in Singapore at a slightly higher price in the hope of whittling away at the deficit. Any losses would have to be declared. That would be embarrassing and worth a rap on the knuckles, or at worst dismissal by head office, but it remained the safest option, but Leeson chose to ignore it.

Instead, Leeson played the markets like a gambler attempting to bluff a win with a bad hand and recover his grub-stake by continually doubling up until the losing streak breaks. In doing this Leeson had committed a fundamental blunder, and ignored the normal currents that underpin financial markets.

It is normal for any financial market to undergo a correction after a steep fall or sharp gain. When a market rises strongly, speculative profit takers move in and cash up, hauling back gains during the ensuing days of trade. Similarly, after a sudden decline, short-term profiteers who believe a market has been oversold enter the fray looking for cheap stocks and in turn help the market to recover lost ground.

The latter, supported by renewed talk of Tokyo injecting up to 5.0 trillion yen into Kobe, which in turn might sustain a stock market run, helped the Nikkei 225 to struggle past the 18,000 mark with a 275.25 point gain on Tuesday. Combined public and private sector spending in the region was expected to reach 10 trillion yen.

To Leeson's relief, the stock market firmed again on Wednesday, rising 98.75 points to 18,159.48, and was on target to minimise Barings losses by returning past the 18,500 mark.

The Thursday edition of *The Japan Times* reflected the buoyant mood. In a report quoting an unnamed broker, the newspaper commented that individual investors had apparently taken a cue from Monday's tumble, triggered by worries about adverse effects of the earthquake that jolted the Hanshin area on January 17.

More than half the buy orders placed at the opening of the afternoon session were for quake-related issues, a Nikko securities official said.

Construction companies surged on a broad front, accounting for nine out the top 10 issues on the first section volume list. Among them were general contractors Taisei and Obayashi, and medium size firms like Aoki Corp and Daisui Construction.

Sumitomo Osaka Cement, the day's volume leader, rose sharply, as did Nihon Cement, Chichibu Onada Cement, Nippon Sheet Glass and Asahi Glass.

It was an accurate report of one day's trade, and for a brief period speculation optimistically forecast the return of bullish investors who would drag the Japanese stock market out of the doldrums. Commentators and analysts were even calculating that Japanese interest rates would have to rise to offset the negative impact that government spending would have on inflation. Even *The New York Times* had reported that global interest rates might have to rise on the back of such moves.

These reasons, and the haranguing from the external auditors over the SLK receivable, determined Leeson's next move. Coopers & Lybrand in Singapore had sought an explanation from Leeson over the missing funds attributed to SLK. Leeson initially told them the problem was caused by a computer error. This explanation bought him some time while he moved on the market. Around January 26, Leeson was continuing to trade in both markets, but had decided to raise the bets in staggering proportions in the hope that the markets would turn in his favour by rising substantially, thereby recouping the losses in error account 88888.

Leeson decided to adopt a long position. He stopped selling and acquired further March 95 futures contracts at between $180,000 and $200,000 each. He again upped the ante by taking out futures contracts in Japanese government-issued bonds known as JGB futures, and the short-term government debt product, Euroyen.

The contracts were acquired from real clients in Japan mainly on behalf of four institutions — three of which were Barings group companies. The long position gathered momentum with the acquisition of 10,814 March 95 contracts, amid dealers' speculation that Leeson was anticipating a recovery in March futures. Not long after, the position ballooned out to 27,158 March 95 contracts. Cross-trading and hiding losses in account 88888, however, combined with the closing out of other contracts, pulled this number back slightly.

As the buying binge gathered pace, the figures themselves were staggering. The entire futures gamble soon reached $7.0 billion and was gambled solely upon the Nikkei 225 rising in response to the Japanese government spending trillions of yen in the Kansai region. Simultaneously the JGB and Euroyen position was heading towards $20.0 billion.

Leeson was going long in Nikkei futures, JGB futures, Euroyen futures and Nikkei options. Barings chief Sir Peter Baring, and the Bank of England's Eddie George, would later claim that an unauthorised $27 billion position had been created.

The position could never have been officially sanctioned — it was daring at best, wildly reckless at worst. If the tide turned as Leeson was hoping it would, he stood to make a bundle of cash, delivering Barings an extraordinary profit, and reaping a bonus that would enable him to retire and be hailed a financial wizard — much like legendary Wall Street hero George Soros, who had made more than a billion dollars through speculative trading against the pound sterling.

Extraordinary profits of well over a billion dollars stood within striking distance. If Leeson was to achieve such a feat, he stood to gain entry into the elite club of financiers who dominated Britain's international investment houses — a circle from which his working class roots would normally have precluded him. Desirable or not, there is no nation or arena where money does not carry prestige and have the power to make people sit up and listen. When Soros, a native Hungarian who fled the Nazis, bemoaned the lack of understanding of what America stood for, he said, 'to put it bluntly the Western democracies have become morally bankrupt'. That comment made the front page of *The International Herald Tribune.*

Fame awaited. All Leeson had to do was ensure his margins calls at Simex were covered, sit tight and maintain his long position until the Nikkei index began to rise. Assuming this was to occur, he would lock in his earnings by offloading the contracts and transfer the profits from Error Account 88888 to a regular house account.

Maintaining margin calls was critical. Simex officials were already disturbed by Barings' rising stake in the their market, and closer daily attention was being paid to the division and to rising margin payments.

As the margin call demands from account 88888 rose in line with falls in the Nikkei, Leeson came under pressure to find ways of reducing the payments on the unauthorised positions. He had already instructed Barings' settlement staff to adjust the positions in account 88888 and another trading account, 92000. Effectively, the long Nikkei 225 position in 88888 was offset against the short position on 92000. Similar adjustments were being made in the JGB position. These transactions were fake off-market cross trades. After a Position Change Sheet was filled out and lodged with Simex, the entries were reversed so that the daily activity statement for account 92000 sent to Barings in Japan did not disclose the adjustments. The trades were reversed the next day and there was no transfer of any profit or loss. The effect of the cross trades transferred a stg13 million profit from 88888 to 92000 and allowed Leeson to report an arbitrage profit of stg5.0 million for the period between January 23 and January 27, when the aggregate loss was stg47 million.[1] This deceived

Simex and slashed margins. On six separate occasions Simex handed back excess margins which in reality were not owed. At one point, Leeson understated his margin requirements by more than stg250 million.[2]

Bax had been concerned about the growing position before the Kobe disaster, and had already discussed the matter in Singapore through the normal course of business. He had also prepared a letter for head office. But Bax and head office believed Leeson was acting on behalf of a client and that the client's position had been hedged. There was consequently no suggestion that the bank could be liable for the futures position, and Leeson's funding demands — while out of the ordinary — were not considered unreasonable.

On the Japanese stock market, the Nikkei 225 went into a period of heavy fluctuation — rising higher on the back of investors who believed the Kobe quake would return a profit before speculative traders, who saw no such gains from Kobe, lopped off the share price gains.

The fluctuations did give Leeson some scope for retrieving the situation — for a small period he had actually narrowed his losses to around the levels of the previous December. But overall, the Nikkei's performance was down and the decline escalated. Trading was complicated by a lack of heavyweight interest from offshore institutions, the Mexican debt crisis, and the sheer uncertainty surrounding the Japanese market that always sidelines buyers and leaves sellers to dominate trading activity.

Unfortunately for Barings, the situation was further aggravated by other futures traders who saw the bank and just one trader going strongly in one direction and therefore decided to speculate that the Nikkei would in fact fall, in the hope of cashing up. This exacerbated the situation tremendously. Leeson was out-gunned by the sheer volume of futures acquired on the Nikkei heading lower and this in turn flowed into the real market and compounded the negative sentiment already overhanging the Nikkei 225.

Like Bishopsgate, other traders had assumed that Barings was on-selling the contracts, or had adopted a hedge that would cover the bank and its clients if the situation went. It also assumed that Nick was still acting on behalf of the still unidentified Big Client, a source of constant market speculation.

They were wrong on all counts.

On the interest rate front, those anticipating a rise were to be sadly disappointed. Their calculations had failed to take into account Japan's high national savings rate, and that the quake itself had had a deflationary impact on the Japanese economy.

Japan could afford to pay for the reconstruction of Kobe without being forced to rely on increased borrowings. Tokyo was also reluctant to lift rates amid the current state of its banking industry, which was facing heavy liabilities. An interest rate hike would simply saddle business with further costs, compound bad debt, and slice off profits while seriously affecting the banks' ability to lend money to quake-hit businesses.

Some forecasts did prove accurate. In the end, the Kobe quake would cost about 9.6 billion yen, but this represented just 0.8 per cent of the national wealth. By way of comparison, costs incurred through Tokyo's Great Kanto earthquake accounted for 1.9 per cent of total Japanese wealth.

Leeson had toyed with the JGB index through an established position just prior to the Kobe quake and acted prudently by liquidating it at a loss of stg5.5 million once the index fell in line with other markets. The day after the earthquake, the JGB index reversed its trend and Leeson built up a short position of 8460 contracts that soon produced a stg3.0 million gain and, like the Nikkei, it continued to fluctuate.

The Euroyen futures book was dealt a fate much like Leeson's overall portfolio. By January 24, a short position of

12,304 contracts had brought about a stg2.5 million loss. Within two weeks Leeson had managed to recoup and generate a small profit, but in the overall performance of account 88888 this was a minor joy.

As the juggernaut gained momentum, Leeson panicked. Individually, bank executives had a vague idea that something was not right, but they were yet to fully realise the risks involved. They automatically assumed big dollars were ahead and were actually impressed by the large number of new contracts Leeson had bought.

The total of 20,000 contracts purchased by Leeson in January was 14,000 more than his closest rivals, and represented a 600 per cent increase on the number of contracts held over the previous month. This significant increase prompted an edgy Christopher Thompson to terminate the informal agreement between Threadneedle Street and Barings in Singapore which had allowed Leeson's exposures to exceed BoE limits placed on international capital transfers. There was simply too much money involved. Over January and February Barings was rated the number house on Simex in terms of volume, accounting, respectively, for 12.72 and 8.78 per cent of turnover in those months.

Unsuspecting senior executives in Bishopsgate remained convinced that all of Leeson's positions were hedged. But the bank's Asset and Liability Committee was concerned enough to order Leeson to cap his current position and when possible scale it back at a profit through on-selling. The committee was not unduly worried about Singapore — moreover, the major point was that business was showing great prospects and attitudes were fairly casual, to the extent that a margin call payment was almost missed. In reality, sentiment didn't count for much — the termination of the agreement with the BoE was meaningless, and the Asset and Liability Committee's instructions were simply ignored.

Within the Asset and Liability Committee, and even at Threadneedle Street, neither Thompson nor anybody else could possibly have understood the full extent of what could

occur, the true situation having been complicated by Leeson's decision to hide his transactions in fictitious accounts
for clients who didn't exist. Much of this appeared as the new
business that had impressed Bishopsgate and would be
reflected in Leeson's annual bonus.

This type of situation was not unheard of.

Coopers & Lybrand had already warned senior executives
that Leeson had hidden losses, but London had failed to act
earlier and were unlikely to act now. The relatively simple
move of enforcing orthodox practice and transferring contract settlement from Leeson's portfolio to another account
would have ensured a closer scrutiny of his operations, and
would probably have revealed the magnitude of the bank's
exposure. As it was, error account 88888 remained unchecked.
No independent checks were carried out. No-one at Barings or
the BoE queried where forwarded funds were going.

Compounding Leeson's dangerous stance was the SLK
position. The auditors had again met with Leeson and Simon
Jones, and a status report was sent to group finance director
Geoffrey Broadhurst in London, who was immediately concerned that such a situation could arise without his knowledge. He spoke to Norris about the missing money and
Norris asked him not to inform the Asset and Liability
Committee because it was premature, and that he, Norris,
would talk to Bax about the receivable.[3]

Over the next three weeks, Leeson would provide the
auditors and different staff at Barings in Singapore and
Bishopsgate with six versions of a contrived story to explain
away the missing S$115 million. They were told the missing
money was related to an options trade between SLK and
Banque Nationale de Paris, that there had been computer
errors, a booking error, that money owed by SLK had been
withheld to be used as collateral. It was even suggested that
the SLK traders at Simex who wore Barings jackets had
booked an error.[4] With each fresh fabrication, Leeson
managed to secure a bit of continued leeway, and continued
hope that the markets would rebound in his favour.

As the lies mounted, so did the Singapore/Osaka exposures, and Barings in Singapore required large amounts of capital to cover their positions. The bulk of Leeson's requirements were met through Barings offices in Tokyo and London where reserves were funded through loans from Japanese banks and cash flow generated by client accounts. As the markets fluctuate, so do margin call payments, and an account holding the capital will rise and fall and indicate variable readings on any given day.

A request for a lodgement of substantial funds had been made by Simex on January 31. It was the Chinese New Year and the holiday would delay payment, but then came an extraordinary move, given the state of Barings' finances, and one made with little fuss. About stg44 million was forwarded in early February to accounts controlled by Leeson — to meet margin calls — along with a note congratulating him on the large amount of business he had written.

This decision proved critical. The trend line shows that for the first two weeks of February, the Nikkei 225 cracked Leeson's safety zone, falling from 18,739.5 to 18,138.5.

Losses that had been recouped were now wiped out, and for each point lost on the index, Barings was the poorer by some $200,000. Leeson's position was now in danger of wiping out the bank's entire capital, an estimated $900 million. More cash was required to meet margin calls and Barings continued to meet them, despite British laws that clearly spell out an obligation on all banks to inform the BoE, in advance, of transfers totalling more that 25 per cent of their capital base. Leeson would request that London 'please pay' the money required into the customer account. A breakdown of the account was occasionally provided and London appeared, perhaps with a few misgivings, satisfied with the explanations. Leeson was by now quite adept at paper shuffling.

It was almost unbelievable that alarm bells had failed to sound in the regulatory offices of either London, Singapore or Osaka. Traders were already aware that something was definitely amiss, and the incessant miming and outcries from the Barings corner of the Simex floor had been the subject of speculation at morning briefings among investment houses around the world, while analysts attempted to decipher the implications for the financial markets.

The concept of a solitary futures trader had raised eyebrows at the Bank of International Settlements (BIS) in Basle, Switzerland. The BIS department had contacted Barings' foreign exchange department asking about the bank's exposure in Asia. The call was based on rumours and did not please Norris. It was nevertheless considered insufficient on its own to warrant urgent intervention by head office.

Speculation on the Simex trading floor was rife. The Big Client theory that was believed to be behind Leeson's dealings was now dominating the bars with each trader attempting to figure out who it was. The more outrageous gossip included allegations that the client was laundering drug money, a prospect made believable by the audacious size of the position Leeson was adopting.

Unsubstantiated money laundering rumours often plague exchanges where client confidentiality clauses override disclosure laws.[5]

No-one wanted to even contemplate that Leeson was in reality involved in unhedged proprietary trading, and he was careful to say nothing that would counter the Big Client speculation. Occasionally, Leeson would simply say he was acting on behalf of a large customer but little else was added. Down at Harry's Bar at the Quay, where dealers would often drink and query Nick and each other about current trading, Jim Gelpi and his head barman, Zulkifflie Ariffin, had noticed Leeson's absence. It was a longer than normal break between beers, though at the time it appeared to be a moot point, given the constant daily flow of traders mixing it across the bar. The other traders hadn't noticed his absence. Leeson could still be heard vomiting in the toilets at Simex and his colleagues still assumed, perhaps incorrectly, that the lad from Watford had been hitting the booze elsewhere on the cobbled path of Boat Quay or at another favourite haunt — nothing out of the ordinary. This may in fact have been one of the few indications that the stresses of his position were taking their toll.

Shortly after the Bank of International Settlements called, a reporter from the financial news service Bloomberg telephoned Fernando Gueler, Barings' head of derivatives in Tokyo, asking what was happening with Barings in the market, given the rampant talk that the bank had adopted very long positions. Gueler's reply added no support to the Big Client theory, but he did say that the bank had a lot of diversified customers, and if there were any suggestions that Barings in Singapore was trading on behalf of the bank, it never rated a mention. And back at Barings' London headquarters, arrogance, ignorance, and greed, in the form of the annual bonus frenzy, were of more immediate concern.

Attempts were being made, however, at some levels, to discover what exactly *was* happening in Singapore. Barings' Group treasurer, Anthony Hawes, had on several occasions urged his seniors to scrutinise the Singapore operation after queries from Simex. Barings' reputation alone had until now allayed at Simex the sort of fears that may have resulted in more decisive action being taken sooner, with lesser-credentialled investment houses.

There was also the additional element of confusion resurfacing from the transaction involving SLK. Executives posed three theories involving the unauthorised brokered deal, including an operational error resulting in an unauthorised payment, and that Barings Securities had been made a counterparty to a transaction through an operational error. The transaction had preoccupied valuable time for executives at Barings and at Coopers & Lybrand. The auditors needed to resolve the S$115 million hole before the end of year accounts for Barings Plc could be signed off although, based on their assumption that a simple typing error may have occurred, their concerns remained limited.

Incredibly, Leeson managed to turn this to his advantage and played for further breathing space by claiming that the deal, which had never taken place, *was* unauthorised after all, and that this was wrong and entirely his mistake. He was sorry and needed help. His duped superiors were sympathetic: Leeson may have been the great trader in the Far East, but he was still a young man, and to make a mistake is, after all, only human.

Leeson was queried on several occasions. He claimed there had been an error in maturity dates on the system deal brokered by Barings between SLK and Banque Nationale de Paris, and that word had been received that the fund would be paid.

In a status report to Barings, Coopers & Lybrand concluded in late January: 'We are informed by BFS (Barings Futures Singapore) that collectability of the said 7.7 billion yen is not envisaged to be a problem'.[6] Coopers & Lybrand did, however, ask whether SLK was a regular client, and credit-worthy.

At Simex, officials had monitored each trade that Barings Futures undertook through the normal course of business, and had witnessed first hand the alarming rate at which the position had grown. As with all exchanges, Simex requires all records of trade, including the buyer, seller, price and time of trade, to be kept, and it is against the law to destroy those records.

The exchange was becoming increasingly irritated with Barings and demanded an explanation from Bishopsgate — reputation was starting to count for a little less as time went on. Market rumours kept circulating that Barings was having problems meeting margin call payments in the Far East.

The Asset and Liability Committee again discussed the growing Singapore position on January 31. The discussion centred around a letter dated four days earlier, sent to Barings in Singapore from Simex, but it was later revealed that this discussion had had the effect of heightening fears among some Barings executives elsewhere in the group, and had created more than a passing interest in South East Asia. James Bax had sent his prepared letter to London on February 3 to, amongst others, Peter Norris, Ron Baker, and Ian Hopkins.

It read in part: 'As you know, recent incidents have highlighted the current operational weaknesses of our Simex business and an urgent need for a new approach'.

'The growing volumes traded on Simex have meant Nick Leeson can no longer continue to run the trading and settlement roles effectively. In any case it has long been acknowledged that there are control weaknesses in this arrangement'.[7]

It can be disputed whether Tony Hawes had failed to gain any solid support for his concerns after he recommended that a Barings senior executive fly out and take a first hand look at what was going on. One such recommendation was reportedly declined. On February 6, Hawes decided to fly out himself with Tony Railton, a Futures Operations Settlements clerk, to have a look at the operations, meet with regulatory authorities and attempt to resolve a number of issues.

By this stage, unreconciled amounts totalled stg306 million compared to just stg22 million in the previous November.

Simex wanted an explanation and while Hawes held his own concerns, he managed to reassure officials that the position taken by the Singapore futures operations was hedged and backed by Barings assets, and that the group was in full control.

The explanation was accepted. Barings was continuing to meet its rapidly growing margin calls through a variety of mechanisms, and there was therefore no need for Simex to suspend the bank from trading. A second letter seeking to allay Simex fears was sent by Barings Singapore executive Simon Jones who assured the exchange that Barings' position was being monitored daily by the bank's risk unit in London.

Hawes had also briefed Railton that he was to improve bookkeeping and treasury in Singapore which would allow London to identify the exact extent of margin payments being required, ensure this was being funded correctly, and that all the information which had been lacking up to that point would in future be provided. Accountants in London were suspicious, but they believed out-of-place figures were more probably the work of sloppy bookkeeping than anything else.

Railton was also charged with arranging larger daylight overdraft facilities with local banks, and it was decided he would remain in Singapore to cover for a colleague who was away on maternity leave. After a week in Singapore, Hawes left. He had not been able to satisfactorily resolve all the issues he had planned to, but a return visit in two weeks time would remedy the situation.

In the meantime, Railton was to prepare a spreadsheet detailing the timing and different types of margin payments made to Simex by Barings Futures in Singapore. Use of spreadsheets is common in investment houses. Typically they are computer models involving columns of financial variables to provide various strategies for different scenarios.

Belatedly, James Bax decided it was better to split the settlement responsibilities held by Leeson. This restricted Leeson solely to back office operations, and meant he would have to answer to Simon Jones. But it was too late. Leeson was already aware that irreparable damage had occurred, and all that remained was for him to be found out.

Leeson steeled his nerve and put up a facade of control to those around him. When confronted by an AP-Dow Jones reporter who was curious about rumours that an Englishman was making huge purchases on the Japanese and Singapore exchanges on behalf of his London-based investment bank, Leeson calmly explained that he was 'buying Nikkei futures here and selling them there'. Nothing out of the ordinary, Leeson assured the journalist.[8] But one of Leeson's colleagues at another Barings branch in Asia told of a different Leeson, with whom he had spoken a few days later.

'He sounded really weird on the phone, like he was in a really good mood', the man told *Time* magazine. 'He asked me: "How's life?". He never asked me anything like that before. It was completely out of character'.[9]

'We talked again later in the day — when he must have already known he was in trouble — but he was still joking around. I asked him to change something in the way he sent reports to us and he said: 'Do you want me to tell you which hand I wrote the report with?"[10]

But while Leeson appeared to be on top of the situation, at Bishopsgate, signs of internal brawling were emerging. Ian Hopkins, who headed Barings treasury and risk department and had warned three months earlier that the control culture within Barings had become 'distinctly flaky', left the department.[11]

Margin calls had nearly surpassed the $120 million mark for the first two weeks of February alone, but the position blowout now required a mammoth shift of funds. Reluctantly, Leeson contacted Bishopsgate and requested a number of tranches of 'top-up payments' to be shifted as loans to clients — in reality the funds were used to cover margin calls emanating from his own trading position.

The demands were placing an insupportable burden on Barings' futures operations in Japan. However, the requests were coming through Nick Leeson, and Leeson was ostensibly Barings' number one trader in the region. Bishopgate's attitude accorded with the matrix system of management, which warns that top levels of management must provide adequate support to ensure success, and must recognise the effect of ill-advised intervention, otherwise the hierarchy would be courting disaster. Borrowings had increased dramatically, and the funds being tied up in Singapore were excessive, prompting the more prudent Asset and Liability Committee to warn Leeson not to increase his position, despite having been previously ignored by Leeson with apparent impunity.

London was also concerned with the way money was being diverted, with Singapore being funded through the Japanese operations, complicating the account books. Leeson's demands were outstripping in-coming funds, and the books were starting to look more like a list of client debtors. Leeson was queried, but he was stern. He had considered London the ultimate 'cash cow' when it came to the funding of the Singapore operations, and had emphasised that the local operations had no formal funding lines. His attitude was not unusual, in fact his response was well-judged: had it been otherwise, there may have been further cause for concern.

Causing yet more anxiety was the situation at Barings Securities Japan, where an equity balance of stg253 million was held on behalf of the Singapore operation, while at the same time Simex margin requirements had reached stg200 million. It was a worrying position, and the Japanese arm asked that some of funds be returned. The number crunchers of the Asset and Liability Committee had little time for personalities, Leeson's image, or the conviction that his position had been hedged. On February 17, the committee again directed Ron Baker to order Leeson to reduce his exposure. Baker was scheduled to leave that Friday for a holiday, so he issued the directive on that Sunday from Switzerland. Some of the funds required by Tokyo were returned, but shortly afterwards Barings Japan's exposure to its Singapore cousin soared to stg300 million.

Barings' total resources were stretched and starting to buckle, with an unrelenting Leeson shifting more offshore funds into Singapore and lodging stg468 million in margin call payments with Simex and without the official notification and approval by the Bank of England. At Barings, executives held onto the assumption that Leeson's position was hedged and, while some sceptics were prodding the accounts, no-one bothered to ask whether the funding was for clients or whether Leeson had created his own portfolio of securities. About stg720 million was eventually sent to cover the rising losses.

Error account 88888 remained tucked away with Leeson's short futures position standing at 24,536 March 95 contracts at February 15. Total losses in the Nikkei 225, JGB and Euroyen futures had reached stg170 million. Even this would prove difficult to hide, and it was later found that Leeson had processed an uncompleted transaction of 7000 March 95 contracts through Baring's transaction system, showing a stg170 million gain. Accumulated losses for the year had thus been offset, and the books appeared to be in order. He apparently reversed the transaction the following day.

Railton continued his investigations with formulated spreadsheets. The first signs of a serious problem had emerged in the JGB position. He had concluded: 'My God, if you close out all the positions there is absolutely no way on God's earth that you could actually return all the yen'.[12] Tony Hawes was informed that a shortfall of 14 billion yen had been discovered, but inquiries later revealed that at this stage no transgression was suspected.

Railton tried another financial spreadsheet, but this also offered no consolation. He found a breakdown of US dollar margins, which were submitted by the Singapore office to London, to be meaningless. His attempts at sorting out the transactions was growing more and more difficult, and Railton eventually confessed to Brenda Granger in London that 14 billion yen could not be accounted for, and he did not know what to do about it.

Granger headed Barings Futures and Operations Settlement in London, and was in constant contact with Railton. On the same day Baker left for his holiday, he told her the hole had grown to $190 million. Railton was worried. He had singled Leeson out for questioning, and the pair agreed to meet the following Monday.

On Monday, February 20, Leeson reported in ill. He took the next day off too, although Railton was successful in tracking Leeson down for about an hour. Railton had intended to elicit more information by steering the conversation towards the trading activities, but Leeson was Railton's senior and this was a cause for some concern, because Railton intended to relocate to Singapore and did not want to be disrespectful towards his potential future boss.

Unable to find any answers, and unaware of the urgency of what was about to unfold, Railton was content with Leeson's suggestion that they discuss the discrepancy when he returned to work, and the conversation soon turned to relocation packages.[13]

By Wednesday, February 22, Leeson had returned to work. He again sidestepped Railton and watched the Nikkei 225 close at 18,106.7. The next day profit-takers made another run on the index and dragged it down to 17,830.0. There were no signs of a turnaround, and Railton was proving to be a nuisance.

That Thursday morning, Tony Railton went in search of Nick Leeson. He wanted hard answers to the $190 million irregularity in the accounts. He found Leeson penned in as usual on the noisy and crowded trading floor at Simex. Railton made several attempts to question Leeson but the usual mayhem on the trading floor made any meaningful interaction impossible. Executives in London were beside themselves. They believed Leeson was reducing his position and were astounded to receive a $45 million funding request to meet another Simex margin call payment. It was blatantly and belatedly obvious that something was awry, and a memorandum sent to Singapore — discovered later — said as much.

Railton later claimed that Leeson had carried on trading despite his presence. Railton left, hoping to clarify the situation with Leeson after the close of trade. He had no way of knowing that Leeson was indeed trading frantically, but to no avail.

※

Leeson was finally forced to confront the truth: he had in all probability ruined his bank. However, it remained his secret that Barings now held millions of dollars worth of useless paper, of which the full value could not be immediately calculated, but when added up, translated into an IOU in excess of the bank's worth.

Meanwhile, the Barings board had met at Bishopsgate to consider the 1994 accounts. They were impressed. A small rise in profits over the previous year — as the market was anticipating — was evident, and senior executives stood to receive their handsome bonuses.

In Singapore, Nick Leeson now knew he would be discovered. Losses had surpassed his own wildest calculations. That day alone, he had lost stg65 million. In the afternoon, Leeson packed his briefcase and telephoned his wife. He then went to the office of Barings Securities on the 24th floor of Ocean Tower, where he met with Railton and Simon Jones. Leeson was told that a large amount of yen was missing, and to Railton's surprise Leeson agreed with him, and added that further information would be provided to resolve the problem. They stayed only briefly before deciding to move to the futures office ten floors below but, before leaving, Leeson spoke with Jones alone.

Jones was reportedly told by Nick that Lisa was suffering from complications arising from a miscarriage and that he needed to leave immediately so he could visit his wife in hospital.[14] As the three made their way towards the 14th floor, Leeson excused himself and said he would return within 45 minutes. He never did.

After his departure, Jones apparently turned to Railton and said: 'I do not blame you for wanting to speak to Nick. This does not make any sense to me'.[15]

It would take another four days to determine the true extent of the one loss-making portfolio, error account 88888, which became known as the 'eights account', and which contained a seemingly endless list of problems and requests to 'please pay'.

CHAPTER NINE

THE LONGEST WEEKEND

'Things started to get very bad at the end of January [1995]. Nick's brother Richard asked me: "Is Nick all right? He keeps on asking me if he can come and work with me and Dad as a labourer. Not even plastering, just mixing cement. Is he losing it?"' Lisa Leeson.[1]

After Leeson left Singapore, the first signs that something was seriously wrong became obvious. Simon Jones was given the task of reviewing documents surrounding SLK. He suspected the documents had been adjusted to convince the external auditors that the SLK receivable had been repaid, when in reality it had not. He noticed that at the top of the confirmation document, a header stated it was 'From Nick and Lisa', leading him to believe the document had been sent from the Leesons home facsimile machine and not the one at the SLK offices, which would bear a Spear, Leeds & Kellogg fax' ID. Jones' immediate surprise was that this had failed to raise the suspicions of the external auditors. By 9:30 pm he decided that Leeson would not be returning for the evening. It was not unusual for Leeson to break appointments. That aside, Jones maintained his faith in the bank's star trader and, after informing James Bax that Leeson was unsighted, he called it a night.

Tony Railton remained suspicious, and reported the matter to London. Tony Hawes was in Japan and had received the memorandum from London querying a funding request from Singapore, made the previous day, for $45.5

million to meet Simex margin calls. London understood that Leeson was supposed to be reducing his position and suggested that something was amiss that warranted a closer inspection. This was several hours after Leeson had walked out of Ocean Towers. Hawes immediately booked a flight out of Tokyo, arriving in Singapore at about 1:30 the next morning. He booked into a hotel and was immediately greeted with a panicky telephone call.

'It was Peter Norris from London asking me: "What on earth is happening in Singapore and where is Leeson?" '[2] Norris was getting edgy. Brenda Granger had already told her supervisor, Tony Gamby, that: 'Nick was coming back to the office later on [Thursday] evening to ensure that the reconciliation was done'.[3] But it was an appointment Leeson had no intention of keeping. Around midday (London time) on that day, Gamby recalled hearing that Leeson could not be located. Later that afternoon, Gamby told Norris that Barings had a $170 million reconciliation problem, 'but, more to the point, we cannot find the trader'.[4]

Overall, what was taking place was cumbersome. Scores of people, many of whom had no relationship with the other except for a business-as-usual telephone call, were desperately trying to ascertain what was going on. Ron Baker was on holiday and Norris, his executives, the board and the BoE had by now well and truly proved their lack of comprehension of derivatives. Their subordinates in London slowly began to conclude that unauthorised transactions had taken place. Fearing the worst — although not knowing exactly what this meant — Norris contacted Mary Walz. He had to find Leeson. Walz eventually spoke with Lisa's mother, who reported the couple had telephoned her a couple of hours earlier to say they were travelling to Bangkok for the weekend. Gamby later remarked: 'That was when the alarm bells started flashing [sic]'.[5]

Back in Singapore, it was about 3:00 am on Friday morning when Hawes met Railton. Railton had also received an unnerving late-night call from Norris. After taking the decision to act immediately, the pair crossed the deserted streets and went straight to Barings' Singapore branch. This was an extreme situation — two executives from London conducting a midnight search in a Far East branch office in the middle of the night to check for unauthorised payments was an uncommon scenario. Warily, the pair began rummaging through the files and through Leeson's accounts in an effort to reconcile the cash position. It was there that Hawes concluded that the apparent SLK settlement 'had been manufactured'.[6]

They were soon joined by Bax and Jones, and their search for unauthorised payments intensified with no-one really anticipating what they might find — especially Jones, who was officially responsible for back room operations. As the sun began casting a morning shadow across the Boat Quay, they stumbled upon it. Tony Hawes started reading a computer print-out and spotted an account labelled error account containing a multitude of transactions. Given the situation, the term 'error account' would have been enough to grab the attention of any budding investigator. And just like in all good detective novels, into one of which these Barings executives must have felt they had stumbled, these ones did contain some answers, perilous ones, causing Hawes to note: 'all of them seemingly standing at enormous losses'.[7]

In London, it was Thursday evening and an urgent meeting of senior executives was convened. Broadhurst, Granger, Gamby, Maclean, Norris and Walz worked through the night, discussing the reconciliation. David Hughes from the treasury department was summoned to Norris' office. 'News was breaking that there was a significant problem,' Hughes said. 'As you can imagine, all kinds of speculation was occurring . . .'.[8]

The executives needed to buy some time, and it was decided that Barings would continue trading throughout Friday in a business-as-usual fashion. No mention of the losses was to be made, and no new futures positions were to be adopted in Singapore. Simex was not told of Barings' exposures, nor were financial markets elsewhere, despite the rights of investors who maintain they should have been kept fully informed. Such a decision could only be made from the very top.

That day, the Nikkei opened at 17,830.0 amid speculation within tight industry circles that something was wrong at Barings. The benchmark Japanese stock index then duly plummeted, compiling losses for Leeson's portfolio and confusing the true nature of the exposures for those trying to sift through a veritable mountain of paperwork.

But the question remained, growing more desperate with time: 'where the hell is Nick Leeson?'. Orders to find him came ringing out of London and Singapore all morning, with the hapless company watching all the while as the Nikkei continued to dive. There was even talk that George Soros had heard that Barings was in trouble and was adopting a short position in order to take advantage of the situation. Whether this was true or not is unknown, but it must have raised a few eyebrows, given that Leeson had at some times left the impression that Soros may have been his mysterious Big Client. Such talk effectively made the bank's position worse, with Japanese share prices continuing to be squeezed.

About seven hours after Hawes and Railton first entered Ocean Towers, a note was sent from Hawes to the Asset and Liability Committee in London outlining the exposures held in error account 88888 as the source of Barings' problems, and that by stashing losses Leeson had been able to inflate profits in account 92000.

But by breaking into Leeson's files, it had taken just a few hours for several people to discover the one account which Leeson had successfully kept a secret for more than two and a half years.

Amid the mounting panic, and the chorus of voices claiming victory for finding the answers first, traders in Singapore, where Leeson had worn the navy and gold stripes of Barings, found a fax from their missing colleague saying he was taking the day off to celebrate his birthday at the beach resort town of Phuket in Thailand. At about 3:00 pm, James Bax received a second fax, this time from the Regent Hotel in Kuala Lumpur. A copy of the letter appeared later in Singapore's *Business Times*.

It read in part: 'My sincere apologies for the predicament that I have left you in. It was neither my intention or aim for this to happen but the pressure, both business and personal, have become to much to bear and after receiving medical advice, have affected my health to the extent that a breakdown is imminent'.

He concluded: 'In light of my action I tender my resignation with immediate effect and will contact you early next week to discuss the best course of action'.

It was signed: 'Apologies, Nick'.

Another letter was reportedly sent to Sir Peter in London detailing what had happened. Again, Leeson apologised and added that he doubted whether the two would meet again.

After receiving the second note, Bax spoke to Norris and they decided that Bax should head for Kuala Lumpur to try to find Leeson and to convince him to return. Barings executives had covered for Leeson before, but this time it was serious. Leeson had fled, and was now a fugitive.

Interpol was alerted.

As Bax flew to Kuala Lumpur, the Japanese stock market had closed for the day with the Nikkei shedding more than 350 points to a dismal 17,472.9.

Sir Peter learnt the grim details when Norris telephoned him on Friday morning at 7:15 am London time. As the chairman made his way to work, he could not have known that this would be the last day of an illustrious history for Barings Plc. In the meantime, Norris ordered Gamby to take the first available flight to Singapore 'to see, hope against hope, if there was some client sitting behind error account

88888 that we were not aware of'.[9] Just like Bax's search for Leeson in Kuala Lumpur, such hopes were futile. Bax had returned empty-handed on the Saturday morning.

Gamby was accompanied to Singapore by Granger and Mike Finlay, who also worked in the Futures and Options Settlements Department in London. At some stage during the weekend, the Barings team sent to investigate prised open a drawer in Leeson's desk.

'There was a stack of paper', Railton said. 'There were holes in some. You could see how [Leeson] had produced [the] confirmation of the SLK deal, I believe, and also I think a bank statement as well.'[10] Granger said Bax had found a fraudulent document in one of Leeson's folders. Gamby said that in Leeson's drawer 'we found some cut-and-paste material for the SLK transaction. There was this SLK letter with a scissor cut around the signature . . . we also found a cut-and-paste of the Citibank statement'.[11]

Evidence was mounting that serious fraud had taken place. The team had to decipher whether a fabrication of payment of the SLK year-end receivable had occurred and, if so, whether this was linked to the unauthorised trading in error account 88888.

They worked through Saturday night, only to confirm what Hawes had already surmised: that Barings Futures Singapore was insolvent. It soon dawned upon them that the biggest problem facing the bank was that the losses were unquantifiable and they had not been capped. A worst-case scenario — the death of the bank — had for the first time, to be considered.

Traders who witnessed the furious toil in Barings' Singapore office during the course of that weekend described the atmosphere as like that of a home where a death in the family is imminent. The unspoken belief was that, whatever the true extent of the crisis facing the bank, the condition would in all probability prove fatal.

Whispers of a potential collapse started to spread. Jack David recalled what turned out to be a 'most uncomfortable

and long weekend': 'I actually didn't get an inkling until the
Friday before the weekend. A Merrill Lynch person on the
legal side had asked the exchange if the Barings customer
had a market call double the worth of Barings equity. I
found out on Saturday night through people here in
Singapore. Then I called my immediate superior, who was
heavily connected with clients of Barings. I didn't sleep well
that night'.

Another trader said he ventured into Simex over the
weekend. 'I went into the exchange to get my software out
and [to establish] whether we were in trouble or not in
trouble', said the trader who, like all those associated with
Simex, spoke only on condition of anonymity. 'I saw James
Bax there. He looked like the closest thing to death that I
have ever seen'.

Bax implored the trader to explain to him how Leeson
did what he did. 'James Bax and I sat in the office and he
asked me how Nick could have done this', he said. 'I told
him that everyone on the floor thought that Nick had a very
big customer'. While this trader, like everybody else, would
have been too preoccupied with his own position too worry
about the fate of Barings per se, he allowed himself an
amused smile at the situation. Nick Leeson had bullied
himself to the top and created for himself a reputation that,
seen in hindsight, had never really been deserved. In the
pubs, Leeson's stories were the ones they always listened to.
How his wins were always more than the rest of pack's. How
his losses were never as bad. It was almost comforting to
realise that it had all been a sham.

The extent of the losses was starting to be calculated in
terms of individual contracts. As at February 23, Leeson had
reported 23,039 Nikkei futures contracts and 8,079 JGB
futures contracts to Simex. In reality, 55,399 Nikkei futures
and 26,079 JGB futures contracts had been accumulated.

The extent of the fraudulent dealings had created the biggest crisis Barings had ever confronted, and Sir Peter knew that unless an outside investor could be found, the bank his family had created, controlled, and dominated for the past 223 years would be lost.

After the close of London trade on Friday, Sir Peter contacted BoE governor Eddie George, who was on a skiing holiday in Avoriaz, France, with his family. Sir Peter wanted a crisis meeting. George had to prove himself a saviour. The chain-smoking governor was astounded by what Sir Peter had to say. George agreed to try to help. The nicotine steeled his nerve and bore out George's nickname, Steady Eddie. He booked the first flight available back to London. Apart from cigarettes, George's other constant companion was a personal Reuters monitor. His days as a free-wheeling marketeer and the lessons they taught him about pure capitalism and the dynamics of profit and loss had not left him, and the Reuters monitor kept him up-to-date with the happenings of international financial markets.

Meanwhile Barings executives were also dispatched to Singapore, Tokyo and Hong Kong for meetings with regulators in an eleventh-hour bid to find a solution.

In George's absence, immediate BoE responsibilities fell to the BoE's deputy governor, Rupert Pennant-Rea, though at this early stage, Pennant-Rea would not officially step in. He would instead oversee talks at arm's length for a proposed rescue package with other British banks, and await George's return. Barings was, after all a privately owned investment bank. The central bank stood ready, however, to provide liquidity in the event of a total banking crisis.

Losses needed to be firmly calculated, while potential British investors with the potential to aid Barings were quietly contacted. There was always the possibility that Barings could use its clout to request that the Bank of England either directly loan enough capital to cover the liabilities, or provide a rescue package of a similar scale to that put together during the Argentine debacle of 1890.

Barings and Leeson were together testing the credibility of the Bank of England. The Barings crisis would prove a true litmus test for the overseer of the British monetary system and lender of last resort. Failure would deal an embarrassing blow to Threadneedle Street, which had already been heavily criticised by outsiders for its handling of the Johnson Matthey and BCCI collapses.

Talks that night faltered, and Barings officials again met with British banking regulators the following day in an effort to find a buyer or a cash injection that would offset Leeson's losses sufficient to allow the bank to open its doors on Monday. It was the first big test for the relatively inexperienced Pennant-Rea. He was an outsider to the British establishment, having been raised in Rhodesia, and despite having been educated at Trinity College in Dublin. His quip that Barings had been struck by a meteor was apt, but no-one quite believed him when he tried to impress that the financial markets had not been struck by a plague.

A former editor of the international weekly magazine *The Economist*, Pennant-Rea had accepted the deputy's post just two years earlier. He could not possibly have forecast the personal cost to himself and his family that the collapse of Barings would eventually deliver, his former mistress also taking this opportunity to make public their affair.

One single hurdle stood in the way: Barings had so far been unable put a final figure on the losses and no-one would absorb an indefinable deficit. The losses were proving difficult to calculate because the nature of futures contracts meant that whoever assumed responsibility for them would have to wait until they were all closed out, and that could take years. Each day the value of the contracts would rise and fall in accordance with fluctuations in Japanese markets.

The role of intermediary fell to Eddie George once he had returned home. George was aghast when told that losses totalling at least stg400 million had been discovered. Barings were the bankers to Queen Elizabeth. Barings had to be saved. The first thing George did was have a stiff drink, which was no doubt accompanied by another cigarette.

George had supervised negotiations with banks for more than 10 years, but soon realised that Barings was facing something graver than he had ever dealt with. The task of finding a local investor seemed impossible.

George seriously considered a direct bail-out by Threadneedle Street. He also had to consider the wider ramifications. The BoE could afford the capital required, even if it reached $1.0 billion, but the politics of the central bank's independence, coupled with his own personal philosophical stance, made it difficult to justify reaching into the public purse to rescue a private bank. Even if it were very much a cornerstone of the establishment. In the event of the bank's demise, the news was certain to ricochet throughout the global marketplace, frightening investors, and throwing the entire system off balance.

A deadline for a final decision was decided on — midnight Sunday, London time, when Japan's markets were scheduled to begin trading.

Finding a buyer was also complicated by the fact that many potential bidders had acquired futures contracts bought against the Barings position. George later remarked that there were simply too many traders who had bet against Barings and hopes that they might settle, short of breaking the bank, were dashed. George began seeking help from outside Britain.

In the meantime, Sir Peter and the board were faced with the most difficult decision of their professional careers, and the most painful in the history of the bank.

The unprecedented decision was made — if a major investor or a buyer for the entire bank could not be found, the Barings Group would be surrendered to receivers in the hope that the bank's assets could be divided and the most profitable assets hived off to cover the losses. This would involve selling the Barings corporate finance team and the fund management operations, Barings Asset Management, BAM.

BAM was considered the richest part of the group with $45 billion worth of assets held on behalf of other big funds and private individuals around the world, while income from the corporate finance team had risen 42 per cent during the second half of 1994 to stg238.8 million.

The search intensified, and at Threadneedle Street George was understood to have come close to securing a deal with Japanese banking authorities. Approaches had also been made to the world's richest man, The Sultan of Brunei, whose personal fortune from oil revenue was estimated at about $70 billion.

Japanese banks were also reluctant to help. They were still reeling from their own massive exposures to bad and doubtful debts, and Barings' unknown futures position was simply too great a risk.

On Sunday morning, February 26, Britons awoke to the news that Barings, the nation's oldest and sixth largest merchant bank, was in deep trouble. *The Sunday Telegraph* carried the story exclusively. International wire services picked up on the *Telegraph's* lead and delivered the story to every major radio, television, newspaper and screen-based service.

Across town from what is left of Fleet Street's international news bureaux, the City's banking leaders met at 10:00 am to thrash out a number of proposals. George started the meeting by asking for volunteers who could offer a fixed sum to bail Barings out.

None were forthcoming.

Instead, it was proposed that certain clearing houses put up stg60 million each, while a number of medium-sized investment houses would each provide stg30 million. The funds could be advanced to a consortium in the form of a loan, which could establish a holding company, using the money as equity to recapitalise the bank. Barings could continue trading, the assets could be sold off responsibly within three months, and the losses could be accounted for.

Bankers feared, however, that their assuming responsibility for the futures position would become common knowledge in the market, leaving them vulnerable to expanding losses at the hands of speculators who could conceivably adopt an opposite strategy, driving down the Nikkei 225.

Such a scenario would be not unlike the plight of Britain's foreign exchange market in 1992 when speculators hammered the pound, forcing it out of the European exchange rate mechanism, and triggering a financial crisis. In Barings' case, a declaration of a $7.0 billion futures position based on a rising Nikkei 225 was an open invitation for fund managers and speculators to hedge against the bank. That sentiment alone would bring about another fall on the key Japanese index.

The meeting lasted all day and considered all the issues, but it was becoming increasingly obvious that a saviour would not be found. At 7:00 pm, George received word that the Sultan of Brunei was prepared to invest half of a stg600 million rescue package if further losses from the futures exposures could be restricted. Several offers had been proposed and rejected, but the Sultan's offer was at least feasible.

It was a cruelly brief moment of relief for Sir Peter and George. The remaining bankers now considered that a flat contribution of 5.0 per cent each would be sufficient to make up the remaining capital. However, George was unable to guarantee the Sultan that total losses could be capped, and at 8:35 pm George informed the bankers that the Sultan had baulked at the bail-out. The world's richest man had faced another negative in the deal: as a financier he would have ranked below the banks as a creditor, despite putting up the bulk of the capital in a deal where losses could not be capped.

It was essential that the Bank of England and its governor acted before the Asian markets opened for trade. World financial markets were already jangled over the Mexican debt crisis and a troubled British government. Wised up traders and investors had spent the weekend glued to their mobile phones. In pubs, on golf courses, and at home, they monitored the escalating crisis through their networks of contacts. Foreign exchange dealers, stock brokers, bond traders, arbitrageurs, fund managers, and investment bankers around the world attempted to gain an inside edge by second-guessing what was happening in London.

For George, resolving the crisis was further complicated by problems at home. The British pound and the stock market had been floundering under pressure from a scandal-plagued government and its Prime Minister, John Major. The pound had fallen the previous week against a basket of the leading currencies, in response to nervousness before an upcoming key government debate on European policy.

On the wider stage, the Mexico debt crisis had ripped through international markets like a plague. Problems with Mexico had been compounded by its central bank decision, made a week earlier, to raise interest rates as part of an overall strategy designed to bridge support for the peso and to control inflation.

Superficially the decision appeared sound, but analysts argued that Mexico City was essentially caving in to demands by Washington, where negotiations for a $20 billion bail-out for the Mexico's problems were being thrashed out.

Short-term rates were driven up by 10 percentage points, putting pressure on Mexico's fragile economy, but the critical point was the further uncertainty being applied to Wall Street, and therefore the rest of the world's markets which take their lead from New York — and in this sense dictated that the BoE had to act quickly. There had to be a resolution, or Barings would be put to the sword. A drawn out Barings saga hanging on the markets would create further uncertainty, George would be vilified for his indecisiveness, and British financial circles would be condemned as ineffectual.

George's attitude had grown simpler with the rising of losses, which now totalled $790 million. A collapse of Barings would further undermine confidence in the government and the financial markets, and would be tantamount to an admission of defeat by the central bank. George faced a haranguing for failing the establishment in an hour of such need. But if the market forces deemed Barings no longer solvent and a collapse could not be averted, then so be it.

The search for an outside investor had failed, and Barings could no longer avoid the inevitable. No institution had been willing to invest in Barings because of the large amounts of money involved, and because of the nature of derivative contracts.

Contracts remained open and the full extent of the losses remained too difficult to determine until all contracts had expired, a process which could have taken up to five years.

The decision was made. Barings would be placed into receivership and the bank's executives and board members would publicly cover themselves by denying any previous knowledge of Leeson's trading activities.

On Sunday February 26, at 10:10 pm, the Bank of England made the following announcement:

> Barings has been the victim of losses caused by massive unauthorised dealings by one of its traders in South East Asia.
>
> It is now apparent that the losses caused by these dealings were in excess of stg500 million by the close of business last week.
>
> The contracts concerned are still open, exposing Barings to unquantifiable losses until the contracts expire or are otherwise closed out.
>
> The British banks were committed to supplying all capital needed to recapitalise Barings, provided it was possible to cap the potential liability on its contracts. In the event, it did not prove possible to meet this essential precondition for the injection of new capital into the firm.
>
> As a result, Barings cannot continue trading and is applying for administration.
>
> These circumstances are unique to Barings and should have no implications for other banks operating in London.

The London markets will open tomorrow. The Bank of England stands ready to provide liquidity to the banking system to ensure that it continues to function normally.

Barings bank had reached the end of the line.

The establishment couldn't afford Barings' bills, and Steady Eddie — an outsider who 'knew the price of everything and the value of nothing' — had let the house of cards topple.

Leeson's identity and his role in the drama had been kept a secret from the public, but the board knew full well that a scapegoat existed on whom the bank's management ills and frailties could be pinned. The press was clamouring for more information and the Barings board made full use of the media's short attention span, diverting to the 'rogue trader' responsibility for destroying one of Britain's most cherished financial institutions.

Behind the scenes, Leeson's guilt had been assumed, conspiracy theories were hatched, and a very public die had been cast.

At Barings headquarters in Bishopsgate, someone had neglected that night to switch off the lights, and they stayed on, as midnight passed, keeping their silent vigil over the 20 storey building which had housed the once proud bank.

1. The trading floor of the Singapore International Monetary Exchange (Simex). Photo provided by The Associated Press.

2. The man who broke his own bank — Nick Leeson. Photo provided by The Associated Press.

3. Nick Leeson is escorted away under custody by German border police after his arrival at Frankfurt airport. Photo provided by The Associated Press.

4. Lisa Leeson at the gates of Number 10 Downing Street on July 19 holds a personal appeal to British Prime Minister John Major for a British extradition of Nick Leeson back to London. Photo provided by The Associated Press.

5. Nick Leeson is escorted through Changi Airport upon his arrival back in Singapore from Germany. Photo provided by The Associated Press.

6. Nick Leeson arrives for sentencing on December 2, 1995. Photo provided by The Associated Press.

CHAPTER TEN

NICK LEESON
DID IT

'I am not a destroyer of companies, I am a liberator of them. The point, ladies and gentlemen, is that greed, for lack of a better word, is good. Greed is right. Greed works. It clarifies, cuts through and captures the essence of the evolutionary spirit.' Gordon Gekko.[1]

As Barings executives handed over the keys to the administrators who were left to determine the true extent of the losses, British investment circles were trying to come to terms with the unthinkable. It was still early and events were only slowly unfolding, but inside tight-lipped establishment banking circles, the finger-pointing had already begun and, at Threadneedle Street, Eddie George, Rupert Pennant-Rea and Brian Quinn were targeted for failing to extend a life-line to the 'victim' of one rogue trader.

The Barings executive management team now fell under the scrutiny of official regulatory bodies. The government had been severely embarrassed by the fall of the landmark bank, and conspiracy theories appropriating blame and responsibility were being hatched, with various factions each moving to cover their own backs, and to make sure the blame fell elsewhere. Nick Leeson's name had not yet entered the public realm but, by skipping Singapore, he had compounded his own problems and the only common assumption was that missing rogue trader, Nick Leeson, *was* guilty despite the traditional presumption of innocence granted under England's judicial system.

While board members were justifiably upset, and retired teary-eyed on Sunday night, international financial markets on the other side of the world had little interest in reflecting on events. They began instead to brace themselves for an imminent series of disasters.

Anxiety was at its most pronounced in real stock markets, where a company's ability to operate is reliant upon the fortunes of its investors and on the lead of indices such as Japan's Nikkei 225, the Straits Times index in Singapore, the FTSE-100 in London, and the Dow Jones in New York.

The first wave of fear was being relayed around the world on Monday morning, when traders and analysts at the centre of this financial storm eagerly grabbed the morning newspapers and readied themselves through pre-trade briefings for the repercussions.

The was no mistaking the gravity of the situation. Barings had to find a buyer or close its doors. Early editions of *The Times* began circulating with the front page banner headline: 'Barings Rescue Attempt Fails — Administrators Called In After Stg600 Million Loss By Dealer Aged 28'.

International time zones divide the world's markets roughly into three geographical groups: Asia, Europe and America. The process of a trading day begins with New Zealand, followed by Australia, then Singapore, Japan, and the rest of the trading region known colloquially as Asian Time. As the day progresses, European markets duly open for business, followed by North and South America, with the Asian Time markets closing, and the process repeating itself soon after. As sure as the passage of these time zones, and much like a row of dominoes, market sentiment overrides international boundaries from one zone to another, compounding domestic issues with problems elsewhere.

As a benchmark for others, Japan now had to cope with the Barings fiasco on top of the Kobe earthquake, escalating internal banking losses, a recession, and a distinct lack of sympathy from Wall Street investors who were preoccupied with the Mexico peso crisis. For traders on smaller stock markets, which take their lead from Tokyo and New York, it was simply one negative wave after another. In London the presumption that markets would be hit hard was as strong as the assumption of Leeson's guilt.

In Singapore, authorities acted quickly. They were incensed that Barings officials had failed to notify them immediately that a problem existed when it had first emerged three days earlier. They were further angered by the Bank of England having taken until Saturday afternoon to alert the Monetary Authority of Singapore (MAS) that things were dangerously awry, giving Simex just a few hours to notify its members that they had barely a day to determine their exposures to Barings, inform their superiors, and prepare a strategy to cope with the market chaos to come.

Prior to the opening of trade in Singapore on Monday morning, Simex suspended Barings Futures and seized control of all the bank's Singapore assets. The exchange was 'obliged to recognise that Barings . . . is and will be insolvent' and, as such, the operations were deemed automatically suspended.

Simultaneously, Simex doubled the initial margin payments linked to Barings' Nikkei 225 contracts to ensure the exchange was financially capable of managing the open positions. Cash-buying positions linked to arbitrage with Nikkei 225 futures were at an historic high during the week ending February 25. This included Leeson's contracts, and at this stage they would remain open and would be subjected to one more day of trading in the Nikkei 225, a day which would sorely test the nerve of all associated with Barings. The prospect of further losses became a conviction.

In Tokyo, the Nikkei 225 began to plummet from the opening bell, tumbling below the 17,000-mark for the first time in 14 months. Trade was hectic. At the midsession, the index was down 809.11 points, or a massive 4.63 per cent, to 16,663 and the doomsayers were forecasting a crash. Such an event would have the potential to throw the fragile Japanese economy into disarray, send businesses bankrupt, wipe out jobs, and upset the global economic order.

While this extreme outlook was most unlikely, the fears of such a scenario were nevertheless real and prompted the president of the Tokyo Stock Exchange (TSE), Mitsuhide Yamaguchi, to take the unorthodox step of issuing a statement which urged investors to remain calm while the TSE trained a close eye on all transactions.

With the suspension of Barings' operations in Singapore, the Singapore Stock Exchange (SES) appointed its executive vice-president, Teng Cheong Kwee, to manage the domestic stockbroking business amid a sliding SES Straits Times index.

Kwee issued a statement claiming that the unit would have no difficulty in honouring all outstanding contracts: 'From a preliminary review of the financial position of Barings Securities (Singapore) Pte Ltd, the exchange is of the view that the company's financial position is sound'. After crashing 92.59 points in the first half-hour of trade to 2022.03, the Straits Times index struggled to recover.

Across Asia Time, the consequences of the actions of a single trader and the ineptitude of his management dominated the markets. Hong Kong stock prices opened sharply lower with the Hang Seng index plunging 170.68 points, or 2.8 per cent, to 8048.27. Hong Kong's quasi central bank, the Hong Kong Monetary Authority, and the securities watchdog, the Securities and Futures Commission, suspended all normal operations of Barings' subsidiary in the territory.

Barings' assets were also frozen in South Korea and Tokyo. In Manila, investors feared that Barings would dump its massive inventory of stocks onto their market. The Philippines market was unaware of how much stock Barings actually held, and the extent to which they would be unwound, and in Manila the main stock index sunk 132.65 points, or 5.1 per cent, to 2455.26.

In Taipei, Taiwan's main stock index closed at 6388.57, down 202.79 points or 3.1 per cent. In Bangkok, the Stock Exchange of Thailand index shed 23.24 points, or 1.8 per cent, to 1270.77. Across Asia, billions of dollars were wiped off the value of publicly listed companies.

In Tokyo, Yamaguchi's statement had had only a marginal impact, but further losses were stemmed. Afternoon trade witnessed the return of bargain hunters who believed the sell-off had spawned cheap buys in Japanese stocks. The Nikkei 225 recovered just slightly from the morning rout to close 664.24 points, or 3.8 per cent, weaker at 16,808. By the close of trade, Barings' known losses had blown out from $750 million and now topped $1.0 billion.

The Osaka exchange also acted, and appointed Daiwa Securities and Nikko Securities to close out Leeson's 16,937 contracts with an outstanding value of $3.0 billion. Barings had deposited $330 million to cover margin calls — enough to cover losses once the contracts were liquidated. A further 4,900 bond futures worth $4.9 billion would also be unwound. Daiwa and Nikko's silent mandate would aggravate further trade in the Nikkei. The pair were among the biggest brokerages in the world, and once smaller traders got wind of what had happened they ditched the market fearing tens of thousands of contracts would be dumped and would devalue their own positions.

Kwee's statement had also helped in Singapore, and the Straits Times index rebounded slightly but still closed sharply lower at 2,070.89, compared with the previous Friday night's close of 2,114.52.

Global trading shifted from Asian Time to Europe, and then to the Americas. 'We'll wait and see what happens tonight', was the sentiment among the disenchanted at Harry's Bar by the Boat Quay on the evening of February 27. The closure of Asian markets was timely for the *New York Times* and Richard Stevenson focussed on the international significance. *The New York Times* headlined its front page: 'Markets Shaken as British Bank Takes a Big Loss'.

The report datelined London, Monday February 27 read:

The abrupt collapse late on Sunday of a venerable British investment bank set off a chain reaction of steep losses in financial markets halfway around the world today in a stark illustration of the global financial system's interdependency.

The bank, Barings Plc, the oldest investment firm in Britain and one of the most illustrious, was left no choice but to seek bankruptcy protection after a frantic rescue effort by the Bank of England, the nation's central bank, came up short'.

Preoccupied with its own problems, Wall Street escaped relatively unscathed but, across the Atlantic in Europe, where Britain's fortunes were firmly entwined with the European Union, financial markets were dealt a harsh blow. The London bourse shed more than 1.0 per cent on February 27 alone, with the FTSE-100 index falling 36.1 points. On the foreign exchange market, the pound crashed to an all-time low of 2.2950 Deutschemarks, compared with a previous record low of 2.2993 marks, with investors fleeing the British currency in favour of the safe havens of the German mark and the Swiss franc.

In Paris, the CAC 40 share index sank 3.57 points, or 0.2 per cent, to 1802.17, while in Rome the demise of Barings added yet another dimension to the economic woes besetting Italy's government. The lira slumped to a new all-time low of 1167 against the German mark, with share prices also taking a tumble amid opposition to Premier Lamberto Dini's deficit-chopping measures aimed at removing 20 trillion lira from the country's budget deficit. Despite these economic preoccupations, even the Italian premier had to take the time to consider the plight of a British bank ahead of a meeting with Italy's budget committee to discuss the economic austerity package, a key plank of his month-old government.

The true cost and disruption of the Barings collapse had become impossible to measure in the trillions of dollars, pounds and yen held by governments and corporations, through to the average worker. Never before had a single operator inflicted damage on this scale.

The mounting chaos forced London onto the back foot. At Threadneedle Street, where public comments are rare, Pennant-Rea tried to react quickly to the rapidly spreading hysteria, attempting to scuttle any suggestion that there was a 'plague at work'. 'It was much more like a meteor striking one bank down', he insisted.[2] George said that what had occurred could strike any bank in the world, at any time.

Under pressure from opposition in Parliament to explain how a single trader could wipe out one of Britain's most revered financial institutions, the Chancellor of the Exchequer, Kenneth Clarke, said that lasting financial damage would not be inflicted on world markets because of the crash.

Authorities had attempted to keep Nick Leeson's identity a secret for as long as they could in a bid to gain control of as much of a runaway situation as was possible. This is a simple strategy employed by public relations firms and media advisers everywhere. By keeping the source of the problem under wraps, enquiring reporters are kept at bay and the prospect of being forced to field a myriad unwanted questions is blocked, allowing them to buy some time for others to get their house in order.

But a missing billion dollars and the imminent meltdown of an international financial institution had sparked media hysteria and a manhunt for the so-called Rogue Trader on a scale usually reserved for wanted terrorists or assassins. Such a mystery was a big carrot for whipped-up journalists in the British and international press and it took barely one day before London newspapers were in a position to name Nicholas William Leeson as the unknown working class boy from 'grimy Watford' who had broken his bank.

George was pushed into following another frequently observed public relations maxim: 'Always tell journalists what they will discover anyway'. This at least allows those under pressure to maintain some semblance of control over the dissemination of information.

George called a press conference and confirmed that Leeson was the missing trader. He told reporters that Leeson had acquired Japanese equity contracts worth $7.0 billion and a short position in Japanese interest rate contracts worth $20.0 billion in the hope of buying them back cheaply. He spoke of the desperate attempts to save Barings, and of the unsuccessful approach made to Japanese banks which had proved fruitless because of the inability to cap the losses. And in reference to Leeson, he shifted away from whole-heartedly supporting Barings management and their arguments by adding: 'There was a failure to control a rogue trader'.[3]

Attempts to quell rising market nervousness were in earnest. However, in the wake of all the more recent derivative and other financial debacles, the demise of Barings had brought to light very real doubts about a financial system which could wreak havoc so rapidly. In Basel the Bank for International Settlements (BIS) took a more sober approach to what was becoming a highly emotional issue, warning that information about derivatives was uniformly inadequate throughout the industry.

The collapse of Barings painted a stark picture of failure and sent bank executives everywhere scurrying into hastily-convened crisis meetings to pose the inevitable question pushed by George: 'Could this happen to us?'. Urgent reviews in the monitoring of internal trading were launched by investment houses amid widespread panic that the Barings catastrophe could easily be repeated anywhere, and at any time. At this early stage, British banks estimated that Barings had borrowed $850 million between the end of January and February 24 and, by their own standards, they were perplexed as to how this could have been done. All that was known publicly was that unauthorised trades by Nick Leeson had occurred, and that this had precipitated the collapse.

'This just makes me feel sick in the pit of my stomach', said Ian Perkin, chief economist at the Hong Kong General

Chamber of Commerce. 'You wonder what's going on in derivatives markets . . . and what's been hidden away, perhaps, and what may still emerge'.[4]

Another banking executive said at the time that unauthorised trades may be specific to Barings but added that anyone not reviewing their security operations today 'must be crazy'.

Barclays, SG Warburg, Morgan Stanley and other banking and investment firms all undertook immediate reviews of their security procedures and risk management systems. They also launched into a serious damage control campaign in an attempt to arrest in the financial system any doubts that were creeping in and threatening to erode investor confidence.

SG Warburg claimed their risk controls were constantly updated, and that these controls were the subject of ongoing special attention. Other banking executives were quick to reassure investors that compliance systems had been beefed up, with some saying that incentives for individuals no longer existed in the same vein as they had in the 1980s and early 1990s and that this had made for 'a better shop'. Also embarking on a damage control exercise was Sir Peter Baring, who was by now attempting to shift the blame away from Barings' management.

The courts, meanwhile, formally petitioned and appointed Ernst & Young as administrators and froze all Barings' deposits and accounts. Justice John Knox had already signed the administration order which gave administrators Nigel Hamilton, Alan Bloom and Maggie Mills the task of deciding whether Barings could be sold or declared bankrupt. Hamilton and Bloom had excellent credentials. They were part of the team put in as administrators of Olympia & York, the Canadian-based consortium and the world's largest property company, responsible for the development of London's Canary Wharf, before it went bankrupt.

The passing of control creates a moratorium which stops creditors enforcing their rights, giving the administrators breathing space to take a sensible look at their options. Barings creditors included Simex and a string of banks.

Hamilton, Bloom and Mills had three months to decide Barings' fate but, realistically, this would have to be done within a much shorter space of time. The latest figures had also arrived from Japan, where losses on Leeson's contracts had widened by a further $280 million. With liabilities now in excess of $1.0 billion, they had to act quickly or Barings would become extinct, taking with it an international banking network and some 4000 jobs.

The bank's board, senior executives and the administrators left no doubt as to where they thought the blame lay. A statement designed to shore up support for Barings as a whole was issued by Ernst & Young. It said the Barings Board and the administrators wish to emphasise that 'the problems are the results of unauthorised dealing in one, and one only, specialised area of activity and in no way reflects the quality of the core activities of the group'.

'It in no way reflects the quality of the core activity of Barings corporate finance, securities research and central banking function, which have been highly successful'.

Administrator Alan Bloom was diplomatically reluctant to compromise the reputations of Barings executives themselves when asked who would bear responsibility for the bank's collapse. 'I don't think it is right to point any fingers at present. We don't know what happened or how it was done. There could be a number of reasons, which I am not prepared to go into', Bloom told a news conference.

As the administrators were making their position known, the Chancellor of the Exchequer, Kenneth Clarke, ordered the Bank of England's Board of Banking Supervision to immediately investigate the events leading up to the collapse. The inquiry was to be headed by Ian Watt, an adviser and head of the BoE's Special Investigation Unit.

The terms of reference were later agreed upon as being: 'To establish in detail the events that led to the collapse of Barings; to identify the lessons to be drawn, for institutions, for the bank's own regulatory and supervisory arrangements, and for the UK system more generally; and to report to the Chancellor of the Exchequer'.

They may not have been mentioned in the BoE's terms of reference, but a number of charities who relied upon Barings' generous donations had been dealt a bitter blow, as had the Eating Disorders Association, which helps victims of anorexia and bulimia. It had been decided by the administrators that all existing commitments would be honoured, but no applications for new funding would be accepted. Those that had come to rely on Barings now feared they would have to fend for themselves.

Charities left out in the cold were not the only ones bearing a grudge against Nick Leeson. There was also a group of bondholders who had acquired perpetual bonds in the previous year as an investment. About stg100 million worth of perpetual subordinated notes were issued by Barings Plc paying an interest rate of 9.25 per cent. Such notes are issued with no maturity date and are favoured by small investors, often retirees looking for a guaranteed income for the years ahead from a long-standing institution.

There are no redemption dates at which the issuer pays out the face value of the bond and if a person wishes to opt out of the investment, he or she has to find a buyer in the market place. And there weren't too many people about wanting to buy bonds issued by a bank that has just been placed under administration. And fundraisers in Britain's Conservative Party were unlikely to see a repetition of the generous stg70,000 contribution the bank had made to party coffers in 1993. Barings was Tory to its crumbling foundations.

The world had turned through one full day, and the sun was again rising over Singapore, where the potential for embarrassment cannot be overstated. Smith Court analyst Mr

Chan Kok Peng expressed the thoughts of many when he commented that the Monetary Authority of Singapore had been embarrassed by the affair, He said "It imposes strict controls, but there seem to be some holes in the regulations."[5] As Nick Leeson was now known as the man responsible, anyone with an interest turned their attention back to Singapore to ponder what would happen next.

CHAPTER ELEVEN

THE FUGITIVE

Q: What's the difference between Nick Leeson and Elvis Presley?
A: Nick Leeson is definitely dead.

The impact of the collapse was felt across the length and breadth of the globe, turning Nick Leeson overnight into a household name, and the butt of jokes of the style normally reserved for celebrities like Michael Jackson, OJ Simpson, or infamous mass murderer Ted Bundy. Those jokes did the rounds of blue-collar and professional pubs alike.

In a manner perhaps typifying the nature of the financial markets in which they trade, dealers in London began trading in Nick Leeson's old business cards. The increasingly rare cards — which boasted Barings embossed winged insignia — fetched stg130 each, a significant improvement on the stg1 ING had formally paid for the entire bank.

In restaurants, tourist resorts, and in offices from Melbourne to Toronto, people made good use of their fax machines and e-mails to send out a string of one-liners that reflected the massive press coverage given to Barings and Leeson, ensuring both names would be etched harshly in history.

Q: What's the definition of optimism?
A: A Barings employee who irons five shirts at the beginning of the week.

Or for the insider:

What does a disgraced trader have to say about all the fuss?
'I may have lost my Barings, but at least I kept my options open!

A mock curriculum vitae for Nick Leeson, advocating Michael Milken as a referee, was circulated with an address c/- the Kuala Lumpur Fraud Squad. The resume stated his university thesis as: 'The impact of inadequate derivative trading on the profitability of UK merchant banks', with Leeson's current occupation given as 'traveller with a story to sell'.

It was also a chance for the Simex traders in Singapore to reveal their lighter side. During the Hong Kong Sevens rugby league tournament a few months after the collapse, patrons and bar staff of Harry's Bar donned t-shirts in support of Singapore's team emblazoned with the slogan: 'All Balls And No Barings'.

None of the puns were likely to win an award at a comedy festival but the fact that people from all walks of life were discussing the demise of a merchant bank demonstrated the extraordinary impact of the case. Almost everybody had an opinion. Even Juan Pablo Davila, the Chilean trader who lost $200 million in bad copper futures a year earlier, was sought out and quoted by Reuters: 'There is one fundamental difference. I didn't turn tail and run'. Santiago's press had dubbed Leeson the English Davila.

Every facet of Leeson's life was scrutinised. The United States media dwelled upon the fact that he hadn't gone to university. His working-class background and his failure to pay a debt was brandished across British newspapers. *Time* magazine managed to get a photograph of a 14-year-old Nick Leeson on a school field trip with his head and hands locked in a set of timber framed stocks which had once held petty offenders in the Middle Ages.

There were erroneous reports that Lisa had worked with Nick in the back office, and exaggerated stories that the couple drove flashy cars, threw extravagant parties, and owned a yacht. The assumption that the Leesons were a yuppie couple and fitted the traditional stereotype of 'new money' people was not totally inaccurate but was, to some extent, misreported.

Back in London, securities authority chief Christopher Sharples commented to the BBC: 'I can't think of anything that's happened in my memory that has struck more to the heart of the City as a financial centre, particularly because of the very British nature of what has taken place'.[1]

Bewildered investigators now had to determine how Nick Leeson had concealed his trading losses, how he had managed to build his extraordinary position without regulatory alarm bells sounding, and how he had managed to pay his margin calls to Singapore exchange authorities on such massive contracts. The sheer complexity of the situation prompted a free-for-all flurry of investigations.

The international agency Interpol was alerted, and in Singapore the domestic police force was handed the more immediate tasks. This was followed by a separate probe launched by the nation's powerful Commercial Affairs Department (CAD) after a Barings report recommended Leeson be investigated for possible criminal misconduct. The CAD answers directly to Singapore's Finance Minister. The CAD's British equivalent, the Serious Fraud Office (SFO), began its own investigations from London, and Britain's Chancellor of the Exchequer, Kenneth Clarke, ordered the Board of Banking Supervision (BBS) to investigate urgently and fully all aspects of the collapse.

Despite the investigations being at such an early stage, it appeared that Leeson's guilt was unquestioned and that his fate sealed. Britain's leading financiers focussed the blame on Leeson's shoulders in a bid to minimise the impact on the reputation of an old and established banking friend. When announcing the BBS probe, Clarke said the collapse was sparked by 'the actions of a rogue trader operating on a desk in Singapore who managed to evade existing managerial and regulatory control'.[2]

The soundness of the internal and management structures of Barings and its system of checks and balances remained unquestioned. Matrix and its installation during the restructuring process failed to become a consideration for people struggling to understand derivatives. It was simply being assumed that the bank and its executives had always acted in a proper and prudent manner, and no-one at this stage appeared terribly interested in establishing the identity of whoever had authorised the capital transfers for margin call payments, either at Barings or at the Bank of England.

This was in part due to the extraordinary pace at which the story was breaking, catching most off guard, and leaving little time for serious questioning by journalists.

In the first instance, this resulted in even the quality press swallowing the Barings line unquestioningly. *The Times* reported as a fact: 'The dealing was unauthorised and Barings had no knowledge of the transactions'. *The Times* was, however, careful to attribute the conspiracy theories. On February 28, the newspaper carried the headline: 'Inquiry Into Stg17 Million Gamble — Singapore Conspiracy May Have Wrecked Us Claims Barings Chief'.

The page one headline on *The New York Times* of the same day was self-explanatory: 'Young Trader's $29 Billion Bet Brings Down a Venerable Firm — 28-year-old Briton Disturbs Financial World'.

Back in the UK, the London tabloid press were typically bold, if predictable, in their treatment of Leeson. The depiction of him as a class warrior was never more evident than in a piece in *The People*, which claimed Leeson was threatening to drag senior members of Britain's ruling Conservative Party into the mire. Leeson was quoted as having said: 'It is a political scandal in the making. Top Tories and supporters of the government were fully aware of what was being done'.[3]

Other mass-circulation newspapers elected to bypass coverage of the bank's predicament in favour of creating a personal scandal around the man they dubbed the 'yuppie anti-hero'. Within a week of the collapse, Nick Leeson had been accused of everything from adultery to loutish behaviour. As Lisa was publicly vowing to stand by her man, *The Mirror* claimed Leeson had been having an affair behind his wife's back. *The News of the World* called Leeson the world's best-paid lager lout when revealing he once blew $11,000 on a night's boozing in Singapore. *The Sunday Mirror* had Leeson begging not to be sent back to Singapore because, 'I'll never get out alive. I know too much — it's as simple as that'.

The Daily Mail wrote that the evidence of 'uncontrolled and unwarranted greed could hardly be clearer'. *The Express* carried the headline: 'Fugitive Bank Dealer's Boast: "I'm So Rich I Could Retire"'. Not to be outdone, *The Star* ran a photograph of Nick and Lisa hamming it up at a party accompanied by the caption: 'Bank Brat and His Blonde'.

Such intense media attention forced Nick's father to flee the family home in Watford, leaving Lisa's parents to bear the brunt of seemingly never-ending queries from journalists across the globe. At this stage, British police had not been asked to interview the parents of the missing couple, and had not even checked to see if Nick or Lisa had telephoned home. Police said they had no authority to question people in Britain because no criminal offence had yet been formally alleged, and Singapore authorities had not asked for the help of Interpol in London.

But although Lisa's father, Alex Sims, was left alone by the police, he was hounded by a press corps desperate for more tales about Nick Leeson. But they weren't about to get any juicy morsels from Sims, who told them Nick was a genuinely nice guy, someone he was proud to call his son-in-law. 'If he is responsible for what has happened it must have been a genuine mistake. He is not the sort who would do anything silly', Sims said.

The pressure of fielding hundreds of queries a day was turning the Sims' modern four-bedroom house into a bunker, and eventually forced Lisa's parents to also go into hiding. The strain was evident in Alex Sims' final comment before leaving the family's home in West Kingsdown. 'I don't know how much more pressure I can take. How do you think it feels not knowing where your daughter is? She is on the other side of the world and has gone missing, and there is absolutely nothing I can do except wait for her to get in touch', he said.[4]

One of Leeson's sisters was quick to rally to her brother's defence, telling *The Daily Mirror* that Nick was without the pretentions of the public school educated type which Barings typically recruited. 'If you knew Nick like we do, you'd know he couldn't have done anything wrong', she said. 'I think he's just very scared. He wasn't one of these . . . types who had it all handed to him on a plate. Nick has worked hard for what he has got and deserves it all'.[5]

Nick's former headmaster at Parmiter's school in Watford, Brian Coulshed, remembered his erstwhile pupil as an affable and well-liked boy who had failed his final maths test. 'He mixed very easily and got on very well with his peer group. He was an asset to the school', he said.[6]

In contrast to the ready comments of confidence and faith offered by Nick Leeson's family and friends, statements from Eddie George, who had initially declined to comment publicly on the scandal, were rare. Britain's central bank governors generally refrain from commenting on banks under their supervision, but Barings was now under administration and the sheer enormity of the situation demanded that George fall into line with his peers. He was also quick to point the finger at one man but his statements were more guarded.

George would soon raise the possibility that Leeson had not acted alone and that collusion must have existed in the backroom, where the transactions were tallied every night. He was clearly unaware that Leeson had held control of both front and back rooms — it was becoming obvious in fact that even senior executives at the bank were unaware of the ramifications of Leeson's dual roles.

When queried by a *Financial Times* journalist, an anonymous senior Barings executive said: 'There is nothing illegal to be in the front and back offices but officially he did not hold both positions'. Such comments may well be technically correct, but they didn't win Barings' management any fans.

Whether the slight change in the direction of blame was derived from some sense of understanding for the situation is doubtful. Talk of collusion in the backroom by relatively low-ranking staff would shortly shift to allegations of bank mismanagement and corruption from the top.

Such allegations followed the widespread public disbelief that just one man could be held accountable for the spectacular breakdown of an institution as distinguished as Barings. It could also be argued that those Barings executives who believed that the public, journalists, rival investment houses, central banks, and politicians and bureaucrats would accept such a line demonstrated precisely the arrogance that had dominated the bank from most of senior ranks down.

Over the ensuing days, the media and Britain's opposition Labour Party became increasingly critical of Barings management. Newspapers and magazines carried page after page of news, comment and background pieces in their attempt to put the situation in context, while the major television stations assigned their best and brightest to grapple with the subject of derivatives and told them to explain in laymen's terms how the complex financial instruments had brought a bank to its knees. Amid the speculation and blame-laying, there was nevertheless in some quarters an element of *Schadenfreude*, the perverse delight at witnessing another's downfall, in this case the demise of such a blue-blooded institution.

In London, Labour's City spokesman, Alastair Darling, entered the fray, saying the real question was whether there was adequate supervision of the derivatives unit and whether adequate supervision existed for the banking industry generally. Tory MPs preferred to downplay the significance of the collapse. Corporate Affairs Minister Neil Hamilton said it was difficult to view the losses as anything other than 'one isolated example of catastrophic misjudgement'.

The Chancellor of the Exchequer made a thinly-veiled attempt to assign the sole responsibility to Leeson during a speech to the House of Commons. 'Mr Leeson has left his desk and no doubt that is because at the very least, he finds it embarrassing to describe his responsibility for a series of investments which has brought down an entire 250-year-old [sic] banking group', Clarke said. 'His explanation will indeed be interesting when he emerges'.[7]

But Leeson was not the only one wanted for an explanation. Pressure on Barings management to reveal more about what had happened, and how, was intensifying. In responding to the clamour, the most direct attempt so far to attribute the sole blame to Leeson's duplicity was made by Sir Peter. In an exclusive interview with *The Financial Times* on February 28, Sir Peter broke his silence to raise the prospect that Barings may have been brought down by a deliberate act of criminal sabotage.

'It's difficult to get a fix on the motivation of this fellow . . . What we are talking about here is hiding financial transactions — you don't have to be in the derivatives markets to do that', Sir Peter said. 'What happened was extremely simple in essence. [Leeson] bought massive amounts of futures contracts, which he hid — everybody is vulnerable to that sort of action'.[8]

Sir Peter claimed that Leeson and a conspirator had combined to destroy the bank. No motive was forthcoming and the allegations were never fully elaborated upon. Essentially, Sir Peter put forward the theory that Leeson could have taken out hidden short positions in the Nikkei to balance the $7.0 billion long futures contracts acquired on behalf of Barings.

This anonymous partner could have then planned to gain on the assumption that the Nikkei would drop, as in fact happened on the Monday. The short position could then be sold at a profit. Sir Peter Baring believed the theory was credible, but market opinion was that there were simply too many parties with whom Leeson had dealt to sustain such a plan.

The theory itself could perhaps be attributed in part to the fact that Barings' rivals had been abuzz with talk of

Leeson's mounting exposure just prior to his disappearance. This had made the search for a financial saviour, particularly outside the establishment of the City, exceedingly difficult. It was a bit like asking a bookie to sacrifice his winnings to bail out a punter who had lost his life-savings. It simply doesn't happen.

The conspiracy theory seemed to be without much substance and if its intention was to further blame Leeson and seal his fate, it failed. The theory was seen by most as an attempt to deflect attention from the inefficiencies of Barings' management, and their ability to control Leeson.

Robin Monroe-Davis, managing director of London-based credit agency IBCA Ltd, expressed the thoughts of countless industry insiders in commenting bluntly: '[Barings] didn't have the controls in place to stop a trader who went mad'.

Simex chairperson Elizabeth Sam backed up Monroe-Davis's assertion. It was metaphorically still early in the day, and Singapore was desperately trying to find Leeson, but Sam made it clear that the blame did not lie solely with Leeson.

'This was a failure of internal controls'.

If Leeson's professional life had been characterised by a lack of controls and inadequate communication, his personal life does not appear to have fared any better. For much of the time leading up to the collapse Lisa had little, if any, idea about her husband's increasingly reckless position, or the distress he was suffering. Nick would simply dismiss any concerns she had. She admired his cool nature, which was providing an effective mask for the problems at work.

With hindsight, others were equally impressed by Nick's nerve. Journalists who had interviewed him during the normal course of work immediately prior to the collapse noticed nothing out of the ordinary. Long-time friend

Michael Sale was equally unaware of any difficulties when
Nick called to discuss the soccer. But Lisa's inability to read
her husband's true mood was something she later regretted.

Shortly before Nick left work for what was to be the last
time, Lisa received a panicky telephone call from her
husband telling her he desperately needed to talk things over.
'He sounded so bad', Lisa said. 'He said things were really
terrible and he was coming home to see me and to talk. I was
alarmed but I didn't think it was a bad position'.[9]

Lisa noted that Nick was 'in a real state' when he arrived
home that day. Nick told his wife he couldn't cope any more,
and needed to get away from Singapore for a few days. To
Nick's relief, Lisa told him to quit, even if that meant
forfeiting their cherished stg445,000 bonus, the nest egg that
would allow the couple to start a family. 'I knew it meant
saying goodbye to the bonus. But it was either that or Nick's
sanity and I knew which I'd rather have', Lisa said.[10]

The Leesons were reported missing from their apartment
the next day and police were ordered to act. They cordoned
off Nick's office on the 24th floor of Ocean Tower while his
condominium near Orchard Road was also quarantined and
searched by CAD investigators. The signs of a hurried
departure from Anguella View were obvious: Nick Leeson's
white business shirts were still flapping on the clothesline,
two mountain pushbikes were perched on the white balcony,
and the weekend newspapers were piled up against the front
door.

Realising that Barings was perilously close to a meltdown,
a scared and confused Nick and Lisa skipped town with the
idea of celebrating Nick's 28th birthday on the coming
weekend. He desperately needed time out to think and plot
his next move. A dinner party for Saturday night was
cancelled, some borrowed golf clubs returned, and a note
plus wages of S$280 were left behind for the cleaning lady.
Shorts and swimsuits were packed and Nick contacted his
friend, Daniel Argyropoulous, from First Continental Trading (Singapore) Pte Ltd (FCT).[11]

Agreeing to drive Nick and Lisa to the airport, Argyro-poulous noticed that Leeson appeared troubled. He and the Leesons had made previous arrangements to spend a week-end in Thailand, and Argyropoulous agreed to catch up with them later at Phuket, a popular Thai tourist beach resort. The Leesons didn't keep the appointment. Instead, from Changi Airport the couple fled to Kuala Lumpur where they booked into an elegant suite at The Regent Hotel, regarded as the city's best. After paying for the room with Nick's company credit card so they could avail themselves of the standard corporate discount, the couple was ushered up to the VIP floor and shown to a room featuring a carved mahogany bedhead and a luxurious en-suite bathroom.

To many, including his wife, Nick Leeson appeared troubled but generally he remained calm and collected before the couple's departure. In reality there is little doubt he was close to a nervous breakdown. Lisa said: 'I told him he had to let his feelings show for once in his life, and that I would support him whatever he chose. I persuaded him to fax a letter resigning from his job'.[12] With those words in mind, Nick addressed a letter of resignation to James Bax and Simon Jones, and faxed it from The Regent.

From Kuala Lumpur's Subang airport, the pair fled to Kota Kinabalu, the quiet capital of Malaysia's eastern state of Sabah on the island of Borneo. It was an astute choice. Borneo is isolated and remote and, by heading to Sabah, the Leesons had to make only one internal flight with no customs gates to negotiate.

Photographs of Nick Leeson were being distributed throughout police stations in the various states along the Malaysian Peninsula amid a flurry of rumours. Initially, police believed the couple had fled to Thailand or were hiding out on a yacht. The most talked about scenario was that the Leesons were hiding out at Phuket, a rumour with some substance, given the couple's plan to meet up with Argyropoulous. Argyropoulous himself remained calm and kept a low profile.

Singapore issued warrants for Leeson's arrest, and Malaysia organised a special police task force to carry out the request once it was learned the Leesons had arrived in Kuala Lumpur. But three days after leaving Malaysia, police admitted the trail had gone cold. All international airports, ferry ports, border crossings and custom officials were put on alert.

Meanwhile, Singapore's CAD concentrated its investigations on auditing Leeson's accounts. His computer equipment and trading screens were seized and scrutinised. Backroom staff, including James Bax, were targeted for questioning and, in some cases, passports were confiscated. It was soon discovered that some records of Leeson's trading activities were difficult to locate, raising fears that they had been shredded.

The press corps was having about as much luck as the police in its quest to locate the elusive Leeson. They arrived at Phuket on Wednesday, March 1. Fresh rumours prompted yet another swarm to head for Manila. 'Leeson's yacht' — quite possibly the company yacht *Baring Up* — had, according to another report, 'vanished from its moorings' in the Malaysian state of Johore. On the same day, *The Daily Mail* delivered a banner headline which posed the question: 'Where In The World Is He?'. It was also suggested the couple had sailed to the Andaman Islands.

Weary of what was proving to be little more than an elaborate goose-chase, one reporter quipped: 'Any twenty-something male who was big, British and balding was fair game. The problem was that that description seems to fit a large proportion of Phuket's tourist population'.[13] Another report had Leeson in a Malaysian hospital, and yet another claimed he had turned himself in to Singapore authorities.

He hadn't. At Kota Kinabalu, the weather was hot and sunny when the Leesons arrived and booked into the Shangri La Tanjong Aru Resort, a seven-storey, 500-room luxury resort set amid tropical rainforests, rolling hills, and views stretching across a sparkling South China Sea. The couple registered under Lisa's name — again using Barings' corporate credit card — and stayed in room 429, which was styled in a Borneo wicker motif, and had access to two swimming pools, three tennis courts, and a nine-hole golf course.

They spent five days at the Shangri La, celebrating Nick's 28th birthday on the Saturday night and covering their estimated S$1100 worth of expenses with cash, using their real names and real passports. There were no disguises and no dramas. Leeson appeared to simply want several days of peace celebrating his birthday with his wife before facing his judges. His judges had in fact by this stage already concluded much of their deliberation.

Lisa would later insist that neither she nor Nick had any clue as to the trouble they had left behind, claiming that it was only on board the flight from Borneo, when every passenger on the plane seemed to have a newspaper with Nick's face on it, that they realised the impact of his actions.

Nick later recalled: 'When I heard the bank was closing, I just thought "Oh My God". My legs started shaking. It was like going into an exam. I knew Barings had lost a lot of money, but I never imagined they were on the brink of disaster'.[14]

The truth behind these claims remains doubtful. It is known that, after leaving Singapore, Leeson had contacted Argyropoulous on several occasions and while the subject of conversation is not known, it would seem highly unlikely that the situation at Barings would not have been discussed.

Realising that responsibility for the collapse of one of Britain's most venerable institutions was being laid squarely at his feet, Nick Leeson telephoned a friend twice, the contents of the alleged conversations later published exclusively by the London tabloid *The Sun*. He was moving to minimise his liability by claiming he was the scapegoat. It remains unknown whether the person he contacted was Argyropoulous.

'I'm the fall guy — I only blew stg200 million. I wasn't acting on my own. Senior people knew what I was doing and the rest is down to others. I was the sacrificial lamb', *The Sun* quoted Leeson as saying.

'Lots of people knew. But I was allowed to carry on. Why? Because if it had worked, the pay day for everyone would have been fantastic. But it went wrong and they're trying to lump all the blame on me'.

'I didn't know that it would break the bank. I was sure it would work. I couldn't believe it when it didn't. I am so sorry it has all gone wrong . . . The losses are not all down to me. A lot of people's mistakes have been lumped in and made to appear all mine'.

'How on earth can one person have done all this on his own behind the backs of everyone else at the bank? I had to have help. Support. Didn't I? But how do I get a fair hearing now? I just can't imagine how to get people to listen to my side of it'.

'I have taken a risk and it has gone wrong. If it had worked out I would have been a superstar, a hero and set up for life — if not, a villain'.

After five days of sunning themselves at the Shangri La, Nick and Lisa prepared to face the music. Naturally, Nick feared imprisonment and he believed any punishment would be more lenient in Britain than in Singapore. The choice between spending time in jail at home or on the other side of the world made London the obvious choice for the couple's next destination. The recent caning of an American teenager had provided Leeson with a chilling reminder of Singapore's intolerance of law breakers. He would argue that he would be more likely to get a fair hearing in London than in Singapore — his problem was whether anyone would *want* to give him a fair hearing at home.

The pair left Kota Kinabalu when reports had them in a Vancouver bank, and boarded a Royal Brunei Fokker

Friendship flight to the Brunei capital, Bandar Seri Begawan, where they spent a day in the airport's transit lounge. This flight would take them to Frankfurt, from where Leeson prayed the couple would be able to travel on to London. They tried to keep a low profile, but a local newspaper had already identified Leeson as a man wearing 'a hat and dark glasses' and discovered they had paid cash for air tickets. Such was the hype surrounding their disappearance, that the media were willing accomplices in the construction of a cloak-and-dagger aura around the pair.

Singapore authorities, mindful of a potential triple-A credit rating in the wings, were furious at the ongoing publicity and again issued requests for Leeson's arrest. They believed the Briton was travelling under a forged passport — certainly, it was almost unthinkable that someone would use their own passport in these circumstances.

There was some substance to the clandestine mystique that had been generated. Interpol did have police on alert at every major international airport around the world, but in the end the reality was quite different.

Over the previous week, Nick Leeson had made a concerted effort to minimise his involvement with the bank's collapse, but at no time did he or his wife appear to be planning a retirement under an alias. In the same report which described Leeson as wearing 'a hat and dark glasses', it was also noted that Nick had corrected the spelling of the name on the ticket to Leeson from 'Lesson'. Taking the trouble to make such a correction hardly represents the efforts of someone wanting to remain in hiding for a long period of time.

Immediately prior to leaving Borneo, a Royal Brunei airline worker recognised the couple, and reported to police that Nick and Lisa Leeson had boarded a flight bound for Frankfurt with a stop in Bandar Seri Begawan before going on to Bangkok and Dubai. Presumably the decision was made to apprehend the couple only on arrival at Frankfurt, allowing authorities time to finalise the necessary documentation. The transit stops made it a long flight across many time zones, affording the Leesons many hours to sit, and think, and hope that they would not be recognised. Each time the plane descended they risked being discovered and handed over to local authorities. And the prospect of spending time in the appalling conditions of a prison in Bangkok or Dubai would not have made the flight a pleasant one for a trader with an acquired taste for the better things in life.

✗

German border police at Frankfurt Am Main airport were ready when flight P1535 touched down and taxied down the tarmac to the arrivals terminal. It was about 6:30 am local time when Nick Leeson and his wife stepped off the plane. Leeson offered no resistance as he was approached by police officers, reportedly greeting them with the words: 'Yes, I'm the man you want'. Cheers rang out on trading floors around the world when news flashed across dealing screens that the financial world's most infamous fugitive was a fugitive no more.

After escorting the couple to the airport's interview rooms, authorities offered Nick and Lisa the opportunity to return to Singapore, but Nick had already discounted this. After drinking some tea and telephoning the British consulate, Leeson rejected the offer. Fearing that Singapore would mount a show trial, he requested that they be allowed to continue on to England. He had made the mistake of assuming the German authorities would allow this. They did not, and the couple was taken into custody where they were placed under arrest without bail, as required under an extradition treaty signed between Germany and Singapore.

Nick Leeson was not the only one with a right to fear Singapore justice. Sir Peter, Tuckey, Hawes, Bax, Baker, and a staff-room full of Barings senior management, essentially anyone who had an association with Leeson's position, could also be justifiably more than a little nervous. They all knew of, or were officially responsible for, the transfer of vast cash sums and someone would have to be held accountable for the breach in regulations whereby these figures exceeded 25 per cent of the bank's capital base. Argyropoulous too would have had cause for concern, given that FCT trades had been conducted through Barings' accounts and that he had aided — however unwittingly — Nick Leeson's escape, which had prompted an international dragnet.

Nick's second and more immediate concern was that Lisa might also be unfairly linked with his activities, and he feared that she also faced the prospect of going to jail.

Television footage of Nick Leeson being taken away under German custody was beamed by the TV networks into living rooms around the world. Nick, tall and slightly balding, carried a backpack casually across one shoulder while clutching the Tom Clancy novel, *Without Remorse.*

Dressed in jeans, an open-neck shirt and a Detroit Tigers baseball cap, Nick Leeson appeared to viewers to be more like just another adventure tourist returning from the South East Asian trail than one of the world's most wanted men. The Leesons had evaded an international manhunt for a week. In doing so, Singapore authorities had been given enough time to prepare an initial case against the trader, and an international warrant was flown by the Singapore justice department to German prosecutors in Frankfurt.

The warrant alleged that Leeson had forged the name of Richard Hogan, a director at Spear Leeds & Kellogg (SLK), onto a document to show that SLK had transferred about $74 million, to Barings Futures operations for speculative investment trading in the Nikkei 225 index. This added a new dimension to the unfolding hyper-drama. SLK is an influential Wall Street investment firm and a favourite of specialist investors, and its involvement could scarcely be ignored. Noted as a market maker in stocks listed on the New York Stock Exchange, the investment house is a major player on the Chicago Board Options Exchange. Many would have wondered where the growing international ramifications of Leeson's crimes would stop.

It was alleged the forged document was used as collateral for a loan from Citibank's Singapore office to conduct trading which contributed to Barings' collapse. More importantly, this was the first time that the exact details of the allegations on how Leeson managed to obtain, hide and trade in vast sums of money became public.

At Threadneedle Street, Eddie George was perhaps being facetious when he muttered to a gathering throng of reporters: 'Perhaps he did a little business he shouldn't have'. George may have been livid about the collapse, but there was no shortage of mirth surrounding the saga. In London, a competition was devised which presented players with a mock portfolio valued at stg800 million, the winner being the first to lose the entire amount through a string of dodgy trades on the Japanese stock market. Fittingly, the winner received an all-expenses-paid holiday for two at the luxury Malaysian resort, the Shangri La. A side trip to Frankfurt, however, was not included in the prize.

Witticisms aside, people associated with Leeson were now contributing to a new myth, one which polarised and popularised Nick Leeson as some sort of working-class hero, abandoned to his fate by the establishment. Arguments that Leeson was made a convenient scapegoat for others have some merit, but the idea that Nick was a hero to his class and an honourable man turned into a sacrificial lamb was starting to take root.

CHAPTER TWELVE

DEATH OF A
BLUEBLOOD

The collapse of Barings is an illustration of how a viable and prosperous group can, in circumstances where controls are ineffective, be brought down by unauthorised activities within one of its subsidiary operations'. UK Board of Banking Supervision.[1]

In the seven days leading up to Nick Leeson's March 2 arrest, the stage upon which events had unfolded had spanned the globe, adding to the confusion. The parameters of the stage were now becoming more defined, with London, Singapore and the unlikely venue of Frankfurt forming the axis.

In London, the Barings board, the Bank of England, the British government, charities, 4000 bank employees, and thousands of big and small investors faced the daunting prospect of a complete meltdown of Barings. In Singapore, Barings staff members were placed on paid holiday leave.

Barings funds were frozen on four Asian futures markets, three of them in Japan — the Tokyo International Financial Futures Exchange, the Tokyo Futures Exchange and the Osaka Securities Exchange. In Singapore, Barings Futures funds were also frozen by Simex, and 62 further principal operating companies across 26 countries and territories were in much anxiety about what would unfold next.

Not all Barings principal entities were wholly owned. Some, such as the Australian broking house McIntosh Securities Ltd, were listed on local stock markets, with Barings holding a majority stake. In such cases, the company was allowed to continue trading but investors had to endure both a steeply eroding share price and capital worth, and the ignominy of the shared fate of Barings in London and Singapore.

In the city of London, administrators faced the same problems as had been experienced by the Barings board and Threadneedle Street. The options were stark: either an entire trade sale, a breakdown and sell-off of the group, enabling the administrators to salvage what capital they could in order to meet the debts or, in the worst possible scenario, a complete meltdown of the group where no buyers could be found and Barings simply closed its doors and sent its staff home.

At Ernst & Young, Nigel Hamilton, Alan Bloom and Maggie Mills were being pressured to act quickly. There was an array of genuine and dubious issues being raised which were adding one complicated layer on another, diverting attention away from the real problem. Among the genuine were Barings' clients who were juggling merger and takeover deals. Such companies were becoming restless. Computer group Misys was justifiably anxious: it had stg10.3 million in a frozen term-deposit account and at the same time was attempting to fund a takeover of its rival ACT Group.

The heat was also being applied from other quarters. In Singapore, authorities were becoming anxious about the unknown damage which might be being felt in Standard & Poor's Tokyo office, where the investment upgrade and a possible entry to the realm of the so-called developed world was being considered. Singapore's public policy of saying as little as possible during a scandal was in place, but wised-up authorities knew full well that its financial integrity was being scrutinised. With this in mind, regulatory authorities were quick to be seen acting decisively, and immediately announced stiffer laws geared towards preventing another Barings-style fiasco.

Singapore's finance minister, Dr Richard Hu, declared that the government would now vet all new contracts introduced by Simex, and would impose stricter criteria on dealers who traded in futures. Simex would also be required by the head office of exchange members to hold a tighter leash on their futures subsidiaries in Singapore.

Asian markets on which frozen Barings funds were traded were also being squeezed by investors. As the major international clearing house of futures contracts, the Chicago Mercantile Exchange and the Chicago Board of Trade contended that by withholding the funds, the Asian bourses were courting a public relations disaster for the already maligned derivatives industry, and should instead release these funds as quickly as possible. This was in itself considered a stunt by some analysts, who argued that the North Americans' real contention was on behalf of their respective investors who were worried that their frozen funds would be used by Asian exchanges to cover losses incurred by Barings.

The United States was showing signs of turning into a legal quagmire for the administrators. In New York, the Deutsche Bank of Germany was attempting to retrieve $48 million from Barings through foreign exchange deals, and French bank Societe Generale had filed a summons against Baring Brothers and Co Ltd to retrieve $1.5 million which had been sent to Barings for two foreign currency trades just prior to the collapse.[2]

Through the Manhattan Supreme Court, Societe Generale said the money was given to Barings on February 27, in exchange for $1.0 million worth of German marks and $500,000 worth of French francs, and that Barings had failed to deliver. Barings was given 20 days to respond.[3]

Meanwhile, the Germans had claimed that Barings had fraudulently induced the Deutsche Bank into a currency exchange while simultaneously and secretly negotiating a potential purchase of Barings. Deutsche Bank executives contended Barings realised it did not have the resources to cover $47.9 million that was deposited into a New York Barings account at the National Trust Corp. In return,

Barings was supposed to deposit an equal sum of Spanish pesetas into a Deutsche Bank account in Spain. This payment had not been made.

One of the few bright spots was the eventual stabilisation of the stock markets which shrugged off the general negative sentiment of the Barings collapse. Investors and fund managers soon turned their attention elsewhere, alleviating the fears of doomsdayers and restoring the faith in those who subscribe to theories of pure capitalism. After fronting up to one financial headache after another, the restoration of market balance earned a reprieve for British Prime Minister John Major's administration and the right-wing economic policies it espoused.

But although the markets bounced back, the unease in trading circles continued as Daiwa began unwinding the futures contracts. They held 6.1 billion yen to cover any losses if Barings' margin call payments fell short. Losses were to be minimised through either selling on-market or by allowing the contracts to expire on March 10 but, for every 1000 point fall in the Nikkei 225, the total exposure had the potential to realise a further stg150 million of losses and until losses could be capped, liability for the exposure remained with exchanges in Singapore and Osaka. It was a delicate task. One week into March, some 8466 contracts had been unwound.

At Ernst & Young, the administrators were running out of time. If a break-up of the group was to occur, a decision had to be made quickly. They faced the dilemma of holding out for a buyer who was prepared to take on the entire group but, in doing so, they risked watching the value of the corporate finance and asset management groups being written back by the hour — particularly if investors began withdrawing their backing or if key staff defected. The latter was already becoming a problem, with many employees around the world openly sounding out alternative work or pursuing previous job offers. Barings' worth went further than its now evaporated capital base. Finance is essentially a people business, and the goodwill value of an experienced and effective staff was pivotal to a successful sale.

Fears of a mass defection of staff members prompted Sir Peter Baring to issue an internal memorandum, in which he said the successful sale of the bank's units would ensure the future careers of most employees. The memo stated in part: 'We must continue to maintain our self-confidence ... Be patient and have confidence that problems will be dealt with, even if not as quickly as would want them'.

Cynics interpreted this as an admission that no-one was interested in buying out the group. Such an interpretation was justified. Some events which precipitated the appointment of administrators were now public knowledge. Staff knew that Japanese banks, the Sultan of Brunei, and their own British institutions had baulked at a capital injection.

The Bank of England had refused a last-minute loan, and the very nature of Barings management had dictated over the previous years that profit was the goal. Most felt they had been deserted and left to fend for themselves and an 'each person for themselves' syndrome was evolving. Those who could, had no problems with ditching any sentimental loyalties and began sounding out alternative employment.

But the massive publicity surrounding the collapse outstripped any of the feeble attempts made by the BoE and bankers on the previous Sunday to find a solution. Every cashed-up bank was interested. Initial inquiries for the takeover of Barings emerged from a consortium led by the largest bank in The Netherlands, ABN-Amro NV. Tentative bids from United States investments houses Merrill Lynch, Bankers Trust, and GE Capital were considered.

Interest was also expressed by Britain's National Westminster Bank, Barclays Bank, HSBC Holdings and Switzerland's Swiss Banking Corp. Barings executives were working hard. Within several days, they had made six complete presentations to potential buyers which, given the scope of the existing problems, was not an easy task.

At the same time, it was believed that ABN-Amro was prepared to pay stg300 million for Barings' corporate finance team and its fund management operations, which were deemed the juiciest part of the crashed group. A sticking point with the administrators was that all the common standards associated with valuations had been discarded amid the fire-sale atmosphere.

BAM was given a loose worth of between stg300 million and stg650 million, an estimate struck on the basis that it had contributed stg32 million to group profits in 1993, but offsetting this valuation was the suspension of redemptions on 20 worldwide unit trust schemes.

Another sought-after operation was the London corporate finance and banking arm, Barings Brothers & Co Ltd. However, as was expected, little interest was being expressed in Barings Securities Ltd, and a trade sale for the entire group was proving elusive.

Still, interest was escalating. Ernst & Young began the bidding for the entire operations at the token level of stg60 million to cover goodwill, including staff. Within four days, more than 10 serious bids were received for BAM. European and United States-based institutions were circling the securities division, but their interest remained lukewarm. Morgan Stanley and Merrill Lynch were understood to be keen on the European fund, while National Westminster and Barclays had firmed as favourites among the candidates likely to take out the entire bank.

Lurking behind ABN-Amro was its homeland arch rival, Internationale Nederlanden Groep (ING), a huge Dutch banking and insurance operation which, with just a short history on the international scene, was a relative stranger. ING's was one of two late tenders. The group had been forged in 1991 through the merger of insurance company Nationale-Nederlanden NV and the NMB-Postbank group and, by the end of 1993, was listed on eight European stock exchanges and the European Options Exchange in Amsterdam. The group had publicly committed itself to 'bancassurance', the concept of marrying the businesses of banking and insurance.

ING — Europe's eighth largest bank and its fifth largest insurer — had expanded rapidly, with principal group companies in 30 countries, but it was not in the market for an investment bank. Instead, ING chairman Aad Jacobs and his team wanted to buy a retail banking operation outside the Netherlands to complement the Postbank operations at home. However, retail banks with home banking, direct sales opportunities and large customer bases do not come cheap. They also tend to operate in mature markets with limited growth prospects.

A geographical breakdown of the group's income indicated ING's relatively limited exposure to growing markets. In 1994, the Netherlands contributed 57 per cent to overall income, with North America responsible for 23 per cent, while Europe and Australia contributed 7.0 and 6.0 per cent respectively to earnings.

Outside those mature markets, contributions from Asia registered a paltry 4.0 per cent, and Latin America accounted for just 2.0 per cent. ING had earned itself a reputation as a pioneer after pushing its way into Cuba and North Korea, and its focus was now on Asia, South America and Eastern Europe. Still, taking out Barings seemed a hugely ambitious task.

Talks continued.

Each party had a team of specialists looking to cut the best deal and circumvent the opposition. Nothing could be finalised and it was becoming abundantly clear that a break-up of the group would have to occur. Viable assets would be sold and the remainder scrapped. Not surprisingly, no-one was interested in taking on Leeson's futures contracts which, by law, must be closed out. An entire trade sale was now unlikely, and the administrators gave the bidders until Friday, March 3, to deliver firm and final proposals.

Ignoring Sir Peter Baring's plea for calm, in-fighting within the collapsed bank was on the rise. Traditional rivalries and old enemies were coming to the fore, with people in each unit fending for themselves. All were blaming the bank's capital markets operations for failing to control Leeson, and for having created the predicament in which they all found themselves.

The securities unit, with Ron Baker at the helm, went it alone and tried to present itself as a cohesive body. But in reality, it all fell into the laps of outsiders. The administrators wanted the best deal and a swift end to the uncertainty. In the most hopeful scenario, the loyal would have liked to have seen the group trade on as a single entity, merged into a bigger operation, and perhaps even retaining the Barings name.

There remained several appealing aspects to acquiring Barings, most notably its exposure to the growing Asian regions. ING had already established Asian beachheads in Japan, South Korea, Taiwan and China through its insurance and banking arms. Since its inception, the group had placed a high priority on risk management, and executives were confident that, had existing ING controls been in place at Barings, the collapse would never have occurred.

The group took the unusual step of listing in its 1993 annual report: 'Fraud and other types of crime are becoming a growing problem for insurance companies and banks. In the Netherlands, government and industry are working together to fight crime'. Insurance fraud, money laundering, and bank robberies were the chief concerns, but the group also made extensive remarks about the group's attitudes to risk management. By way of comparison, risk management rated barely a mention in Barings' 1993 annual report.

ING's 1993 report to shareholders also noted: 'ING Bank will also continue its policy of responding actively to economic recovery in Latin America and to the opportunities presented by growth markets in South East Asia'. ING was celebrating its return to China after a 60-year absence by the banking division, and its last recorded full-year net profit had reached 2.03 billion guilders, up 10.9 per cent from the 1.83 billion guilders registered in 1992.

Jacobs was savvy, having begun his career in investment management, but while he wanted Barings keenly, he was forced to contend with a second late bid from the sidelines. ABN-Amro had placed a $US475 million bid on the table for the asset management and corporate finance arms of Barings, ensuring a position as favourite. With a break-up of the group still looming large, US broking house Smith Barney entered the race, but both Smith Barney and ING remained outsiders to ABN-Amro.

Smith Barney was the second largest retail brokerage operation in the US and was headed by the aggressive Robert Greenhill. He was a well-known deal cutter, poached two years earlier from Morgan Stanley and analysts considered his performance at the helm 'outstanding', given the difficult market conditions which prevailed during his tenure. It was in part Greenhill's reputation which was behind Smith Barney winning the confidence of the market as a takeover aspirant.

Jacobs' team needed a ploy: specifically, one capable of locking out ABN-Amro's offer for part of the group while at the same time nullifying any eleventh-hour bid by Smith Barney which might also involve ABN-Amro. Some quarters were not taking the British offers too seriously because they had passed up their chance in the two days prior to Barings being handed over to the administrators when they had had an exclusive opportunity to pick up a rival.

It took the Barings family 233 years to build the company into the formidable financial house which had so dominated its arena, but ING needed barely one day to lay the plans to seize control of the bankrupt giant. ING negotiators homed in on what the administrators, Hamilton, Bloom and Mills wanted — a complete trade sale of the entire Barings group.

They reached an exclusive agreement that ING would acquire the entire operations under the condition that competing bids were precluded from further talks while ING management undertook their own initial investigations into Barings' true worth, and ascertained just how much money it would take to recapitalise the bank and enable it to resume trading. ING was cashed-up and confident. The administrators were equally confident that ING was in the best position to make a firm offer for the entire Barings group — losses and all — and make it an addition to ING's 75 principal operating companies.

On March 6, ING struck a deal with Ernst & Young and agreed to acquire Barings Plc for just one British pound, a nominal price later seized upon by many satirists. British cartoonist Kipper Williams sketched a man begging on the streets who, when glancing at the coins in his hat, tells his friend: 'Seven pence more and I'll have enough to buy Barings'.

But the real cost of the acquisition was a capital injection by ING of stg660 million, a payment necessary to resuscitate the institution whose losses were still steadily growing. Jacobs was still on a knife-edge. He had calculated that Barings' losses were now in the vicinity of stg880 million. The estimate was conservative to say the least: a solicitor for the bank's administrators put the figure as high as stg916 million. The Dutch bank had calculated that after the restructuring and writing-off of losses, Barings would retain about stg200 million worth of shareholder funds, and Jacobs was confident that this, combined with the capital injection, would prove enough to kick-start Barings under Amsterdam's control.

The sheer weight the deal had placed on the Dutch bank's shoulders was underscored by credit rating agency Moody's Investors Services announcing that it was considering reducing its rating on about US$1.1 billion worth of the group's debt because of the potential risks involved in the purchase.

A further cause for concern was ING's agreement to return all frozen assets and reimburse 100 per cent of all liabilities, although liability claims dated after March 6 were rejected. On the same day, ING's director in charge of investment banking, Hessel Lindenbergh, realised that Barings losses could blow out to $1.46 billion, 50 per cent above the anticipated $1.0 billion loss. While Lindenbergh pondered the latest headache, outsiders were relieved to hear that frozen trading funds — margin and equity money — from the four Asian futures markets had been released.

A communique was issued which expressed ING's desire to retain all of the bank's employees, together with the Barings name and shingle. However, the deal still had to be approved by several regulatory authorities, including Threadneedle Street, the central bank of the Netherlands, and the court which had ordered Barings be placed under judicial administration.

Still, Jacobs was confident, despite the possibility of escalating losses. He said the strategic fit between Barings and ING was compelling. 'I'm delighted. It's a fantastic fit with our plans and will give us an enormous boost', he said.[4]

Once the necessary approval was granted, ING stood to emerge as a genuine new powerhouse on the world financial stage, a strengthened institution in a prime position to take on its main rivals — ABN-Amro and Robobank — on the Dutch trail into Asia. With 50 per cent of the Netherland's gross national product tied to trade, ING was champing at the bit to make serious inroads into Asia.

The road to approval was neither long nor arduous. Just four days later, Barings' administrators completed the sale of virtually all operations of Barings Brothers & Co and Barings Securities to ING.

'The joint administrators are delighted to relinquish control of the business operations so rapidly', they said in a statement. ING established Barings Holding Co Ltd to run all Barings operations.

In an irony no doubt not lost on the new Dutch owners, control and ownership of Barings bank had returned to the

birthplace of its founder, Johann Baring. Bowed and demo-
ralised, Barings and its staff now faced an unknown future
under their new masters.

✄

Three ING executives were put in charge: Hessel Lindenbergh, the chairman and chief executive of ING capital in
London, Onno van den Broek, and the chairman on ING
capital in New York, Lane Grijns. These three, along with
another ING executive, Ted de Vries, also made up the new
board of Barings Securities.

The much sought after Barings Asset Management and its
stg30 million of funds under management was kept intact,
with John Bolsover being retained as the unit's chairman.
One Barings employee quipped: 'Now we can see the light at
the end of the day . . . there really are no conditions on this,
other than we have to be good boys'.[5]

Barings Plc had ceased to operate under family control
for the first time in its esteemed history. The entrenched
culture and family influence at Barings was not lost on Philip
Ziegler when he completed his biography of the bank and its
dynasty several years earlier. In his epilogue, he noted:
'There is nothing in the constitution of Barings or of the
foundation which requires family involvement, and its con-
tinuation depends on a flow of suitable individuals. However, there is no lack of up-and-coming Barings in the wings,
and this, together with the interest of other members of the
group in seeing the traditional spirit of the house maintained,
gives good reason to hope that the business will continue to
have a distinctive feeling for some time yet'.

Contrary to Ziegler's opinion, ING obviously felt that
there was a serious lack of up-and-coming Barings in the
wings. Sir Peter Baring was promptly denied any senior
executive role as the bank's new owner reshaped its management structure. Sir Peter's earlier offer to resign was rejected
by Aad Jacobs, who said he should remain until after the

Bank of England inquiry, adding: 'If it finds something wrong, we will take appropriate action but I hope it does not'.[6]

As early as March 17, 1995, Sir Peter was relegated to a 'liaison' role but he fared better than Ron Baker, the former head of the financial products group, who had no role in the new structure. Peter Norris was demoted to the position of adviser to the co-chairman of Barings Securities. A further six members of the bank's risk committee also faced the axe, as did key directors of the treasury department. John Bolsover was virtually the sole survivor of the shake-out of the main board. A Dutch source said: 'It is difficult to keep people on who are responsible for what happened when we are trying to make a new start. ING might be forced to take further action if the Bank of England report is delayed'.[7]

Lindenbergh was content not to undertake any mass sackings — at least for the time being. ING had adopted a policy of treating Barings executives as innocent until proven guilty. Any purge of those responsible for the fiasco would have to wait until after authorities had completed their investigations. This was understandable and made commercial sense. ING needed people who were au fait with the bank's key operations.

The transition to Dutch control had been undertaken with unprecedented speed, and Lindenbergh was keen to complete the change as smoothly as possible. Generally, staff were relieved when the deal with ING was announced. A meltdown had been avoided and most jobs seemed secure. However, many senior operators had initiated talks elsewhere with rival banks and institutions, sounding out alternative employment in case the worst-case scenario presented itself. Barings' rivals were delighted that senior staff were defecting.

This was underscored by the poaching of 11 stock market analysts based in Tokyo by Smith New Court one day after the London High Court approved the ING takeover. They were key analysts operating in core sectors of the bank's Japanese securities operations covering chemical, industrial and the smaller companies sector as listed by the Nikkei-225 index, an area requiring specialised expertise.

In an effort to retain staff, ING made the extravagant gesture of agreeing to pay out stg90 million worth of staff bonuses. It may have been an ironic twist that staff be rewarded for their work for a bank that had just lost in excess of $1.0 billion, but Lindenbergh had little choice. Some senior executives waived their entitlements, and ING was suitably selective in allocating rewards to those who may have been involved with the collapse.

Barings' bondholders fared less well. They had been virtually frozen out of any reimbursement of their investments by ING. ING had argued, with legal justification, that people holding such notes were no different to people holding common stock in companies and therefore were not entitled to a return. ING did not buy Barings Plc, the company which issued the notes, though they had agreed to effectively pay all creditors stg7.5 million.

For the bondholders, this was a paltry sum when compared with their initial investment, and most of it was expected to be spent on fees. This was cold comfort for investors in a bank brought down by the illegal activities of one man and, at the very least, the mismanagement of others. For the noteholders — who had formed the Barings Perpetual Noteholders Action Group — it was an insult to reward those responsible for their investments sliding into the abyss. The group intended to raise 0.25 per cent of their initial total investment, or about stg250,000, from noteholders to mount a legal challenge in the hope of obtaining a higher return.

As the former Barings board watched ING assume control and exert its influence from across the English Channel, they could only stare with envy as rival merchant bank Standard Chartered Plc, which does most of its business in Asia, Africa and the Middle East, posted a record stg401 pre-tax profit. Like Barings, Standard operated a futures division, including a branch in Singapore, but Standard had steered away from speculative derivatives trade, opting instead to concentrate on traditional banking and newly developed franchise operations.

Barings' former board was also keeping a close eye on the investigations being carried out. As details began to emerge, it was becoming apparent that Leeson's claim of management support had serious credence.

A conference called by Simex on the day that ING secured control of Barings revealed that Leeson had operated on behalf of only four companies, including the three Baring institutions.

'The failure of internal controls within the Barings Group has allowed the general manager of Barings Futures (Singapore) to commit the Barings Group to substantial positions which now account for the loss sustained by the group', Simex chairman Elizabeth Sam told the news conference. Her comments followed supportive statements by Singapore Prime Minister Goh Chok Tong, who blamed a lack of internal controls, and stressed that local regulators saw the catastrophe looming and had warned those involved.

James Bax had also moved into damage control and attempted to, at least in part, exonerate himself. Simex called a press conference to brief journalists on the running issues surrounding Barings from their perspective. At the conference, Simex authorities released a copy of the memo Bax had sent to Bishopsgate prior to Leeson's arrival, warning of the inherent risks associated with allowing Leeson to control both front and back offices.

Some of the answers were beginning to emerge. On the same day ING secured the agreement, Reuters quoted an official from the Bank of Japan as claiming that 20 Japanese commercial banks had lent 60 billion yen to Barings Securities (Japan) Ltd, cash used to cover Leeson's margins on the derivatives splurge. This would at least serve to explain how Leeson was able to meet his margins on trade and carry on without raising the suspicions of exchange authorities. Aad Jacobs said he believed Nick Leeson may have had help from someone in London.[8]

But failings within Barings itself were now emerging as the critical factor in the collapse of the bank, and the first reports had broken that Bishopsgate forwarded stg44 million in emergency funds to help meet margin calls. There was more to come, and the conspiracy theories forwarded by Sir Peter Baring were now looking decidedly weak.

In Preungeshelm Prison in the Frankfurt suburb of Hoechst, Leeson — who by now had been dubbed by the press 'the screen jockey from hell' — awaited a hearing for extradition to Singapore on cheating and forgery charges. Lisa had been released from custody shortly after their detention at Frankfurt airport.

Singapore had alleged that Leeson had forged a document for a fictitious deal with Spear, Leeds and Kellogg (SLK). The document was to confirm a deal that apparently never took place. This allowed Leeson to transfer $80 million into his trading account from another Barings account.

The charges were denied, and a court subsequently found that there were sufficient grounds to hold Leeson temporarily for an extradition hearing on fraud charges and possible return to Singapore. Leeson was given no explanation for his detention but, behind the scenes, there existed a mountain of evidence supporting the Spear Leeds allegation.

A further 800-page formal request for his extradition arrived soon after and he now faced 11 charges, which both German and Singapore authorities refused to publicly detail. After initially examining the 11 charges, German prosecutor Hans-Hermann Eckert formed the opinion that most of the charges each represented a strong case for Leeson's extradition.

But in the meantime, Leeson faced an indefinite stay behind bars in Germany. One of the warders at the 300-inmate prison said Nick had worn a 'look of desperation' as the door slammed for the first time on his spartan 3.6 by 2.4-metre cell. Leeson's letter of resignation, in which he claimed he was on the verge of a nervous breakdown, and his obvious depression, led prison officials to place him on suicide watch, requiring wardens to check on him every 30 minutes while a psychological profile was compiled and a program of activities arranged. Lisa's visits were virtually all Nick had to look forward to. One of his few other thrills was the arrival of a letter from the Manchester City Football Supporters' Club, a show of solidarity which served to lift his flagging spirits.

Once he was removed from suicide watch, Leeson was given a choice between learning Latin or German, playing the guitar, practising yoga, or writing for the prison newspaper, *Seen Through The Bars*, in his spare time. He was also allowed to buy sweets, cigarettes and coffee in the prison shop, but spending was strictly limited to about S$149 a week. Perturbed by Nick's steady weight loss, Lisa supplemented his supplies by bringing food during her one-hour weekly visits.

She also brought her husband a television set, which Nick was allowed to keep. But, in stark contrast to the halcyon days in Singapore, such luxuries were few and far between. Each morning, with the regularity of the opening bell on the Simex trading floor, Leeson was awoken before first light with a 5.45 am alarm call. He had to wash using the basin in his cell and was allowed the privilege of a shower only once a week. He had his own toilet.

Amid heavy posturing from those who stood to lose and those given the task of seeking the truth, an endless procession of opinions continued to be trotted out. Most were well-meaning; others questionable, but whatever their motives, the isolation of Nick Leeson continued. As did the media's willingness to feed the appetite for Leeson trivia which the case had spawned.

Mark Duncan was a dealer at Barings Securities in Singapore and Leeson was apparently godfather to his children. He said he had no indication about what could happen. 'I did not expect this', he said.[9]

Max Clifford — the undisputed ruler of the London tabloid kiss-and-tell brigade, and a man renowned for hawking stories to the more sensational areas of the press — also jumped on the bandwagon. At one stage, Clifford claimed to be 'helping' Leeson deal with the media. He described Leeson's position: 'It's like a tidal wave hitting you. You're angry, you're numb, you're shocked. It's a very emotional experience to be hung out to dry worldwide'.[10] However, sources close to Leeson later claimed Clifford had never contacted Leeson, nor Leeson Clifford.

Even a former Australian model turned London-based futures trader, Catherine McBride, made it into the newspapers by saying she had worked and lunched with Leeson a couple of years earlier in Barings' London office. In a Sydney newspaper, she received a billing under the headline: 'A Lunch That Could Have Saved Barings'.

'It was staffed by really smart, bright people with PhDs from the best universities, and then there were others who were like East End barrow boys. Nick was one of the latter', she said.

McBride was said to have had lunch with the managing director and three other directors. When asked how things were going in the derivatives department, she told them it was in trouble because people there lacked either qualifications or experience. It was also claimed that McBride was invited to Singapore to manage the operations there. She inspected the operations and Leeson — which the newspaper claimed was 'then a phone clerk' — showed her around. It was said McBride declined the job and later quit.

Unlike many others, McBride was not prepared to single Leeson out: 'Now the bank's senior executives are saying they didn't know what was going on. To me that makes them doubly culpable,' she said. [11]

The benefits of hindsight didn't escape *The International Finance Review* either. Its editors were mindful of their earlier efforts in burying a story on Leeson's drunken exploits and 'the dropping of the pants' episode after the Simex dinner six months earlier. Somewhat cleverly, they published in March: 'We have a tragic footnote to the collapse of the Barings dynasty. Without wanting to sound too self-important, the whole thing may have been avoided had we published last autumn a hair-raising tale on the antics of Mr Leeson'.

The *Review* then posed the questions: 'Would Barings still be around if we had run the story? Would Leeson have been expelled from Singapore with his tail between his legs and sent off to run derivatives in Mexico? And would his fatal trades thus have happened?' In answering its own questions, the *International Financing Review* said: 'We have a horrible feeling that the answer to all three questions is "yes".'[12]

Leeson had already beed fined and punished through the Singapore judicial system for those antics. While it was admirable to a point that *The International Finance Review* admitted it may have been lacking journalistic endeavour to publish without fear or favour, it was quite ludicrous to suggest that it could have prompted a harsher punishment and thus have saved the bank.

Much was made of every snippet of news or trivia involving Barings. As the secrets of the Eights Account began to reveal Leeson's unauthorised trades, the irony of what constitutes lucky numbers was not lost with those who dabbled in Chinese astrology. Some wondered what Peter Norris would have thought. On the eighth day of the eighth month in 1988, Norris supposedly arranged for a feng shui practitioner to exorcise any evil spirits lurking in his Hong Kong home, and he gave each employee at Baring Brothers 88 Hong Kong dollars.[13]

Each new twist delivered a new turn in the Leeson and now ING-Barings saga. The Eights Account was now public knowledge, Sir Peter's theory of a conspiracy had been dismissed, and investment houses were aghast to learn that Leeson held control of both front and back offices in Singapore. It had also been gleaned that someone in London had transferred vast sums of money to Singapore to cover Leeson's margin call payments.

With the exception of bondholders, ING had met nearly all of Barings' obligations. Most of the legal issues had been settled, Barings' fate had been decided — although it would continue to trade under name only within the ING stable — and many of the major and peripheral issues that had dogged the previous week had been resolved. The emphasis was now on apportioning blame.

In Singapore, authorities embarked upon a two-pronged strategy. First, there was the investigation into the collapse and, secondly, a legal case had to be mounted to successfully extradite Leeson from Germany. In Frankfurt, Leeson had decided to push his bid to be returned to London and to fight off the efforts of Singaporean justice through the courts by means of an extensive propaganda campaign.

In London, investigators began their own probe. Everything seemed to be in order when, suddenly, presumptions went out the window and London authorities stunned the financial community and the general public with its stubborn reluctance to support Leeson's bid to be returned home to stand trial.

It looked like Leeson was going to be stitched up alone.

CHAPTER THIRTEEN

DOGS THAT DON'T BARK

'People [at Barings] talked about [Leeson's rising profits] almost incessantly. I have to say that a load of people — all of us, really — found it very puzzling. But I have to say, equally, and maybe you will say naively, we accepted it'. Barings director George Maclean.[1]

Barings' new owner, ING, tried to act swiftly. Under the stewardship of Hessel Lindenbergh, an internal inquiry was launched, but the insurance and banking giant was taking a steady approach with Lindenbergh preferring to let the proper regulatory authorities independently assess and lay blame for the debacle.

At the time, it was noted that Lindenbergh's attitude was considered charming evidence of old world Dutch etiquette in a sea of corporate cut-throats, but it was this attitude that was stalling the relaunch of the now Dutch-owned and controlled British institution.

Lindenbergh had optimistically anticipated that the Bank of England inquiry would take about a month to complete. Should any Barings executives be found to have been directly connected with the collapse, ING would then be in a position to purge the guilty and proceed with the task of rebuilding the battered bank. Amsterdam was duly furious when BoE governor Eddie George said the inquiry could take until June to complete. The central bank's Board of Banking Supervision did not even plan to complete the first stage of the inquiry detailing the sequence of events until May. The rest may have to wait till late June or early July.

But George was having a difficult time. If having to endure criticism from the establishment for not throwing a life-line to Barings was not enough, a sex scandal from within the bank's hallowed halls probably was. In an extraordinary turn of events, George's deputy, Rupert Pennant-Rea, came under public fire over an extra-marital affair he had ended a year earlier with Mary Ellen Synon, a journalist with whom he had worked during his tenure at *The Economist*.

The spurned Synon chose to go public with sordid details of their clandestine relationship — including the revelation that they once had sex in George's dressing room at Threadneedle Street — when she had seen Pennant-Rea on television discussing Barings as the BoE's acting spokesman while George was still on his skiing holiday in France. 'Seeing him like that brought back all the hurt', she was quoted in *Vanity Fair* as saying. 'I just wanted to see him pay the price for how he treated me'.

The price was high indeed. Pennant-Rea had his dirty laundry hung to air in every quarter of the insatiable British press. It was a bizarre case of life imitating art: in 1979, Pennant-Rea had written his first and only novel, *Gold Foil*, the steamy tale of an affair between a Bank of England official and a female journalist who 'learnt at an early age that money and sex make fools of intelligent men'. (She betrays him in the end).[2]

The press had a field day. Banner headlines such as 'The Bonk of England' were commonplace. Even the high-brow *Financial Times* went as fas as: 'Bank Called to Act on Matter of The Heart'. The racier tabloids dredged up a host of letters Pennant-Rea had written to the cooperative Synon during their three-year affair, the most sensational being a note dated November 1993 in which Pennant-Rea told his lover he sat in formal BoE meetings imagining her *sans* underwear.

'I spend quite a lot of time at meetings thinking of you: sometimes practical thoughts, but mostly pretty carnal ones', the newspapers quoted Pennant-Rea as having written to his former lover. And: 'Perhaps it's a natural reaction to all the men in suits sitting round the table; it leads me to imagine you with no knickers, just those lovely suspenders and beautiful white flesh. You are v. (sic) beautiful; when so much of me is drained of emotion, I still stand in wonder at the sheer physical delights of you'.[3]

Still reeling from the collapse of Barings and having barely recovered from the BCCI debacle, the probity-obsessed central bank eagerly accepted Pennant-Rea's resignation from his stg180,000-a-year position on March 21.

Hessel Lindenbergh was not interested in the bedroom — or dressing room — antics of others. His own camp was disturbed by headlines like: 'Barings Chiefs Face Purge'. Sir Peter Baring and Andrew Tuckey alleviated some of the strain by bowing to the obvious: both resigned on April 3. Lindenbergh wanted hard answers from the BoE inquiry and threatened that unless the central bank's board of banking supervision produced initial findings by the end of April, ING might start to dismiss the Barings executives it believed to be responsible for the collapse.

Aad Jacobs was furious, pointing out that ING had not agreed to pay about stg700 million to acquire a 'people business' if the group had not expected Barings people to remain: 'We are not going to fire anyone'.[4]

Jacobs and Lindenbergh's discomfort surrounding the positions of Barings directors remaining within the group was understandable. Already, preoccupation with the Barings acquisition had diverted the attentions of ING management away from other areas of their operations, and had placed on hold the potential purchase of the Budapest Bank of Hungary. ING had also been hand-tied by an order from Britain's Securities and Futures Authority (SFA), which temporarily banned ING from appointing Barings directors to the boards of the two new companies established to take on the new Barings business until after the Bank of England had completed its inquiry.

As head of the derivatives operations in London, Australian Ron Baker was coming under intense pressure to resign, with the British media leading the campaign at every opportunity. But Lindenbergh had apparently taken a liking to Baker and, the Singapore debacle aside, was impressed by Baker's track record. Nevertheless, when asked whether Baker was likely to leave Barings, Lindenbergh answered: 'I'm afraid so'.

Lindenbergh's firm belief was that Baker may not have been actively involved in the fall of the bank, but the Dutchman had already concluded the first line of responsibility was within the Australian's group.

The Bank of England had formally served notice on ING under section 42 of the 1987 Banking Act. The section is reserved for only the most serious probes. It allows the BoE to subpoena witnesses and a list of 20 executives to be interviewed was provided, although Lindenbergh said up to 40 could be questioned. His comments triggered a wave of speculation of a hit list within Barings and that blame for the mess might not be levelled solely at Nick Leeson after all. Barings staff were becoming increasingly agitated. Paranoia was on the rise, with bank staff having to put up with clients asking questions such as: 'Will you still be here in three weeks?' or, 'Are you on the list?'. The latter was becoming a standard insult and received an impetus from reports in Singapore contradicting London by saying that Leeson may not have acted alone.

Sighs of relief were almost audible when, the day after Sir Peter Baring and Andrew Tuckey resigned, Britain's Serious Fraud Office concluded that Leeson had acted alone and was not part of a criminal conspiracy. However, at the same time, a copy of an internal Barings report was leaked to Britain's *Independent* newspaper, revealing a morass of gross incompetencies.

These included allegations that:

- Leeson had shredded documents on his trading activities and had falsified information provided to Coopers & Lybrand and Singapore exchange authorities;
- Leeson had ordered the shredding of the Eights Account while he held onto a sole copy;
- Barings had advanced more than twice its own capital, stg760 million, to Singapore to fund Leeson s trading activities.

Two questions, however, remained unanswered:

- who was responsible for the transfer of capital from London (an obvious breach of the law)?; and
- why were the investigators and authorities apparently not overly interested in establishing this person's identity?

Leeson was aggravating matters from Frankfurt by refusing to cooperate with British authorities unless they attempted to extradite him home. It seemed, however, that investigators had by this time decided to leave Leeson to his own fate. London authorities would again cleverly argue that he was the sole contributor to the bank's collapse and, more importantly, that his crimes were committed in Singapore, and that consequently Singapore was where he should be sent for trial. On the face of it this made matters easier for authorities in Singapore seeking his extradition, and it now appeared possible that Leeson could be back there by Christmas. Whether others would pay for their sins now depended upon the results of regulatory inquiries by both London and Singapore.

SFA chairman Christopher Sharples said the regulators would decide whether former directors of Barings were, in the terminology of the 1987 Banking Act, 'fit and proper' to sit on the new boards after the inquiry was completed. This was widely believed to reflect concerns about the inaction of those Barings executives who had failed to act on the internal report which claimed Leeson held too much power.

Sharples' view of the collapse had been blunt: 'It seems to me that Mr Leeson pulled the trigger, but the bank gave him

the gun and the bank gave him the ammunition, and when
he wanted more ammunition they gave him as much as they
could give him until they ran out and then the bank was
bust'.[5]

Sharples later told a conference in London it would be
unfair to lay the blame for the demise of Barings at the feet of
regulators, and warned that any move to do so would be
contested.

If all the senior people in an organisation . . . claim they
couldn't see what was going on and couldn't stop what was
happening, how on earth can anyone expect regulators to
prevent what was going on?'

Sharples said the futures authority was then meeting
regularly with senior managers of financial firms in anticipation of the publication of the Bank of England's inquiry
report, which Lindenbergh was anxiously awaiting. From
London, this interpretation of events was becoming dangerously familiar. Regulators there were claiming for themselves
the mantle of innocence, while pointing the finger at Leeson
and as yet unnamed managers within Barings. The latter
were contributing nothing more than hot air.

Lindenbergh was never forced to act out his threat to fire
Barings executives involved with the collapse, unless the
Bank of England published its initial findings by the end of
April. On May 1, 1995, the resignations of 21 executives
based in London, Tokyo and Singapore were accepted. ING
resisted laying blame on any of the 21, but Barings' former
top-brass were duly labelled by the press 'The Dogs That
Didn't Bark' for their part in the derivatives fiasco. Peter
Norris, Ron Baker, Simon Jones and James Bax were among
them.

'Our review has confirmed that the problem stemming
from Singapore was extraordinary and not endemic. It is a
problem we have put behind us. We now turn our attention
to the future', Lindenbergh said. He added that the goal was
to restore the pre-eminence of the Barings name, and build
the business through providing clients first class service from

a first class organisation. 'It is with no pleasure that we have said goodbye to those who have left. Those who have departed have given many years of loyal service', he said.[6]

🦊

James Bax was justly upset. He had given the former board a clear, written warning of the looming disaster. His warnings had gone unheeded, and he still had to negotiate Singapore investigations, with little alternative but to remain there after his passport was held while local investigators carried out their inquiries. In early June, authorities allowed Bax to return to Britain for six weeks.

ING remained committed to the ideal that all Barings executives were innocent of wrong-doing until it had been proven otherwise. But the investigations underway behind the corporate facade were being frustrated by an unprecedented bureaucratic maze of corporate entanglement. The remnants of Barings management, ING executives, Interpol, and national police and regulatory authorities in Britain, Germany and Singapore were still arduously trying to expose what had become one of the greatest international financial debacles ever. Conspiracy theories remained, but little, if any, real evidence had surfaced.

In a deliberately blunt statement, Lindenbergh said in reference to the resignations: 'Those leaving comprise the executives of Barings with functional responsibility (whether direct or indirect) for the Singapore derivatives business'.

Ernst & Young were also becoming anxious. They were given the task of recovering as much of the approximately $700 million in losses as possible, and were canvassing the possibility of suing Barings' auditors Coopers & Lybrand. Ernst & Young administrator Brian Singleton argued that despite Coopers & Lybrand's decision not to sign off the Barings 1994 accounts, its accountants should have been aware of the weaknesses of internal controls within the bank. Given the immensity and unauthorised nature of Leeson's dealings, Coopers & Lybrand would be justified in disputing this assertion.

Agitation was also on the rise between Threadneedle Street and Singapore investigators. Their working relationship deteriorated following an acrimonious meeting in April over access to documents. The British were incensed and would continue to blame the Singapore authorities for hindering their efforts to discover what had really happened.

It was being assumed that underpinning the British inquiry were the exact motivations behind Leeson's trading position, and verifications were needed to substantiate losses in the Eights Account. The British claimed they were being denied access to James Bax and Simon Jones, and that it was proving increasingly difficult to prove or discount whether there were any third parties involved with Leeson in either Singapore or Osaka. They were therefore forced to concentrate their efforts on accessible people who had been 'directly concerned' with the collapse.

On March 7, British investigators met with the Judicial Managers to explain the scope of the inquiry and to present a list of preliminary information requirements. The Judicial Managers said it would be difficult to disclose information without approval from the Court.

Three days later, they met with Rajah & Tan — who had been retained as legal advisers to Singapore investigators — and were informed that inspectors had been appointed by the Minister of Finance in Singapore, and that the Judicial Managers and the inspectors would be requesting assistance from the UK authorities. Rajah & Tan provided information on the funding of BFS and its trading positions.

But on March 16, British investigators were told by James Bax that the Inspectors and Judicial Managers had ordered him and other employees at Barings Futures in Singapore not to disclose any information to the UK inquiry. Rajah & Tan later confirmed the restriction and told the team it should obtain approval from the Court before any disclosure of documents or access to BFS employees would be allowed.

The wrangle over access would drag on until April 8, when British investigators were finally given the green light to inspect the Court file. They were, however, still being denied access to Barings documents, and they applied formally to the Court on April 20. This was declined on May 3, but Rajah & Tan suggested the exchange of notes should take place after both parties had completed their respective investigations.

Simex authorities in Singapore were incensed by a report that the exchange had lost documents listing deals made by Leeson over the previous two months. Their own investigations had revealed that the documents had been shredded, and Simex now believed that enough evidence had been gathered to support possible fraud allegations. A request for an inquiry, to be conducted by Price Waterhouse, was made. Shortly afterwards, on March 9, Singapore's Finance Minister Richard Hu reacted to Simex complaints and requests, authorising a Price Waterhouse investigation to be conducted by Michael Lim and Nicky Tan, targeting allegations of fraud within Barings to complement investigations already being carried out by Singapore's Commercial Affairs Department.

Life inside ING-Barings was difficult in the extreme but, in Singapore and Malaysia, a new twist appeared, driving morale to its lowest ebb yet. About $2.0 million worth of share scrips had gone missing. An international courier had transported eight courier bags containing company shares held in trust for investors from Singapore for settlement of transactions to Kuala Lumpur on Saturday, March 18. But when the bags were sent out on the Monday, three were empty. Barings was quick to reassure investors that their stakes were safe and the bank's operations in Kuala Lumpur were quick to blame their frequently-used courier, arguing that tighter security measures should have been in place. The police did not rule out the possibility of an inside job and, while investors' scrip would be replaced, it was yet another headache that London, and Amsterdam, simply didn't need. It was the first time such an incident had occurred.

Meanwhile, members of Ian Watt's Board of Banking Supervision (BBS) unit were travelling extensively. Primary interviews and documents were being sought from London, Singapore, Hong Kong, Japan and the United States. While they had been frustrated by Singapore's own efforts to conduct its own inquiry, Watt's team had also been unable to interview Nick Leeson in Frankfurt. Acting through his lawyer, Stephen Pollard, Leeson was frustrating the inquiry with continued refusals to co-operate unless London authorities granted his request for extradition. It was his only bargaining chip.

Leeson was being difficult in a very calculated fashion. While so many issues hung in the balance, one thing to emerge with clarity in the direct aftermath of the bank's collapse was a propaganda campaign which was executed with almost military precision by Leeson, Lisa, and a man named Rod Tyler, who was appointed by Pollard to advise him on how to handle the media.

In one corner was Nick Leeson. Surrounding him was a legal team headed by Pollard, of the British firm Kingsley Napley, a leading specialist in white-collar crime. His German representative was Eberhard Kempf. Leeson's Singapore counsel was a man named John Koh, a 40-year-old former deputy director of the Commercial Affairs Department (CAD) who had been educated at the distinguished law schools of Cambridge and Harvard.

There were the immediate realities that needed to be faced. Lisa was broke. Rod Tyler arranged the media deals and sold initial exclusive interviews to *The Sun.* One estimate put the figure at stg50,000 and the money went straight towards the defence fund. Tyler also dealt with press inquiries and arranged for Lisa to speak with only particular journalists he considered might be at least fair or at best sympathetic to her plight. The lawyers would fight on the front lines. Tyler and his PR team were allocated the somewhat more delicate task of winning the hearts and minds of the British public, a nation of people renowned for their fiercely loyal support of the underdog and a healthy disdain for its establishment. It is understood that

Pollard decided against using Leeson's father in the campaign because of past difficulties.

In the opposite corner stood ING, the Bank of England, the Serious Fraud Office, and Singapore's Commercial Affairs Department, headed by director, Lawrence Ang. The British contingent had worked on a plan of action, cleverly contrived, waging a war not of writs and laws, but a war of greater subtlety and risk. A war of strategically manipulating the media and public sentiment.

The Leeson camp's strategy of disseminating a steady stream of painstakingly-manipulated statements designed to win an empathy for a stranded Briton who was prepared to be judged by his peers if only the authorities would bring him home. This was in stark contrast to the campaign waged by the Singapore camp.

On the island-state, credit ratings-conscious authorities maintained their low profile in seldom commenting publicly on the debacle. Press statements were rare and and those which were released were deliberate and designed to limit the negative fall-out emanating from the collapse. Nevertheless, the situation with Standard & Poor's, and the collapse of international markets, demanded that Singapore politicians be seen to be acting.

Prime Minister Goh Chok Tong distanced his country from the affair by saying Barings had only itself to blame through internal problems stemming from a lack of control. He also pointed the finger at senior management for failing to act on the warnings issued by Singapore regulators.

To the relief of many, decades of cautious economic management triumphed — Singapore's fiscally sound reputation had easily offset any damage that Barings could inflict upon Singapore in the eyes of Standard & Poor's. The ratings agency granted Singapore its debt upgrade, and welcomed the nation to the sovereign borrowers club.

In a glowing report card, Standard & Poor's said Singapore was stable with 'risk averse and visionary political leadership which underpins financially-conservative economic policies'.

The Barings debacle was not mentioned in the dispatch from the Tokyo office of Standard and Poor's, which described the country's transport, communications and banking facilities as 'top-notch'.

The devastation of the British-based Barings might have had little influence on Standard & Poor's decision, but it was proving a nightmare for those appointed to ensure that the world knew Singapore could mix it with the world elite in the sovereign club. The long-awaited announcement was well and truly overshadowed by the antics of Nick Leeson and his bank, and Singapore's establishment wanted to ensure that the Leeson affair was handled correctly and that this was seen to be done.

Investigators from Singapore were playing hard ball. The UK inquiry was asked to 'establish in detail the events that led to the collapse of Barings ...' by the Chancellor of the Exchequer, Kenneth Clarke, whereas in Singapore Michael Lim and Nicky Tan were charged with duties their British counterparts were not. As gazetted by the Singapore government, their brief included 'allegations of fraud, misfeasance or other misconduct'. The differences would eventually prove critical for Nick Leeson's stable.

The unravelling saga also stole centre stage at ING's annual general meeting in Amsterdam in May. Chairman Aad Jacobs told shareholders he was disappointed with the tardy response of the BoE and its failure to deliver its findings on the collapse.

'We can't wait too long. Staff and clients are asking for measures ... from our side we are working on that', Jacobs said, adding that ING was prepared to take its own measures if the BoE failed to produce its report within a month.

On a more positive note, Jacobs was able to tell shareholders that most of Barings' clients had remained, and that no clients had been lost from the prized Barings Asset Management unit. Keeping John Bolsover at the helm had silenced any critics.

Shortly afterwards, Singapore's High Court allowed ING to begin settling outstanding debts with known creditors of

Barings Futures Singapore. The court appointed three Price Waterhouse partners as judicial managers to carry out the task. The managers now had 60 days to present a repayment plan to the company and the known creditors, leading to the eventual winding-up of the Barings futures operation in Singapore in July, and a mass-sacking of its former staff. The entire dealing and back-room team, who used to work with Nick Leeson and who had been on paid holiday leave since March, had their services terminated at the end of June.

The court decision also cleared the way for the repayment of losses expected to top S$126 million from the division. Citibank, the largest creditor, was owed S$86 million, while Bank Nationale de Paris was owed about S$36 million. ING eventually reopened a futures division in South East Asia, trading under the name of Barings Futures International.

Only the bondholders were still out of pocket.

CHAPTER FOURTEEN

NICKED

'It's a chapter in my life that I'm looking to forget.' Nick Leeson.[1]

After four weeks of good behaviour, Nick Leeson was allowed to swap his blue jail-house garb for civilian clothes. He also became eligible for a prison job: he could choose between filling envelopes for the German military, packing containers for local companies, or working in the kitchen. Earning a token wage of eight deutsch marks a day, Leeson would have to spend more than 700,000 years on the job to repay the amount of money he lost while trading for Barings.

Leeson was the only British national in Preungeshelm Prison but about 70 per cent of its inmates were foreign, and there were plenty of English speakers. Not that there was much time for socialising. The only contact Leeson had with his fellow prisoners, mostly young offenders also accused of white-collar crime, was made during a brief morning exercise session in the courtyard. Although his comforts were limited, he was allowed to open his cell window to let in some fresh air, and could gaze through the metal bars, the mesh grille, and beyond the 7.6-metre walls into the outside world.

Across the Continent and the English Channel, Lisa was surviving off her family's generosity and some savings. They helped her pay for a weekly airfare to visit Nick. Her income was bolstered by money earned as a waitress at Elizabeth's Tea Room in Maidstone, and funds raised by the media interviews organised through Rod Tyler. The sandwich shop job, which paid stg25 a day plus tips, filled in her days, leaving her little time to feel sorry for herself.

'It certainly strengthens your relationship. It makes you realise how much you mean to each other', Lisa said in an interview with London's *Sunday Telegraph*. 'He was never very open about his feelings before, but now he tells me everything. Nick's scared and I'm scared — we are together in our fear'. Asked if, in her lowest moments, it had occurred to her to leave Nick, she replied: 'I love Nick. I want to spend the rest of my life with him. I married him for better, for worse, for richer, for poorer . . . .'.

The latter pledge was certainly being tested to its limits. The Leesons' once-assured financial security was being eroded rapidly as hefty legal fees began accumulating. Through Stephen Pollard and Rod Tyler, Nick Leeson began negotiating deals to sell his jail-cell interviews in a bid to recoup some costs, but this was proving trickier than first envisaged because technically, Leeson remained a potential witness yet to go before the British courts. Under UK conventions, such witnesses are not allowed to receive payments for interviews. The convention was also a convenience in ensuring that Nick kept his mouth shut.

In May, Leeson requested that a British journalist be allowed to visit him for four hours so he could give an interview which would be made available to the whole British press. Although the director of Hoechst prison agreed to Leeson's request, the courts initially declined to give permission, arguing that such a visit went well beyond the normal scope of prison procedures. The lower court also argued that it would have been difficult to refuse other prisoners a similar right. But in the German Constitutional Court, judges overruled saying that the granting of an interview would not upset domestic precedents and that given the world impact of his case they believed such a move would be worthwhile.

Whether or not Leeson stood to profit financially from an exclusive interview was less important than his desire to tell his side of the story, in the hope it would aid his quest to be returned to the UK and ease his frustrating silence. In fact, this notion may have been self-defeating. The more he protested that others were involved with the collapse, the greater the fear he generated and the greater the resolve, no doubt, in certain quarters to see him kept out of London. There was, however, little else that could be done, and Leeson's camp began scouring Britain for the right journalist to carry out the exclusive interview in Frankfurt.

In the interim, German lawyer Eberhard Kempf was preparing Leeson's case in the German courts to fight against the extradition warrants, and he intended doing so by mounting his case on grounds of human rights, Singapore's perennial sore point.

Kempf's argument was that the charges were insubstantial, and that Leeson would not receive a fair trial in Singapore. The German prosecutor's office opposed the argument on legal grounds, with prosecutor Hans-Hermann Eckert arguing that there was no problem with the extradition from a legal point of view.

In London, Pollard went on a different tack, arguing that his client had been made a scapegoat for an ailing and mismanaged bank, and he continued to push British authorities to initiate their own extradition.

Although German authorities had denied Leeson's request that he be allowed to return to London, he had not lost all hope that his case would be heard in an English court, where Leeson claimed he would receive a fairer trial and quite probably a lighter sentence. However, as it became more obvious that London had no real intention of bringing him home, Pollard was strengthened in his strategy of continued non-cooperation with British authorities investigating the collapse unless they moved to extradite Leeson.

Talks with the Serious Fraud Office (SFO) started but stalled, with the SFO claiming it lacked enough evidence to mount an extradition, given that the alleged offences committed by Leeson had occurred in Singapore and concluding that Singapore was where he would have to go. This was proving effective on the home front. By mounting this argument, the same could be said for any offences committed in Britain by Barings executives — therefore the onus of prosecution of such offences lay purely with British authorities and people such as Eddie George and Kenneth Clarke. Preliminary criminal investigations had already decided that Leeson had acted alone and that no conspiracy had existed. It seemed also that no-one was much impressed by the attitude in Frankfurt where the Leeson camp was still attaching conditions in return for co-operating with investigators.

Delays in Germany were brought about mainly by the time-consuming translation of documents for Leeson's extradition which had been prepared in Singapore in English. This was an added burden for German authorities who were responsible for translating the charges within the correct context of German law, while remaining true to the wishes of Singapore and interpreting some 800 pages of evidence. A requirement of the extradition was that allegations against Leeson from Singapore must be punishable under German law.

A hearing on May 2 found that sufficient evidence had been presented to support the initial charge of forgery, but Kempf had decided to fight this. His argument was that the allegations involved Leeson cutting out another signature and photo-mechanically transferring it onto another paper that had been prepared by him.

Kempf also contended that evidence presented was photocopies of the original forged letters, which are not admissible as evidence under German law. He believed the public prosecutor's office and the regional high court in Germany would support this argument, and demanded that the detention order jailing Leeson be withdrawn.

In the prosecutor's office, Eckert may have been inclined to agree with Kempf, but there were still a further 11 charges which needed to be processed and, while one Singapore request might be rejected in a German court, there was still a maze of legal avenues which the Republic had every right to navigate. In the meantime, Singapore had been given 40 days to complete and submit its full extradition request. Singapore's Commercial Affairs Department believed this was ample time to prepare their case.

⚔

Kempf failed in his next attempt to have Leeson freed on bail. A three-member court ruled in favour of Singapore's extradition request, and Leeson was ordered to appear before a Frankfurt judge where lawyers could air their arguments against the extradition.

Legal procedures would then be reviewed by the court to establish whether Singapore's extradition request was valid under German law, a process which was expected to take a further month. The final decision on whether Leeson would be extradited would be made by the German government. Leeson had every right of appeal up to this stage, and the entire process was expected to take months.

But Leeson and his team were planning on a long fight while pleading to British authorities to mount a rival bid for his return to London, challenging them to prove false Leeson's statement that his homeland was 'happy to throw me to the wolves'.

Leeson wanted to go home. For this push, he prepared a letter from his jail cell and gave it to Lisa, who called a news conference on July 12, in the faint hope that British authorities would be sympathetic to Nick's plea. Lisa was also planning to appeal to the sympathetic side of the media, and the tears she shed were captured by the cameras for a world-wide audience.

Amid sobs, Lisa read out Nick's words for the gathered reporters: 'At the end of the day, there are only two things that are precious to me — they are my wife and my family. I only ask that I be returned to the UK so that I can take my punishment and continue to see the people that are dear to me'.[2]

The letter continued: 'I did not steal any money. I hope that this is very clear to everybody. Everything that I did was done in the hope that it would be for the ultimate benefit of the bank. I acted unwisely and exceeded my authority, but never with the intention of improperly enriching myself . . . the British authorities seem happy to throw me to the wolves. Please, please help me'.[3]

Stephen Pollard was insistent that his client be returned. 'The only place for a trial is Britain if there is any serious and genuine wish to get to the bottom of what happened', he told the news conference.[4] Pollard also claimed the Serious Fraud Office had declined to interview Leeson in Frankfurt, and that a Singapore trial would not provide the answers for the collapse.

'There could be a narrowly-restricted trial in Singapore dealing with technical offences and carefully avoiding the issues raised by the collapse of the bank and the responsibility of parties other than Mr Leeson', Pollard said. 'It would be embarrassing if Leeson came back to London. The City would be embarrassed, Barings would be embarrassed, the Bank of England may be embarrassed, all sorts of powerful people may be embarrassed'.[5]

'Despite all the arguments, both legal and emotional, indicating that he should be dealt with here, it appears that the authorities are determined to ensure that this will not happen. I think it's completely misconceived'.[6]

British authorities continued to baulk and were annoyed at Leeson's continued refusal to be interviewed by the Serious Fraud Office unless he was extradited home. Still, the SFO maintained its position. There was simply not enough evidence to support his extradition to the United Kingdom.

Nick Leeson was becoming desperate — no-one had really bargained on British authorities completely ignoring his calls, and after consultation with his lawyers, a plea-bargain was offered. Leeson would plead guilty to the charges if his case was heard in London. Arguments to support Leeson's fears of Singapore-style justice became more strident. Leeson now claimed that if extradited back to the Far East, he would be subjected to a show trial and therefore a punishment far harsher than he stood to receive in the United Kingdom.

Lisa Leeson argued that her husband was not a murderer and therefore did not deserve a jail sentence which realistically could stretch 14 years. She continued the claim that if he was extradited to Singapore, the full story would never come out because authorities there would make her husband the prime issue — as opposed to focussing on Barings itself.

As panic gave way to desperation, the Leesons went so far as to personally lobby Prime Minister John Major to assist in their campaign to bring Nick home. Lisa hand-delivered a letter from Nick to the security gates near number 10 Downing Street. However, she was prevented from personally taking the letter to Major's front door, presenting photographers with the long-awaited opportunity to take a picture of at least one of the Leesons behind bars.

'I am a very ordinary British citizen who made some very silly mistakes', Nick's letter to John Major read. 'But I am British and it was here in Britain that most of the damage was done. Most of the people hurt by [the] collapse are in Britain. I caused it to collapse. I can be charged in Britain. I will plead guilty'.

Leeson's letter argued that in Singapore — 'where little damage was done' — he faced 'a nightmare trial and nightmare prison conditions'. Leeson said the Singapore charges were designed for a quick trial and a long sentence.

※

Evidence to support theories that others within Barings had also broken the law was starting to emerge. On April 5, 1995, Eddie George has stated bluntly that Threadneedle Street had had no idea that huge sums of money had been transferred to Singapore prior to the collapse, and that Barings had broken British law. He told the House of Commons' Treasury and Civil Service Select Committee that Barings had broken the law by exceeding the 25 per cent limit on risk exposure to offshore stock exchanges. (Barings had incidentally also broken Simex's exchange rules and collected a neat little S$6.95 million fine for its troubles.)

'It is a criminal offence to advance money without notifying us', George said. 'I can be absolutely certain to tell you that we did not know as of February 27 that stg443 million plus stg317 million was advanced to the bank'.[7]

While distancing the BoE from the affair and leaving Barings solely responsible for the transfer of funds, George also defended the BoE's investigations against claims by ING that the central bank had been dragging its feet. 'I can't think of a method that would be more rapid', he told the hearing. 'I won't come out and accuse people of negligence, or worse, without being absolutely sure of the facts'.[8]

By this stage, dozens of inquiries had been launched into the collapse of Barings and other areas of the banking industry.

It is difficult to determine whether measures adopted by regulatory authorities in the aftermath of the Barings collapse were effective. Certainly, the public and corporate relations departments from all types of organisations were kept busy as further losses occurred elsewhere, and the interest Barings had generated guaranteed any further derivative debacles were exposed in the media.

Shortly after Leeson's arrest in Frankfurt, another trader, this time in South Korea, was branded a rogue. Lee Nam Yol was blamed for losses totalling more than $20 million incurred by the state-run National Federation of Fishery Cooperatives. In a separate incident, a Deutsche Bank employee was dismissed without notice after being arrested on a comparatively small derivatives charge involving $12.0 million.

Report followed report. While the Bank of England took
its time deliberating on its inquiry, other banks were eager
to voice their own opinions on the matter. The Basel-based
Bank for International Settlements (BIS) conducted a survey
of 26 countries and recommended that major derivatives
markets should consider a market reporting system in the
same vein as the procedures undertaken by stock markets.
It asserted that the collapse of Barings made abundantly
clear the need to overhaul management and market procedures.

In a report released in May, the BIS said the Barings case
had revealed shortcomings in internal risk management, the
traditional separation of front and back offices, and in
customer trading. 'For the organised markets, the event
raised the issues of regulatory arbitrage between competing
exchanges, as well as the inadequacy of information sharing
and coordination between supervisory authorities', the BIS
said in its report on international banking and financial
market developments.[9]

In early July, the City was abuzz with rumours that
authorities were finally prepared to act and that more senior
heads would shortly roll in response to the collapse. Anxious staff had just completed giving evidence against
Leeson, and for many the attitude was 'bring it on'. People
had grown tired of Barings and more financial mismanagement laid bare in London's centre. Some suggested the
purge would begin with Barings and extend as far as the
Bank of England and the Securities and Futures Authority.
Within the secluded walls of Threadneedle Street, Christopher Thompson, who had monitored Barings after April
1991, had been wearing most of the internal flak for his
informal concessions in allowing Barings to at times exceed
exposure limits.

Word had leaked that Thompson had either resigned or
had been asked to. Eddie George and company refrained
from commenting as the anxiety set in ahead of the release of
the independent report undertaken by the BoE's Board of

Banking Supervision (BBS). This was the one everyone was waiting for. It landed on July 18.

The report laid the bulk of the blame for the fall of Barings squarely on Leeson's shoulders, but said it could not rule out the possibility that other Barings employees or outsiders had broken the law. The report found that Barings managers, auditors and regulators had all missed the danger signals emanating from Leeson's activities in Singapore. Leeson refused to co-operate with the inquiry. His attorneys disputed some of the findings but refused to give any details at the time. However, it was understood that their problems with the findings of the report stemmed from the failure of the BBS to obtain important documents from Singapore during the course of the official inquiry.

In handing down the 337 page report in parliament, the Chancellor of the Exchequer was generous in apportioning censure to those who could have made a difference but preferred to do nothing.

He said that those responsible for supervising and regulating Leeson were, at worst, complacent. 'It never actually crossed their minds that they might be playing some small part in such a huge and systematic process', Clarke said in his summary of the bank's investigation to the House of Commons.

'The management of Barings did not question the extraordinarily high levels of apparent profitability of supposed arbitrage dealings in Singapore, which were regarded as being without risk'.

'In the Board of Banking Supervision's view, these profits should have been viewed as abnormal and questionable, and the extraordinary profitability reported in 1994 should have attracted the close and thorough attention of the management long before the collapse'.[10]

The BBS was never charged with identifying any criminal violations and it pointed out it could not determine Leeson's motives. Still, some blame was apportioned: 'Barings' collapse was due to the unauthorised and ultimately catastrophic activities of, it appears, one individual that went undetected as a consequence of failure of management and other controls of the most basic kind'.

'Management failed at various levels and in a variety of ways ... to institute a proper system of internal controls, to enforce accountability for all profits, risks and operations, and adequately to follow up on a number of warning signals over a prolonged period'. And, almost unnecessarily: 'Neither the external auditors nor the regulators discovered Leeson's unauthorised activities'.[11]

In reference to market rumours and the telephone call made to Barings by the Bank of International Settlements, the report noted: 'While management may initially have been justified in taking no steps with regard to these market concerns, given their perception that the positions in respect of the "switching" activities were fully matched, nevertheless we consider that at the beginning of February 1995, it would have been appropriate for steps to have been taken to investigate the foundation for them'.[12]

BBS investigators commented belatedly through Clarke's report that Leeson could not have built up such a massive unauthorised position had there had been effective management, financial and operating controls within Barings. They said the money required to cover those losses was sent forth from London to Singapore without independent checks on the requests or any attempt to link them to any known trading position.

'If management in London had sought to examine the information from Singapore to support the requests for funds, they should have discovered the information was meaningless', Clarke told parliament.[13]

In the main, the Bank of England escaped relatively unscathed from the BBS report. Although the central bank was reproached for a lack of rigour, the inquiry made it clear that no fundamental change was needed in the UK framework of regulation. However, while contending there was no evidence that the BoE could have prevented the collapse, the report added there existed 'some areas in which the Bank's performance could have been better'.[14]

The central bank was obsessed with matters of probity and was anxious to be seen reacting to the inquiry. Shortly after the report was handed down, Eddie George confirmed reports that Christopher Thompson had resigned. In parliament, Kenneth Clarke branded Thompson as the official 'mostly responsible' for the collapse and George added that Thompson resigned willingly as he felt the 'criticisms' in the report made his position untenable.[15]

The report stopped short of demanding any drastic change to the system; instead the BBS proposed a number of improvements. In essence, the Bank of England was urged to try to undertake the following measures:

- Consolidate and extend its role as Britain's banking supervisor.
- Gain a comprehensive understanding of banking businesses that are not considered core banking activities. Understand their risks and how they are controlled. This included holding formal meetings.
- Review staff numbers, their skills and demands for on-site visits in regards to capital market issues.
- Establish internal guidelines to assist its staff in protecting depositors by identifying risks.
- Learn the key elements of management and control structures within banking groups. The BoE should be fully informed of any significant reorganisation or shift into new operations.
- Review information received by the BoE from banks under its responsibilities.
- Make one senior director in each bank responsible for the accuracy of returns. Especially in regards to the most important prudential returns.
- Consolidation of any one trading unit within a bank must gain formal approval of the executive director in charge of the BoE's Supervision and Surveillance Division, or obtain similar approval from a BoE governor.

- Establish internal guidelines for BoE staff on procedures in respect of consolidation of individual banking units.
- Review of the BoE's memoranda of understanding (MOU) with the Securities and Futures Authority and other British regulatory authorities.
- Expand international co-ordination between regulatory bodies and where possible instigate MOUs with non-banking regulators.
- Hold further meetings with the internal audit departments of banks. Where the BoE is the consolidated supervisor these meetings are to include internal audit functions. The BoE was told it should also meet with the chairman of each audit committee at the larger UK-incorporated institutions.
- Where necessary, instil more flexibility in the use and scope of some reports that move outside the bank and the UK.
- The scope of commissioned reports into systems and controls by authorised institutions could be widened to cover the input of data from major overseas locations.
- Require existing concessions in respect of large exposures be formally reported to relevant divisional heads annually while breaches should be reported to superiors regularly.
- Comfort letters and guarantees should be examined and there should be international talks between supervisors on how to account for attendant risks.
- Obtain an independent review of its supervision of banks on quality assurance with regular reports to be made to the Board of Banking Supervision.

For Barings detractors, the BBS recommendations were wanting. The report itself was convoluted and to a large extent simply stated what was already common knowledge, and emphasised the importance of banking practices which many assumed would already have been in place. While it did criticise the BoE and Barings' auditors, they escaped by and large with a metaphorical slap on the wrist. For those who felt that the central bank's approach was compromised by its clubbish ties to the City's old boys' network may have taken some comfort in the BBS investigators' comment that the relaxed attitude of BoE was due largely to the continuity of Barings' management.

'All those with whom we discussed the matter were of the view that, while its controls were informal, they were as good as those in comparable institutions and were considered effective', the report said. 'Both Quinn and Foot referred to the continuity of Barings' management as being one of the factors which justified the informal control culture'.[16] [Michael Foot was the deputy director for supervision and surveillance. He and Quinn both held more senior positions than Thompson.]

While the BoE's independent investigators let Thread-needle Street off with some harsh words, the Opposition Labour Party, taking seriously its duty as the Queen's loyal opposition, responded far more vigorously. The report's assertion that no fundamental change was needed within the UK framework of regulation was challenged by Opposition Treasury spokesman Gordon Brown, who argued there was a strong case for banking supervision to be hived off to a new banking commission, leaving the central bank alone with duties associated with monetary policy.[17]

Brown slammed the report as a 'damning indictment on the Bank of England's whole approach to the supervision of the banking system', which he said relied too heavily on informal contact. 'We now know that the entire capital of Britain's oldest merchant [bank] was transferred out of the country against the law without any supervisor or regulator either noticing or finding out', Brown said.[18]

In parliament, Kenneth Clarke was subjected to more than an hour of questioning over the actions taken by the government and the BoE in the wake of the collapse. Responding to Brown's position that the supervision of the UK banking system should be transferred to a new commission, Clarke said: 'If a policeman makes mistakes it does not mean that the common law is defective and that the law should be changed by parliament'.[19] This may well be the case, but a policeman who makes a mistake is at least admonished. The resignation of a single BoE official who had been lax in observing regulatory requirements seemed to be a slight punishment for an institution which had 'supervised' the demise of Barings.

It was in response to this assertion that Conservative MP Teresa Gorman said it would be preferable for Leeson to be tried in the UK 'rather than have him hung out to dry while people in this country are able to walk away from their basic responsibility for this whole business'.[20]

Such comments put Eddie George on the defensive. The next day he angrily attacked as a political 'witchhunt' the storm over the BoE's lapsed regulatory role in the collapse of Barings. His outburst came during a heated exchange with members of the all-party Treasury and Civil Service Committee, during which he admitted the central bank's role in the collapse of Barings was 'hardly a success'.[21]

George also complained that the BoE was having trouble recruiting new supervisors in their late 20s and 30s with experience of the banking industry. 'Actually getting people to do the job is becoming damned difficult', he said. 'How on earth do you think we get people to do this job when you go through this kind of procedure every time there is a problem?'

Accusing members of parliament of 'wanting blood', George said: 'You have to take account of the fact that if there is a witch-hunt every time something goes wrong, it is going to make it very difficult to get people to do the job'. Amid impassioned argument about the accountability of the BoE to Westminster, one Labour MP fired at George's offsider Brian Quinn: 'Maybe you should put your head on a platter'.[22]

Such criticism was widespread. In an editorial published shortly after the release of the BBS report, *The Financial Times* asserted that if one thing had emerged with clarity, it was that the real issue had very little to do with derivatives.

'The problem at Barings arose not from the complex nature of the risks being run in new-fangled financial instruments, but from a failure of old-fashioned internal control', the newspaper said. 'The losses . . . started building up over a very long period without anyone — management, auditors, regulators — noticing'.

The Financial Times did not stop there. Also on its hit-list was the Bank of England. 'Equally striking is the fact that the shortcomings of the Bank of England in supervising Barings were not primarily to do with a failure to keep abreast of new financial instruments. Rather, the BoE has been slow to recognise that its approach to supervision needed to be overhauled to cope with financial conglomeration'.

At regulatory level, the system is too fragmented, the editorial lamented. 'Yet ensuring that banking supervisors understand the full range of risks the financial conglomerates in their charge are running may be as important as reforming the structure itself. That said, the case for separating supervision from monetary policy is worth reconsidering — if only to ensure that those in charge of monetary policy are not tarred with the supervisors' brush.

Indeed, the release of the report sparked a chain reaction of moves by regulators around the world, resulting in a series of surveys of banks and companies with treasury departments which dealt in derivatives. The findings were that while all organisations professed to be security aware and to have procedures designed to minimise risks, the majority did not follow them.

By the time the British report was released, the relationship between Singapore and London investigators had all but broken down, with London authorities claiming that access to Nick Leeson and information in Singapore had been limited.

Friction between Singapore and British authorities was noted in the BBS report, prompting Kenneth Clarke to remark: 'It is regrettable that there remained serious legal obstacles which prevented all the relevant documents being provided to our board'.[23] He also implied that, had there been closer co-operation, Leeson's motives may have been determined.

There is an old political line about never holding an inquiry unless you know the results. While the BBS report was accurate, it was more intriguing for what it left out than for what it contained. Leeson's guilt was largely taken as read, the greed of Barings' executives was widely implied, the confusion generated by the matrix system and group re-structuring was explained. The regulatory authorities were found wanting, and it was determined that there was no conspiracy.

What the report, conspicuously, did not explain in its limited scope was who was actually responsible for breaching the law and transferring more money than the bank was worth to Singapore. It did note: 'There is no clear explana-tion as to why Barings' management did not question why BSL [Barings Securities Ltd] should be apparently lending over stg300 million to its clients to trade on Simex, when it had only collected some stg31 million from clients for those trades'.[24] The argument was essentially that capital had been transferred through so many individual transactions on behalf of clients that no-one had noticed.

On September 6, 1995, Singapore's CAD investigators, Nicky Tan and Michael Lim, finally delivered their report into the collapse of Barings to the Minister of Finance, Dr Richard Hu. Dr Hu issued a statement announcing the completion of the investigation and said that the report would now be considered in consultation with the Attorney-General. The investigative team was believed to have gathered more than 6000 pages of evidence after interviewing 35 people, including the former Barings chairman.

With Leeson still clinging to the hope that his extradition to Singapore might be rejected by Germany's constitutional court or the government, Dr Hu faced three options. He could release the report publicly, table it in parliament, or wait for the German legal process to run its course before announcing the investigators' findings. He elected to hang on to the report.

Speculation surrounding the contents of the report was as intense as that which had greeted the Bank of England's own investigation when its findings were unveiled in July. Security surrounding its findings were tight and confirmation of its actual contents was difficult to ascertain, However, local journalists were quoting sources who said the report included an examination of whether there was a high-level attempt to cover up the losses. Meanwhile, Britain's Serious Fraud Office finally agreed to interview Leeson.

※

Leeson's long-awaited chance to outline his own motives before the general public came in September when he was interviewed in prison. Tyler and Pollard had decided that Sir David Frost would be the ideal choice, and Sir David accepted.

Leeson's hotly anticipated interview with Sir David was beamed into houses across Britain and transcribed in countless newspapers across the globe. The interview itself was limited in detail, and Leeson's lawyers knew there was a very real chance their client would be returned to Singapore. Nick had to be careful with what he said. Speaking publicly for the first time since the collapse, Leeson was articulate and alleged the blame for the bank's demise lay with the Bank of England and Barings executives for exacerbating the scale of the losses.

Leeson said incompetence by the BoE and his former bosses had brought Barings to its knees when they unwound part of his loss-making futures and options position into a falling Japanese stock market. And he said the upper echelons of Barings had only their own ignorance to blame.

'If I can summarise what I see as the problem at Barings, it was a business that they'd got into too quickly with not enough experience and not enough personnel', Leeson said during the interview.

'A couple of the people who were in the core places within Barings that should have been administering a high level of control had what I would describe as almost no understanding of the fundamentals of the business they were supposed to be controlling. Futures and options is a relatively new business. You need somebody controlling it who's grown up with the business and understands the real intricacies of it. And they didn't have that'.

A tanned and relaxed-looking Leeson described the collapse as 'a chapter in my life that I'm looking to forget' but said he accepted the prospect of being made to serve a prison sentence for false accounting. He claimed Error Account 88888 was opened under order from Barings management because they did want errors and mismatched trades going through a London account.

But about three months later executives had decided against this and requested that all trades be booked through London, and the account remained dormant.

However, a crying colleague led Leeson to reactivate the account, he said. Leeson told Sir David that a young woman working for another Barings trader had mistakenly sold 20 futures contracts instead of buying them. This had cost the company around stg20,000 and Leeson found her after work distressed and sobbing at The Hard Rock Cafe. Leeson decided to shift the losses into the account 88888 and it was then, Leeson said, that losses began to spiral out of control. Such uses for error accounts are not uncommon. Traders and back room staff can easily make a simple and honest mistake just by hitting the wrong key on a terminal. It is common but unspoken practice for such errors to be placed into an unused account where they can be reconciled at a later date, and this may well involve rectifying the mistake at no cost.

'There were days when I could lose stg25 million to stg30 million. There were days when I made stg50 million. Not every day is a down day. So it adds to your belief that you can do it', Leeson said. 'Taking a futures position is a 50–50 gamble and the laws of probability had to say that I would win some. Unfortunately, I lost more than I won'.

Asked by Sir David if a secret account would ever be discovered with, say, stg10 million stashed away for Nick Leeson, he replied: 'No, definitely not'.

'I have nothing to hide. I'm the guy who wants to go to jail now', Leeson said. 'I understand what I've done. But I don't think of myself as a criminal; I didn't steal any money. I've certainly misled people. I didn't mislead them because I was trying to profit myself. I was trying to correct a situation. I was also working in the best interests of the bank'.

Leeson made use of the interview to again outline his reasons against being extradited to Singapore. He cited family ties as his main reason for wanting to be returned to the United Kingdom, saying he 'lived from week to week' between Lisa's visits. However, the harsh criticism of Singapore justice which had featured in his arguments to date was noticeably absent.

'The most difficult thing for me at the moment is only seeing my wife weekly and then only for an hour', he said. 'If I'm returned to Singapore, the maximum that she's going to be able to see me is probably monthly. The rest of my family, there are chances that I will not see some of them ever again'.

Nick Leeson was determined to use the interview to further his bid to be extradited home. Emotional issues aside, Leeson told Sir David: 'On a more logical basis, the Singaporean request says nothing about the collapse of Barings. That's what this is all about. The only place that is going to be correctly tried in a court is England'. In some respects the interview was disappointing. Leeson's threat to name names and reveal who was ultimately responsible for the transfer of the bank's capital out of London was never carried out.

Hopes of a return home were dashed a few days later. Britain's Serious Fraud Office finally confirmed what the investment and wider community had widely expected, and what Leeson had feared most: The SFO would not attempt to extradite him to the United Kingdom.

After lengthy deliberations, the SFO had decided not to alter its view that Singapore remained the principal jurisdiction for a criminal prosecution, despite legal protests from Leeson's camp, and his emphatic desire to be tried at home. 'Consequently the SFO has decided not to put in an application to the German authorities for extradition', said an SFO spokesman, using barely a dozen words to end what hope Leeson still clung to.[26]

The SFO was disappointed by the information they had obtained from interviews with Leeson in his German prison cell. They claimed that nothing substantial had been added to earlier inquiries. The SFO also pointed out that it believed that senior Barings executives in London were not criminally liable for the collapse and said there would be no charges against other bank executives.

Stephen Pollard was defiant, claiming that the SFO continued to ignore the real issues of the case. 'The SFO claims to believe that Singapore is the best place for Nick Leeson to be tried, but will not explain how they reach that conclusion. . . . It makes no sense, unless there is a non-legal explanation and they are coming under political pressure to resist his extradition'.[27] Pollard vowed to maintain the rage, saying he would battle to 'overturn this irrational decision' and to defeat the Singaporean extradition request in Germany.

Unconvinced, and unwilling to let matters lie, the push continued. Leeson's publicist, Rod Tyler, indicated that perhaps not all the cards had been laid out when he trotted out the well-worn expression: 'It ain't over until the fat lady sings'. But SFO officials stood equally firm, arguing that Singapore was the location of the crime, most of the documentary evidence and the key witnesses.

All roads led to Singapore.

CHAPTER FIFTEEN

FACING THE MUSIC

'A Barings Master of the Universe Who, it Turns out, Wasn't'.
Headline in The New York Times, February 28, 1995.

The unfolding of the Barings epic provided one high note after the other, spinning a tale which bemused, entertained and astounded audiences around the world. As dealers traded Nick Leeson's old business cards for stg130 a piece, a punk rock single about the fall of the bank was released, and an opera was composed on the same theme.

Even the creation of a board game was in the pipeline. Inspired by Leeson's attempts to avoid the extended arm of international law, businessman Gordon Tan planned to market *In The Nick Of Time*, a game which pitted players against police in the negotiation of an escape route from Singapore to London via Frankfurt. Not to be outdone, a Singapore businesswoman printed 2000 T-shirts emblazoned with the message: Barings Learns Its Leeson.[1]

In a different league altogether, and playing for much higher stakes, Sir David Frost hoped to cast the high-profile British actor Hugh Grant as the character of Nick Leeson in a Hollywood movie about the collapse of Barings. The *UK Mail* estimated Leeson could receive up to stg3.0 million for the film. Faced with the prospect of not emerging from prison until in his mid-40s, Leeson was said to be thrilled with the prospect of his character being portrayed by the considerably less follicly-challenged Hugh Grant.

Sir David must have uncovered some well-hidden secrets when he interviewed Leeson in Germany. Of all the anecdotes and superlatives used to describe the 'barrow boy from

Watford' by those who knew him, Frost was the first to consider Leeson 'fascinating'. Frost described his movie project as 'a modern morality tale with flashes of comedy'. Hugh Grant must have been a carefully considered moral choice in light of his less-than-salubrious encounter with a Los Angeles prostitute several months earlier.

'It's very early days yet, but Hugh Grant has expressed an interest. And he would be excellent. He is an incredibly in-demand actor at the moment. He'd be absolutely perfect for this', Sir David said.[2] The combination of Hugh Grant and Nick Leeson was enough to ensure another front page Barings tale. And they kept coming.

While the Hollywood film was said to be in an embryonic stage, some dismissed it as most unlikely. Meanwhile, the English-language rights to Leeson's side of the story were snapped up for stg450,000 at the 1995 Frankfurt Book Fair, in the most spirited auction seen for years. A triumphant Phillipa Harrison of Boston publisher Little, Brown said the hefty advance for the book, which was to be ghost-written by Edward Whitley, was a sound investment. She promised Leeson's story was 'full of revelations' which were 'likely to embarrass a number of people'.[3]

'It's the most compulsively readable story I've seen for many years', *The Publishing News* quoted Harrison as saying. 'The son of a plasterer, he opened his famous account to help a friend and he got involved in a greater gambling binge than any fiction writer could possibly imagine in their wildest dreams'.[4]

But while they may not have penned the saga, artists of a broad range of genres were dreaming up ways to depict what Harrison called 'one of the most remarkable stories of our time'. With the creative work complete, the composers of the opera about the bank's collapse applied to the charity arm of Barings to help fund their production.

But Phillip Parr, the artistic director of Spitalfields Market Opera in London's financial district, obviously didn't view Leeson as an integral character in the plot.

Unlike Sir David Frost's stg20 million plan for a Hollywood epic, Parr had no intention of using the character of Nick Leeson in *A City Opera*, by composer Geoff Westley and librettist Paul Griffiths.

However, at the opposite end of the musical spectrum, Leeson played a supposedly starring role. A British punk rock band claimed that Nick had turned his hand to another profession: singing. Through the Dusseldorf-based Gun Records, The Bollock Brothers released a compact disc single called *Selling England For A Pound*, with Leeson purportedly crooning Frank Sinatra's *My Way* over a telephone line to lead singer Jock McDonald.

The recording was mixed with screeching back-up sounds from The Bollock Brothers and 5000 initial copies went on sale in Germany, with Leeson starring on the CD's cover superimposed beside Queen Elizabeth II on a one-pound note. Liner notes offered special thanks 'to the officers at Frankfurt Jail'. The Bollock Brothers had no qualms about dealing once more with an infamous character. Michael Fagan — the man who created headlines around the world when he broke into the Queen's bedroom at Buckingham Palace — had sung on the band's version of *God Save The Queen* just a few years earlier.

The recording of *Selling England For A Pound* took place in August 1995, prior to the Sir David interview and at a time when Leeson was allowed few visits, a scant number of telephone calls, and while he was still pressing the German courts to be allowed to tell his story. Still, some scribes had enough faith in The Bollock Brothers — who pledged to donate stg1.00 to London's homeless from every CD sold — to put through a telephone call to Leeson's lawyer.

Stephen Pollard was quick to scotch the band's claim that it was Leeson's voice on the recording. 'This is entirely false', Pollard was quoted by the Press Association news agency as saying. 'Mr Leeson has never had any contact with the band whatsoever. The suggestion that he sang down a telephone line from Hoechst prison is frankly laughable'. He dismissed the claim as 'nothing more than an attempt by the band, in the absence of any discernible talent, to gain free publicity'.

Leeson's notoriety was being seized upon by people everywhere, to the point where he had became literally the laughing stock of finance industry participants around the world.

At the launch of a derivatives book in Sydney, a Nick Leeson look-alike made a cameo appearance wearing an orange and green futures jacket emblazoned with 'Frankfurt Correctional Institute' over a crossed-out Barings. The look-alike made his staged entrance as one speaker was recounting his experience with derivatives when he presided over the AWA foreign exchange case. 'Nick' got down on his knees and grovelled to the speaker, saying he was in desperate need of a few tips on how to suck up to a judge and jury. 'Get a knighthood and all will be well', was the speaker's acid rejoinder.[5]

Certainly, he had penetrated every facet of the media, where he kept illustrious company. *The Times* compared Leeson with the Princess of Wales, because both Nick and Diana had a penchant for wearing baseball caps and both were deemed icons of a new-age Britain in the 1990s. In Leeson's case, he was listed as 'another new-age failure'.[6]

Many artists may have taken pleasure in making a song or an opera out of the Leeson saga, but there was yet a finale to be sung, and an epilogue to be delivered. A world away from the musings of writers and musicians, Leeson's real story was still being played out on the axis crossing London, Singapore and Frankfurt.

※

While Leeson had been counting on capitalising on his international notoriety, there were those who were justifiably ready to thwart such moves. Barings' bondholders were appalled at the possibility that Leeson could profit despite their losses, and in mid-September the bank's administrators

initiated legal action to prevent him from benefiting financially from the collapse.

Filed in England's High Court, the writ claimed 'damages
for fraudulent and/or negligent representation in the advancement of funds not repaid and the use of funds and
dealing on exchanges'. The administrators claimed for 'deceit
and/or negligent misrepresentation' and demanded an account of and repayment of money or other profit or benefit
made as a result of Leeson's 'deceits and breaches of duty'.

The claim was based on fraudulent and/or negligent
misrepresentation by Leeson that led to Barings in London
sending him funds in Singapore. The liquidators also obtained a separate Singapore High Court order allowing them
to examine all the accounts relating to any deals made by
Nick, Lisa, and Stephen Pollard concerning the downfall.

The order, issued on December 1 by Justice Lai Kew
Chai following an application by Rajah & Tann on behalf of
liquidators, called on the trio to 'produce all books in their
joint or individual custody, power or control' relating to
Barings Futures Singapore.

It included documents which provide evidence of assets,
contracts and arrangements entered into by either of the
Leesons or their agents 'for the sale, assignment or disposi-
tion of any rights in respect of properties, books, films,
television and/or newspaper projects'. The authorities were
at least attempting to ensure Leeson did not prosper where
others had lost. In reality, this would prove difficult to
enforce.

In Singapore, traders and authorities experienced mixed
feelings, but they all wanted the final issues resolved. Reputations were at stake. Immediately following the collapse of
Barings, traders put up a united front, arguing out of a sense
of loyalty and self-preservation that a peer was being used as
a scapegoat to hide the ineptitude of others. They were right.
But, as the facts unravelled, many were forced to confront
the realities of their industry and the prospect that Leeson
had cheated, and was not the only trader in the Far East who

had controlled or manipulated both front and back offices, and had abused the power to hide secret trading accounts.

Honest traders wanted Leeson — and anyone else associated with the fiasco — brought back to Singapore, tried and used as an example for other investment houses whose traders deliberately misled head office and abused the ignorance of senior management.

Publicity surrounding Barings was relentless and left a bad taste throughout the entire derivatives industry: in Singapore, the trade had virtually died over night. But short-term profits were not underpinning desires to see Leeson in court. Ironically, press coverage focussing on the fiasco in Singapore had reached regions of the world where investors thirsted for new investment strategies. Those in eastern Europe were particularly curious. The nouveau riche of the old communist bloc had found difficulty in finding alternative investments.

Derivatives do not require companies to establish a physical presence, take on local partners or make capital injections in plant and equipment. There are no requirements to tangle with complex tax laws though in Singapore, such laws are considered friendly. The fruits of unwanted press coverage for 'squeaky clean' Singapore were surprisingly borne on the bottom-line of Simex's own accounts as new money began drifting into the island republic.

Simex normally only issues full-year profit results, but the windfall and the continued bickering and after-effects of the collapse of Barings prompted Simex chief Elizabeth Sam to take the unorthodox step of issuing the exchange's interim results to demonstrate Simex had survived the events of the preceding months.

Simex declared an after-tax profit of S$15.2 million for the first half of the 1995 calendar year. This compared with a net profit of S$19.6 million for the full-year ended December 31, 1994. According to financial statements audited by Price Waterhouse, turnover for the first half of 1995 reached S$26.3 million against the 1994's full-year result of S$39.8 million.

Sam said it was important to reassure members of the financial community that the integrity of the exchange had not been affected by the Barings crisis. 'Simex weathered the Barings storm without needing external financial assistance and has continued to perform strongly in subsequent months', she said.

Just as it appeared that the Leeson and Barings saga was drawing to a close, events took yet another turn on two fronts in the last week of September. Fears held by traders on the Simex floor that some less honest dealers might be hiding losses in secret accounts proved correct, and the conviction that Leeson would face his day of reckoning in Singapore was now waning after yet another legal joust, this time in London.

The first development occurred on September 26 when Japan's embattled financial system was hit by its own rogue trader. Daiwa Bank, which had taken a lead position in unwinding Leeson's exposure, announced a $US1.1 billion loss arising from fraudulent trading spanning 11 years in the New York bond market. Forty-four-year-old trader Toshihide Iguchi admitted to forging and concealing documents to hide losses in the US Treasury bond market.

'We entrusted him with everything — we really trusted him and evaluated him too highly'.[7] This could have been any one of a thousand quotes from the many people who witnessed the collapse of Barings but this time, a few brief months later, the words were those of Daiwa president, Akira Fujita.

Daiwa was the world's 19th largest bank and Japan's 10th biggest, with assets in the vicinity of 5.0 trillion yen. Its financial strength meant it could avoid a Barings-style collapse and write off the losses in the fiscal half-year ending September 30, 1995.

There are some striking similarities between Iguchi and Leeson. Both had relied on their flair and skill in trading circles to rise quickly through the ranks, with Iguchi becoming an executive vice president in New York, allowing him to take charge of both back and front office trading operations, to falsify documents, and to hide losses which began with a $200,000 loss on margin trades in 1984. It had been alleged that he forged statements from a Bankers Trust account linked to securities held by Daiwa on behalf of clients.

Comparison between the two was easy fodder for a media which had been handed on a platter its second international banking and securities scandal in less than seven months. In the same way journalists had focussed quickly on Leeson's working-class roots, they were equally hasty to point out that Iguchi had once been a car salesman and held a degree in psychology, not the usual qualifications considered relevant to a career in high finance.

Iguchi was considered very good and likeable, and was well respected by his peers, after beginning at the bank in 1976 in New York. Traders thought Iguchi was fearless. They watched in awe as he would scramble through hundreds of millions of dollars worth of trades within seconds. Rivals and colleagues had nicknamed him 'Tosh', pronounced as 'Toast'. Though Iguchi had never worked in Japan, his corporate rise was rapid, with the native from Kobe becoming head of Daiwa's prestigious US government bond trading outfit, landing him a position of trust and control of auditing his own accounts, and his own destiny.

Just like Leeson, Iguchi could order up to $100 million worth of paper from any number of firms. As word leaked that Iguchi was active, bond prices would rise and Iguchi would start dumping the stock he had just acquired back into the market at a profit. And like his British counterpart, Iguchi's world was a lie. There never were any profits, only losses which remained, for the time being, out of sight.

Total losses inflicted on Daiwa were just shy of those experienced by Barings, but once again Japan was proving itself a powerhouse in the global banking game as just 1.0 per cent of the bank's capital base had been lost, enabling it to easily recoup and trade into the future. Behind this capital base were the government and Japan's 11 major banks standing ready, willing and more than able to lend.

The most fearsome comparison of all was that, like Barings, Daiwa believed it had sufficient risk controls in place to prevent such episodes. Given the speed at which its revelations followed the Barings collapse, it was almost another knock-out punch to those who had insisted that controls within financial markets were sufficient.

Japan's Finance Minister, Masayoshi Takemura, strongly reprimanded the bank which, along with Iguchi, was being threatened with legal action over what it knew about the losses. But despite a long series of blows in Japan's banking industry, with bad loans causing regional banks and credit unions to fail, Takemura was able to confidently and quickly reassure investor faith in the nationl's banking system.

Takemura said the scandal was deeply regrettable, but added that it would in 'no way' endanger Daiwa's overall financial position. When the $1.1 billion losses were actually written off, it was reported that Daiwa had already amassed more than $3.0 billion in unrealised profits from its stock portfolio alone.

As authorities moved in, it appeared Iguchi had replicated Leeson's activities over a much longer period, having punted wrongly for several years over the direction of US interest rates. An estimated 30,000 transactions were involved, with Iguchi allegedly forging custodian statements to continue unauthorised off-balance sheet trades in US Treasury bonds. Iguchi was hauled before the courts almost immediately and was accused of doctoring Daiwa's accounts. His fate served as a sobering example for Leeson, his lawyers and frustrated Singapore officials seeking his extradition from Germany.

Leeson's touted 14-year maximum sentence for charges arising out of Singapore, while considered extreme in many quarters, was a source of anguish for his supporters. Now, that stretch of time appeared modest when compared with the predicament of Iguchi, who shuffled his way into Manhattan's District Court with his wrists shackled. In the US, Iguchi was facing up to 30 years in jail, fines in the vicinity of $1.0 million and the prospect of being forced to make restitution to his former employer. And like Barings executives, Iguchi's former employers were also being viewed with deep suspicion.

The second twist occurred just two days later and was delivered at the hands of irate bondholders and their Perpetual Noteholders Action Group. The City of London Magistrates' Court issued eight summonses against Leeson, requiring him to appear before the court on October 30 to face a series of allegations. The court said that after the summonses were issued, it would ask the UK government to make a formal extradition request to the German government. It now appeared that Leeson might after all slip through Singapore's legal cordon, through no deliberate act by either the Commercial Affairs Department or Leeson's legal camp.

In the charges of obtaining property by deception it was alleged that Leeson had obtained by deception a total of around $US320 million from Barings Securities. 'These alleged offences are within the jurisdiction of the Central Criminal Court and there is substantial public interest in their being tried in this jurisdiction', the group of bondholders said.

Holding out for a reprieve, Leeson's support network was hopeful. They appeared to have won the support of independent fraud specialist Brian Spiro, a partner in the law firm Simons Muirhead & Burton, who publicly stated: 'The normal procedure would be for the defendant to appear before the UK court . . . If he does not appear, he would be issued with a warrant of arrest. Since he clearly can't appear in court, the UK authorities would have to apply for his extradition and it would be up to the German authorities'.[8]

Emphasis on the bondholders action soon became the last and only focal point for Stephen Pollard, even though he was not an active player in the litigation. On October 5, Germany's High Criminal Court in Frankfurt handed down a 13 page ruling clearing the way for Leeson's extradition to Singapore. The court allowed 11 of the 12 charges brought by the Singapore authorities. The one charge which was rejected was the initial forgery allegation which Singapore authorities had rushed to Germany to keep Leeson behind bars.

Leeson's lawyer, Eberhard Kempf, began pursuing an appeal against the decision in the Constitutional Court. Kempf said the Constitutional Court could take anything from less than a month to almost two years to rule on Leeson's last-ditch appeal against being returned to the scene of the crime. The final decision to hand Leeson over to Singapore rested with the German government, and it was unlikely that Bonn would rule against the High Court.

Twelve days later, the results of the Singapore investigations were handed down and the case against Leeson was established publicly. The liquidation of Barings Futures Singapore was ordered by Finance Minister Dr Richard Hu, and Singapore authorities began what had previously been considered unimaginable — looking into possible criminal charges against Barings employees other than Nick Leeson, if a criminal act had been committed in Singapore.

CAD director Lawrence Ang kept the department's chief suspects under wraps though he said charges could be based on violations of Singapore's Companies Act and Penal Code. Peter Norris had been singled out for criticism and for appointing Leeson in the first place, allowing him to accumulate the losses, and continuing to finance his operations.

'We will investigate and prosecute anyone who has committed an offence under our purview', Ang announced.[9] 'We are investigating all those who are involved and all those who may be involved'.

The reporting of the affair heralded a fresh, albeit sometimes questionable, wave of variable journalistic standards with newspapers breaking their own stories through the use of unnamed sources. Sometimes the identification of source was omitted completely, leaving the reporter to take the risks involved with breaking a story solely under his or her own name.

Such stories included the possibility that Leeson's friend Daniel Argyropoulous — the First Continental Trading (FCT) employee, found by investigators to have driven Nick and Lisa to the airport when they fled Singapore — could be charged. The investigators had discovered that between June and November 1994, Leeson had on six occasions helped Argyropoulous close out his trades in Japanese Government Bonds and square the books through error account 88888.

The investigators found that this had been used to inflate profits and whittle back gains. On five occasions adjustments totalling S$1.8 million had been made to the FCT's detriment but, in all, the Chicago-based investment firm had registered a net gain of $700,000. It remains unknown what had happened to the money. For his part, Argyropoulous made himself unavailable for comment to reporters, and his colleagues at FCT were instructed to do likewise. He has since been completely cleared of all allegations.

In response to the findings of the Singapore investigation, which were publicly released on October 17, Eddie George described the report as fair and consistent with Britain's central bank's own analysis. 'I think the Singapore government's report is very, very consistent with our own. I think they reveal essentially the same story', George told reporters in Kuala Lumpur, where he was giving a speech to local bankers.[10]

He added that there was nothing in the Singapore report which invalidated the conclusions of the BoE or the recommendations for the central bank which flowed from it. 'The contributory factor was the failure of management to control his activities. That was in essence the story', George said.[11]

Months later, in the following January, the BoE's executive director in charge of banking supervision, Brian Quinn, underscored the need for tighter regulation in publicly calling for more international co-operation between regulatory authorities, and for the possible introduction of entry requirements for certain high-risk financial markets in order to avoid another Barings-style collapse.

In a speech in New York, Quinn said the international financial community would be 'dangerously complacent' if it failed to update certain safeguards. 'Had information about Barings Futures activities in both Singapore and Osaka been exchanged and subject to a common and single scrutiny, it is less likely that the group would have failed', he said.[12] Eddie George also expressed his support for closer international cooperation. 'We must get to the point where there's a habit of communication between financial institutions and market regulators at home and abroad', he said.[13]

But despite George's earlier insistence that the Singapore and London investigations 'reveal essentially the same story', the relatively compact 183 page Simex report in fact went considerably beyond the BoE's inquiry. Contending not only that Barings executives should have halted Nick Leeson's fraudulent trading activities, the Singapore probers suggested they had been embroiled in a deliberate and systematic cover-up.

Singapore further accused Peter Norris and James Bax of understating the significance of the stg50 million accounting discrepancy which turned out to be part of

Leeson's losses. The inquiry also accused the two men of trying to discourage investigations of the discrepancy, hinting that a 'plausible motive' for Norris' action might be that Christopher Heath had left the firm in 1993 when the losses were accumulated.

The report stated that Norris had taken the helm at Barings Securities when Heath departed after losses, and he clearly had an interest in concealing the much larger losses that the Baring group had incurred via error account 88888 in the course of the three years that Leeson had been in Singapore'.[14]

Although Singapore inspectors felt that 'the question of motive remains conjectural',[15] they suggested that Norris and Bax's actions had hindered Barings from finding the losses held by Leeson in error account 88888 and, like the BoE report, concluded that 'timely action'[16] could have prevented the collapse.

A critical factor setting Singapore investigators apart from their British counterparts, was the former's ready access to the records of Barings Futures Singapore. The Singapore report's criticisms of Barings executives was split between two timeframes, the first being the period between July 3, 1992 (when Leeson opened error account 88888) and the end of 1994.

The second time span was the months of January and February in 1995, immediately preceding the collapse. Echoing the BoE report, Singapore cited poor reconciliation procedures as being the reason Barings was not wise to the existence of error account 88888 or to Leeson's secret trading activities.

However, Barings' claims that it was unaware of error account 88888 implied that key individuals were either 'grossly negligent, or wilfully blind and reckless to the truth',[17] the report contended, adding that the way in which the matrix management structure was implemented was conducive to a less than complete supervision of Leeson.

Still, the report concluded that whether or not Barings' management knew of error account 88888 was 'hardly crucial', arguing that if executives were not aware of it from the outset, they would have discovered its existence as soon as they undertook a number of simple steps to analyse Nick Leeson's trading activities.

'For three years, account 88888 purportedly escaped the notice of the entire Baring group management', the report said. 'Yet within hours after . . . Leeson had fled, Baring Securities personnel working in London and Singapore with incomplete documentation uncovered error account 88888 and identified it as the immediate cause of the collapse'.[18]

Also in the Singapore inquiry's firing line was group finance director Geoffrey Broadhurst. The report accused Broadhurst's department of adopting a blinkered view of its own role, asserting that it had 'never properly tracked the cost of funding' Leeson's trading and had failed to complete an attempt to do so in 1994. And while margin payments on Leeson's trades in error account 88888 were registered by Barings Securities as loans to clients, Singapore investigators pointed out that no attempts were undertaken to verify their identities or creditworthiness.

Singapore investigators contended that during 1993, Baring Securities was aware that between stg15 million and stg20 million of funds remitted for margin payments could not be reconciled; in 1994, the unreconciled sum blew out to stg100 million and, in the first two months of 1995, the sum spiralled to about stg320 million, without any satisfactory explanation.

Two key warning signals were ignored, the Singapore report said. The first alarm bell sounded in the form of a letter written on January 11 by Simex to Simon Jones, questioning some problems with margin payments on error account 88888.

But while London executives denied knowledge of any such letter, a reply had in fact been sent by Simon Jones. However, Jones told Singapore inspectors that he had 'no knowledge' of the contents of the reply, which had been drafted for him by Nick Leeson.

That letter was followed by a second which arrived on January 25 and questioned Baring Futures on its capital resources to meet potential losses and margin calls. The reply sent by Baring Futures — this time written by Tony Hawes — said the whole assets of Barings stood by the unit.

According to the Singapore investigators, the second warning signal materialised in the discovery by Coopers & Lybrand Singapore of the stg50 million discrepancy in Baring Futures' accounts. (Leeson had first told Jones that the amount had arisen from the transaction between Spear, Leeds & Kellogg and Banque Nationale de Paris.)

The Singapore report alleged that Norris and Bax attempted to discourage investigations after being told of the problem: 'Within the next few days, at least six different versions of how the receivable had arisen circulated among Barings management', the report found.[19]

Singapore investigators were incredulous that a company's senior executives could claim that 'it never occurred to them that such explanations could have been fabricated or untrue', or that they felt any discomfort about the differences.[20] The report contended that Norris 'downplayed the significance of the matter and discouraged all independent investigations into the transaction, and the circumstances in which Barings Futures had supposedly paid such a large sum'.[21]

Further, they said Norris 'took steps to conceal this matter from the other Baring directors, and to discourage Coopers & Lybrand in Singapore and London from including the matter in their audit management letters'.[22] The report said Norris specifically instructed Broadhurst not to inform Barings' Asset and Liability Committee in London, which oversaw trading risks, about the discrepancy. (When it was discussed by the Committee on February 8, Broadhurst said it was an operational error and requested that the discussion not be minuted in detail.)

'In concealing the problem, Norris was assisted by Bax, who tried to divert investigations by external auditors and (Tony) Hawes, the group treasurer', the report said, alleging that Bax encouraged Leeson to present the external auditors with authorisation of the trade.[23]

Inspectors said Ron Baker authorised the transaction in a letter. They added that Bax had urged Leeson to show Coopers & Lybrand this letter although he knew the contents to be false in light of the fact that the transaction was unauthorised.

'Norris and Bax have denied being involved in any plan either to underplay the significance of the discrepancy or to discourage independent investigations into the matter', the report stated. 'However, we are unable to accept their denials. Had Mr Norris and Mr Bax not taken such steps and, as a result of proper investigations, the flow of funds to BFS been curtailed, this may have averted the collapse of the Baring group'.[24]

Also under the microscope was the meeting between Norris and Leeson in Singapore on February 16. Although Norris had claimed their rendezvous lasted only three to five minutes, the report cited testimony from four witnesses who claimed that Leeson had spent about 90 minutes in a room with Norris.

Immediately after this conversation, Leeson had written to Hawes stating that after his meeting with Bax and Jones, he had been told not to respond to Hawes' further questions on the SLK transaction until the external auditors had signed off BFS's audited financial statements for the year ended December 31, 1994.

But while Norris denied the existence of such a conversation to the Singapore inspectors, Bax and Jones admitted that the meeting had taken place. They claimed that the decision emanated from Leeson's suggestion that further investigation into the matter ought to be postponed until the completion of the external audit by Coopers & Lybrand Singapore.

The Singapore report cited several witnesses, including Broadhurst and Hopkins, who asserted that Norris had wanted to take personal charge of resolving the issue. However, the report found that only days before the collapse Norris had, as a result of his conversation with Nick Leeson, actively discouraged efforts to bring Barings' positions down in order to ease the funding pressure faced by the group.

'In our view, Mr Bax played an active role to conceal the significance of the matter raised by the external auditors and to discourage independent investigations into the matter', the report stated.[25]

In particular, the report accused Bax of having actively sought to divert Hawes from his investigation into the incident and of having been anxious that Hawes' direct access to Leeson be restricted. They also queried Norris' actions on the night when Leeson fled Singapore, expressing surprise that he was one of the first to conclude that there had been unauthorised trading when he did not possess a detailed knowledge of the operations and trade settlement procedures of Barings Futures Singapore.

According to the inspectors, when Bax received Leeson's resignation fax on February 24, he spoke with Norris and they decided that Bax should fly to Kuala Lumpur in an effort to find Leeson. The investigation team concluded that this was a 'remarkably optimistic venture' which turned out to be futile.

Accompanying the release of the report was a fresh bout of speculation that Nick Leeson would not be the only Barings employee to face criminal prosecution. *The Straits Times* carried the headline: 'Inspectors' report shows high-level conspiracy over fraudulent trades — Top Barings officials helped in cover-up'.

No individuals were singled out, but the newspaper report pointed out that James Bax, Peter Norris and Geoffrey Broadhurst had been the high-level executives dealt the strongest criticism by the Singapore investigators. *The Business Times* asserted that the unnamed senior officials were 'almost certain to face criminal prosecution in Singapore'.

※

In late October, Simex announced it would more closely monitor large customer accounts to prevent them from spiralling out of control. The exchange was also said to be considering requiring exchange members to appoint a senior manager to 'a position of authority' for all of the firms' activity on the exchange.[26]

A hastily convened international advisory panel had just handed down six recommendations of ways to improve Simex and its procedures in the wake of the demise of Barings. 'Simex wholeheartedly endorses the findings of the advisory panel and has already implemented or is in the process of implementing the panel's recommendations', Simex chief Elizabeth Sam said.[27] Additional changes included upgrading Simex's computer system, improving clearing policies to reflect the rapid speed at which transactions occur, and sharing more sensitive information about positions with other exchanges.

Simex announced it would step up its monitoring of large trades 'so that reports of large positions would apply to all accounts'. 'Additionally, positions which are owned or controlled by the same person will be aggregated to monitor and assess the overall exposure of the exchange', Sam said.[28]

Still, even the panel's chairman was unconvinced. John Gilmore, a former chairman of the Chicago Board of Trade, pointed out that while implementing the recommendations would improve the chances of avoiding a Barings-style collapse, they would never totally eliminate the potential for disaster. 'People will say never, but it can always happen, it can always happen', Gilmore noted.[29]

※

Singapore's case against Leeson was established. There was a faint hope the British Home Office might support the bondholders' action and launch a rival extradition. There was also a faint hope that either Germany's Constitutional Court or the Bonn government would overrule the High Court's decision, or that Europe's Human Rights Court might prove the saviour. But if all options bore no fruit and Germany's Ministry of Justice approved the extradition, prosecutor Hans-Hermann Eckert would be forced to liaise with Singapore authorities to decide a date upon which Leeson would be flown back to face the music.

Leeson's hopes of being returned to London finally dissolved in the face of the indifference of the British Home Office. No competing extradition request was made on behalf of bondholders. The stance of the UK authorities did not waiver. Although the Serious Fraud Office held the power to take over extradition proceedings, it chose not to budge from the view that Singapore remained the principal jurisdiction for Nick Leeson's crimes, and the magistrates' court's plan to extradite him for criminal fraud essentially fell by the wayside after it ruled in favour of the SFO and dropped all summonses.

Efforts to secure support from Bonn and the European Human Rights Court were dubious. Singapore had justified its case in the German court, which also found Singapore's legal and judicial system was on par with European standards.

Arguments that Leeson would be confronted by wolves and that he deserved sympathy proved as ineffective as Barings' risk controls. London was no longer an alternative, and the growing realisation of this sparked a sudden and significant change of tune. Leeson would shortly be forced to dance to Singapore's music but first he had to alter and adapt his steps. Responsibility for Leeson's legal matters was passed from Stephen Pollard and Eberhard Kempf in Europe to John Koh, who had been handling Leeson's defence from his native Singapore.

Leeson's camp promptly issued a news release in London and Singapore. 'After consulting my legal advisers, I am satisfied that I will be fairly tried and judged in Singapore', Leeson said in his about-face statement. 'I wish to apologise to all Singaporeans for having doubted that I would receive a fair trial'.

Nick Leeson agreed to go quietly, and pledged to co-operate.

He also prayed for leniency.

CHAPTER SIXTEEN

BANK BREAKER

Bank Breaker: An amber-and-green cocktail, comprising layers of scotch whisky and Midori liqueur topped with Cointreau and soda, created by and served at Harry's Bar in honour of its most infamous former customer.

Nick Leeson left his German jail cell on Wednesday, November 22, 1995 — 38 weeks after his incarceration. Under tight security, he was driven in a police car right up to the flight steps of a Singapore Airlines jet at Frankfurt Am Main Airport, and handed over to officers of the Commercial Affairs Department who were waiting on board the plane. He was escorted to the business-class section of the upper deck, where he was joined by Lisa.

Watchful cabin crew firmly protected the Leesons from the dozen or so journalists who had also caught the commercial flight. If the jet-setting reporters were counting on getting the scoop of their careers during the long trip, they were to be sorely disappointed. The only in-flight information they were able to elicit came from Leeson's German lawyer Eberhard Kempf, who, when asked how Leeson was feeling ahead of the trial, told them: 'He seems to be taking it okay'.[1] John Koh provided the newshounds with a few more quotes, commenting that Leeson was 'not scared but is certainly apprehensive'. 'There are a lot of things going through his mind, but he's not worried that he'll be made a scapegoat and he's comfortable that he'll be treated fairly'.[2]

There was not much else to note except that the once bespectacled, high-flying futures trader now looked more like a Los Angeles homeboy, dressed in a baggy green Adidas tracksuit over a Manchester City soccer shirt, and a reversed baseball cap. Others wondered whether the designer sweatshirt that Lisa wore, emblazoned with a picture of the statue of liberty, was a carefully considered choice.

The tedium of such a non-eventful flight resulted in some of the scribes organising a call to Adidas to check if Leeson's choice of attire for his first public appearance since the David Frost interview stemmed from a sponsorship deal with the sportswear manufacturer. Though promptly dismissed, the queries were legitimate. The use of Nick Leeson's name for commercial ends had gone on unabated. A print media advertisement for an upmarket model car showed a picture of the car with Leeson's once-staple command to 'buy, buy'. The right-hand side of the ad counsels the prospective customer to 'lease, lease', the instruction being from: 'Your accountant, the voice of reason'.[3]

Throughout the 13-hour flight, Nick and Lisa nestled together in their business-class seats, deep in conversation, with gin and tonics at hand. Their privacy was limited. A Singapore security official sat on the other side of Nick and two others were close behind as the airline screened its in-flight movie, *Bad Boys*.

In Singapore, the anticipation was great. Whether or not Nick's quest for freedom would be furthered upon arrival remained to be seen. One of the few things which was clear was that of the traders still plying their trade at Simex, the attitudes towards their fallen brother were divided. 'Some traders don't like him and hope he hangs, and some people think he's the greatest thing since sliced bread', Jack David said.

When flight SQ325 touched down in Singapore the next day at 4.13 pm, Leeson was formally arrested as he alighted from the aircraft. Singapore's most infamous expat was back, and more than 150 journalists and photographers from around the world turned out to record the occasion. As a pale and weary-looking Leeson appeared through the customs gate at Changi Airport's Terminal One, he was deluged with questions from journalists, each trying to out-shout one another much like traders in the Simex pit: 'Give us a smile!', 'How do you plan to plead?', 'Say something!', they begged him.

Leeson did not oblige. As more than a dozen police officers whisked him through the corridors of Changi Airport, it was only an onlooker's yell of 'Keep your chin up, mate!' which drew a half-smile, but there were no words. There was plenty of talking to be done upon arrival at CAD headquarters. Outside the airport, Leeson was ushered into a white Mazda police car which sped off, sirens blaring, and was tailed by two other unmarked cars and a cavalcade of media vehicles. He was driven first to the Criminal Investigation Department, where he was fingerprinted and photographed. Leeson arrived at CAD headquarters at Winsland House on Killiney Road at 5.20 pm. There, his questioning began and he was kept under police guard at the building overnight.

The following morning, Leeson was escorted to the Subordinates Courts dressed in a white shirt with cufflinks, a red-patterned tie and dark trousers. Lisa was not present. Once again, he did not reply to the shouted questions of the dozens of reporters who had gathered outside the court. Before District Judge Tan Siong Thye, a sombre looking Leeson was charged with eight offences of fraud and three of forgery — a non-bailable offence — with the intent to cheat.

The twelfth charge, one of forgery, was dropped because it was not a punishable offence under German law. Leeson, who was not handcuffed but had a Singapore security official beside him, uttered only one word during his remand hearing. When asked if he understood the charges, an expressionless Leeson replied: 'Yes'.

It was a one-hour ordeal rather than the five-minute remand hearing legal experts had foreshadowed. Most of the charges were long, and packed with technical details, including those of individual trades. CAD chief Lawrence Ang told the court his officers required time to question Leeson and said it was not necessary for an immediate response to the charges from the accused. He said CAD investigators would question Leeson before his next hearing. 'As the accused has just been brought back to Singapore and CAD officers have not had sufficient opportunity to interview him, I'm applying that his plea not be taken at this stage', Ang told the court, before the charges were read out.

Justice Tan ordered Leeson be held at the Tanah Merah prison, a maximum-security facility on Singapore's east coast.

The circus surrounding the Leesons' return was over, and matters were now turning serious. The Singapore courts were again the venue for an internationally scrutinised trial, and the ramifications of such an event were not lost on the Republic's leaders.

However, officials were firm in their belief that the West placed too great an emphasis on the rights of individuals, neglecting the right to economic development, the rights of the community as a whole, and cultural rights. Chief Justice Yong Pung How argued that public opinion favoured law and order, and the deterrent value of punishments was what instilled public confidence and respect for the legal system.

But unlike Singapore's detractors, Leeson had to consider self-preservation, and he went to great lengths to express his confidence in being able to get a fair trial — a sentiment which demanded much back-pedalling from his previously harsh stance on Singapore's judicial system. Throwing himself on the mercy of the Singapore courts, he had co-operated with officers from the Commercial Affairs Department and agreed to give evidence against James Bax. Leeson was certain that such co-operation would weigh in his favour when it came to sentencing, and the prospect of prosecutors dropping some, or the bulk, of the charges was an overwhelming one.

The opinions of legal experts only served to reinforce Leeson's optimism. Walter Woon, a member of parliament and law professor at Singapore's National University, was quoted in London's *Daily Mail* as saying that if Leeson pleaded guilty, co-operated fully and there was legal evidence which showed he was 'just a pawn in a larger game, he might get off with a sentence of only 12 months'.[4]

It was with this in mind that Nick Leeson started to adopt some of the traits which had so characterised his persona during the days when he reigned supreme as the King of Simex. He was confident to the point of cockiness when he reappeared in court on December 1 for his sentencing hearing. In the best possible scenario, he could be out in as little as six months' time. At worst, he would have to spend two, maybe three, years behind bars.

Leeson pleaded guilty to reduced charges, admitting two charges of cheating, and the prosecution dropped nine other charges of forgery and cheating, following what it referred to as 'representations' from Leeson's legal team. Leeson was delighted.

Of the remaining charges, the first claimed that on or about February 2, Leeson had cheated Barings Futures' auditors Coopers & Lybrand by making them believe that Spear, Leeds & Kellogg had paid 7.778 billion yen into a Barings Futures Singapore account when it had not. This was done by doctoring statements to conceal the actual payee's name, and the charge was amended to cheating from forgery. This reduced the maximum penalty from seven years in jail to one year.

The second charge carried a possible eight year sentence and alleged that on or about February 1, Leeson had cheated Simex through misrepresenting the number of Nikkei contracts held by Barings Futures Singapore, allowing him to

obtain US$114.96 million from Simex through excess mar-
gin payments.

Leeson's lawyers had devised their strategy designed to
mitigate the coming sentence. John Koh stated that the
prosecution was not seeking a deterrent sentence, which is
typically an enhanced sentence for repeat offenders or for
violent crimes that society abhors and wants stamped out.
This was not denied by Lawrence Ang, who said in his
subsequent closing statement that he was 'leaving the question of sentencing to the court'.[5]

Ang outlined how the auditors had discovered the 7.778
billion yen discrepancy in October and that this had led
Leeson to concoct an option deal to balance his firm's books.
Computer entries were faked and false statements made.
Four and a half hours later, the court adjourned for lunch,
after which the hearings continued.

At 2.00 pm, Koh began an eloquent plea. He depicted
Leeson as an 'extremely remorseful' man who had, in effect,
returned to the scene of his crime with his tail firmly between
his legs, ready to atone for his mistakes. Pleading for
leniency, Koh told the court his client was not a crook who
had sought to enrich himself. 'What he did was a cover-up of
losses, not a cover-up of crimes', Koh said. '. . . He ran away
from the situation, not from the law. He left because he could
not cope with the pressure'.[6]

The defence team emphasised Leeson's precarious psychological state at the time he fled Singapore, stressing that
Nick had been traumatised by Lisa's miscarriage. They were
also at pains to portray Leeson as a struggler, describing him
as a Londoner of modest means who started work following
his A-levels to support his three siblings in the wake of his
mother's death from cancer.

Emotional issues aside, Koh and company made its bid to
spread the blame, pointing out that error account 88888 was
'never a secret' because Barings' management knew it held
large positions. 'If they wanted to . . . these large positions
could have been analysed and appropriate action taken. It

would have been at least equally the responsibility of Barings to manage the positions he had taken and to rectify the situation', Koh said.[7]

Citing 'overwhelming' mitigating factors, Koh also stressed that Leeson was not a common criminal who had committed a common offence. 'He was not taking personal positions against the company or against a client to make money. What do the facts show? Recklessness. Our client is not a crook. If he was, he could have enriched himself', he said.[8] Koh said Leeson was now willing to accept responsibility for his misguided actions, and contended that his remorse was manifest in his plea, his voluntary return, and his co-operation with the CAD in its investigations.

Koh also pointed out that his client did not stand to gain from his deeds. He said any proceeds from Leeson's account of the saga, *Rogue Trader*, 'will go to the agent, the ghost-writer, English and German lawyers and Singapore counsel'. Prosecution costs of $S150,000 were expected to be covered by properties owned by Lisa. Koh also earned a few sniggers from the public gallery when he pointed out that 'there is no Hollywood movie with Hugh Grant' and he reminded the court that a Writ of Summons had been served on Leeson in Britain to prevent him from gaining financially from the bank's collapse.

Still, the words Leeson had tapped out on a laptop computer in his Frankfurt prison cell would not go astray. The book's ghostwriter, Edward Whitley, himself a former banker, was busy weaving them into the finished product, together with material gathered from four sessions of interview with Leeson.

In a last-ditch attempt to soften what still threatened to be a nine-year jail term for Leeson, Koh offered one precedent. He said the only case he could find was the sentencing of the chief foreign options trader for the New York branch of ABN Amro Bank to 21-months' imprisonment for a similar crime.

Koh had held the floor for an hour, and on the surface of his campaign Leeson had a right to be optimistic. He faced only two charges. He had pleaded guilty. He had co-operated. The prosecution team was seeking neither a deterrent sentence nor a maximum term. The one precedent which was offered suggested an optimistic outcome. Events were forging towards a dramatic conclusion for the thousands of observers who had followed Nick Leeson's fate over the previous nine months.

Leeson was convicted of the two charges, and sentencing was postponed until 9.30 the following morning.

While Lisa was comforted by friends back home in England, her husband had only his thoughts for company that night.

Judgement day was swift. Judge Magnus had listened to the pleas and the evidence. He examined what had happened in Singapore for more than two and a half years before the collapse. Judge Magnus concluded that Leeson had 'spun a web of deceit' that was 'deliberately designed to beguile' Simex authorities, external auditors, and his employer. 'The sentence must be sufficiently substantial to indicate the gravity of the offence to the public', Judge Magnus said.[9]

All eyes in the court room flickered from Judge Magnus towards Leeson as his sentence was handed down.

Six and a half years in maximum security.

Leeson bit his lip and gazed skyward.

The sentence began retroactively from March 2, 1995 — the date of his arrest in Germany — and was due to expire in September 2001. The maximum-security provision was enforced because Leeson's term stretched beyond five years. Criminals serving shorter periods are sent to medium-security facilities.

Those close to Leeson confirmed that Nick was shocked at the severity of his prison term. Koh had done his best.

What once threatened to be a 14-year jail term had been cut by more than half. With remission for good behaviour, this could be further cut to three and a half years. Still, as Leeson was escorted away, he realised that it was perfectly feasible that he would not taste freedom again until into the new millennium.

The more pragmatic were not surprised. Legal expert Walter Woon said: 'Six and a half years is way above the precedence in proportionate terms. I won't be surprised if they appeal'.[10] Lisa's father, Alec Sims, described the length of the sentence as disappointing, but said the conclusion of the trial had at least resolved the uncertainty which had been plaguing the family since Leeson's arrest. 'It's all been a bit of a nightmare really but at least now we know it's over and we know he will be doing three or four years', Sims said.[11]

Nick had little to look forward to. Only visits from Lisa could provide some comfort. Lisa, for her part, could have done with some spare cash to help finance her promise to visit Nick in Singapore once every four weeks. Quite apart from the prospect of spending endless hours on the London to Singapore route, it was estimated that Lisa could spend upwards of stg50,000 on air fares if she kept her vow.

It was a long way to travel every month, in light of the fact that prison visits were strictly limited to one hour. Lisa spread this into two 30-minute sessions. The couple was separated by a glass screen which required them to use microphones to converse. After each visit, Lisa prepared for the 12-hour haul back to England, where she was living with her parents. Lisa also continued to work part-time in a sandwich shop to help support herself.

There remained some cynics who believed that before Nick fled Singapore, he had stashed away assets for himself and Lisa to collect upon his eventual release from prison. Despite neither the British nor Singapore investigations uncovering any evidence suggesting that Leeson had siphoned money out of Barings, forensic accountants and investigators were said to be continuing their hunt for a possible pot of gold. Their previous efforts had included tailing Lisa when she visited her husband in Frankfurt. The search for a link in banking centres in the Caribbean, the Channel Islands, and Switzerland continued, and shortly after he was jailed *The Sunday Times* quoted sources as confirming that bank accounts had been connected with Leeson in offshore centres.[12]

The extent of these accounts and their purpose remained a mystery. But if a dubious purpose existed for their use, it would be a long time before Nick gained any benefit. Less than a month after his sentencing, Leeson decided not to appeal against his sentence. There was always the very real possibility that his six and a half year term would be increased: he would instead sit out his time on the chance of an early release.

However, he had not abandoned the possibility of resuming a business career, and he planned to start a relevant course with Britain's Open University, which teaches through television and radio programs. Others thought this would provide some much needed therapy and remove the boredom.

Stephen Pollard said Leeson had inquired about taking a course through Lisa but he stressed that Nick was not gearing up to resume a career in high finance. 'He has chosen business because that is all he knows. He may want to do something relating to law as well', Pollard said.[13] But undertaking a course through the OU's affiliate in Singapore, the Institute of Management, was limited, as it offered neither OU business studies nor law as subjects, prompting one OU spokesperson to point out wryly that: '. . . it might be difficult for him to attend the summer schools'.[14]

Back in the United Kingdom, those associated with Barings were licking their wounds. Some sought to distance themselves from the fiasco. Peter Norris, who remained under the suspicion of Singapore authorities, broke his long-held silence by denying any attempt to conceal unauthorised trading by Leeson. Norris said that if the accusation levelled against him in the Singapore inquiry had been published in Britain, he might have sought a judicial review of its fairness.[15]

Despite Leeson's claim that he did not gain from his fraud, Norris contended that he was 'unable to see a real distinction' between Leeson's actions and theft, as both involved taking money from its rightful owner.

Arguing that there was 'no truth in the conclusions' of Singapore's Price Waterhouse investigators, Peter Norris said they had depended on 'a sequence of conjecture and circumstance'. He added that he did not believe Leeson's claim, made in the David Frost interview, that he started by concealing the blunders of other traders in a hidden account, and that these losses had spiralled out of control.

Claiming he could only speculate on the real explanation, Norris said he did not find it credible 'that an ostensibly well-intentioned, misconceived, limited act could turn into the systematic fraud and deception which destroyed Barings'.

The bondholders' action group did not subscribe to such theories. Spokesman Jonathan Stone was considering another lawsuit which could include former Barings managers, directors, and former auditors Coopers & Lybrand, seeking damages for the group's combined losses of stg100 million.

Christopher Heath, the founder of Barings Securities, was busy launching a new Luxembourg-based investment bank. Launched under the name Caspian, the new group was set to focus on agency broking, corporate finance, and asset management within selected emerging markets in Asia and Latin America.

Peter Norris's comments were closely followed by a similar statement by Masahiro Tsuda, a former general manager of Daiwa Bank, which, like Barings, had tested the mettle of regulatory authorities. Tsuda, indicted on charges that he helped conceal the $1.1 billion loss stemming from unauthorised deals by hiding records and failing to report the losses, said through his lawyers that his indictment was 'unwarranted and unjust'.[16]

At Daiwa, business had also thrown up a number of unexpected surprises. Tsuda, the former manager of Daiwa's New York branch, had already been charged by the Federal Bureau of Investigation in the scandal that resulted in criminal charges against Daiwa Bank and a shutdown of its 15 United States branches.

The indictment described how Tsuda allegedly concealed the scandal after learning that Toshihide Iguchi had traded illegally for 12 years. But his lawyer, Stanley Arkin, said Tsuda had simply 'followed what his employer and the Japanese Ministry of Finance determined was the only appropriate course: that a thorough investigation of Iguchi's extraordinary trading loss be conducted before a report was filed with US regulators'. 'What happened was a good-faith misunderstanding, not a crime'.[17]

With the man who had blotted their reputation finally behind bars, Singaporeans soon turned their attention to Christmas. An early present had arrived in the form of international recognition. Singapore's economic clout had delivered it out of the ranks of developing nations. The republic's average annual per capita income reached $22,300, the ninth highest in the world. Singapore was rich.

The one question which remained unanswered was, what was Leeson's motive? Leeson had a good head for figures, but was never considered bright. He had no formal education in his field, nor was he reared for any lengthy period within the sort of culture that could provide the imprecise antecedents for holding a position of trust. His common sense gave way to greed and failed him.

In trying to determine why people behave the way they do, philosophers have argued that no rules exist to enforce good sense, and we cannot rely on instincts to reach sensible conclusions. Instead, common sense stems only from culture and education.

Leeson did have his day in court, and was justly punished. What remained disturbing was the silence in London. The Bank of England, the British government, the Serious Fraud Squad, the Securities and Futures Authority, and Barings' management had sealed Nick Leeson's fate by arguing that he committed his crimes in Singapore, and that it was therefore Singapore's duty to prosecute.

This was true, but conveniently served a second purpose. In doing this, they set the precedent that any crimes committed by Barings employees in London would be subject to the same rationale. This meant that those who were responsible for the transfer of more than 25 per cent of the bank's capital base — an illegal transaction in that it was made without central bank approval — should be prosecuted in Britain.

This never happened. No-one was ever prosecuted, and just one middle-ranking BoE official resigned.

The BoE had failed noticeably in its duty, as had the SFO, the SFA, and Barings' management. Those who had provided Nick Leeson with about $1.0 billion in illegal capital in two tranches were neither named nor admonished.

They remained secure at home, among their own, and out of harm's way.

GLOSSARY

abnormal items: profits or losses which are incurred through the normal course of business but are considered extreme and unlikely to be repeated. These are stipulated as an abnormal item inferring that such profits or losses are unlikely to be repeated.

arbitrage: trades yielding profits by switching from one market to another — stocks, bonds, currencies, futures — to take advantage of price fluctuations between markets. Traders in this field are called arbitrageurs.

back office (room): office responsible for settling financial transactions initiated in the front office.

Bank of England (BoE): also known as The Old Lady of Threadneedle Street, Britain's central bank and lender of last resort.

Bank of Japan: Japan's central bank.

bond: similar to an IOU, a bond can be issued to investors by banks, companies or governments in return for cash. Interest is paid to the investor during the life of the bond.

central bank: a government agency overseeing a country's monetary and banking system. Is a lender of last resort to authorised dealers and banks with the ability to heavily influence interest rates and exchange rates.

clearing house: a house that processes trades on behalf of exchanges, and finalises settlement.

clearing member: person who is a member of the clearing house; also a member of a related exchange, responsible for the processing of transaction settlements.

client accounts: accounts for security trading maintained by a clearing member; must be completely segregated from house accounts.

Commercial Affairs Department (CAD): Singapore's powerful investigation squad, handles corporate fraud and white collar crime, answering directly to the finance minister.

cross trade: the acquisition and sale of the same security by a dealer between two clients or between a client's and a house account. The dealer may also be required to offer the cross trade to the market as a safeguard.

derivative: financial instrument intially used as a hedge against fluctuations in real markets, but traded in secondary markets for products. Generally comes in three forms; see also futures, options, and swaps.

error account 88888: a hidden trading account established by Nick Leeson which enabled him to carry out unofficially sanctioned trades.

Euroyen: Japanese financial instrument, not under the control of Japanese monetary authorities.

futures: a contract linked to the price of a particular commodity or another form of financial security for a specified amount and date in the future. The contract expires at that date.

front office (room): where business is initiated on behalf of a financial institution.

hedge: a form of insurance designed to reduce risk.

house account: maintained by securities firms for dealers to record and maintain their own transactions on behalf of the house; kept separate from clients' accounts at all times.

JGB: Japanese Government Bonds.

long position: in futures, this indicates that a trader has acquired more contracts than have actually been sold.

margin call: a request from a clearing house for a trader or investment house to provide funds to cover adverse price movements in the futures market.

market maker: a bank or financial institution prepared to quote buy-and-sell prices (two-way prices) in securities, financial instruments, or derivatives.

Monetary Authority of Singapore: regulating body responsible for Singapore's money supply, and for implementing montary policy.

Nikkei 225: Japan's index of the top 225 companies as listed on the Tokyo Stock Exchange. Japan's most popular index, and the basis for that country's equity derivative contracts.

open outcry: trading taking place on the floor of an exchange, with traders restricted to designated areas; prices are agreed to, and the deal struck on the floor.

options: contracts which enable the holder to sell or buy a financial security such as shares or a commodity during a period of time; a call option is the right to buy from the person or company who granted the option at a set price during the life of the contract; a put option is the right to sell to the issuer of the option; to buy and sell is known as a double option.

Osaka Securities Exchange (OSE): a derivitives exchange dealing in Nikkei stock contracts; where major foreign investors trade in futures linked to the Nikkei 225 index, and where Nick Leeson traded on behalf of Barings.

preference share: holders of this type of security, issued by companies to raise cash, claim a special dividend payment and, in the event of a company being wound up, rank ahead of ordinary shareholders.

proprietary trading: a term sometimes used to define a risk position adopted by an account held by an institution, as opposed to an institution's client account.

screen jock: industry jargon for a trader who sits behind a desk and trades, communicates and receives the news via electronic screens.

security: essentially paper money, written to secure the repayment of money such as a company share certificate, bond, bill, promissory notes.

Securities & Futures Authority (SFA): authority which regulates British trading in securities and futures.

Serious Fraud Squad: Britain's investigative body, established to monitor the nation's financial world, similar to Singapore's CAD.

SES: Stock Exchange of Singapore

short position: when a trader has oversold, or has sold more contracts than made purchases.

Simex: Singapore International Monetary Exchange, established in 1984 as a commodity futures exchange.

straddle: a position of combined put and call options on the same underlying price with the trader speculating it will remain close to the strike price of an option when it is sold.

strangle: the simultaneous purchase and sale of a call option and put option with the same expiry date, but different strike prices.

strike price: the set price of an option when it can be settled.

swaps: banks or companies can swap interest rates, or their types of borrowings, if both parties agree their loan costs would be lowered; currency swaps are also traded.

Tokyo Stock Exchange (TSE): Japan's oldest and largest share market which began operations in 1949 with the leading Nikkei 225 index.

TIFFE: Tokyo International Financial Futures Exchange.

NOTES

CHAPTER 1

1. Ziegler P, *The Sixth Great Power*: Barings 1762–1929, Collins, London, 1988.
2. Ibid.
3. Ibid, p. 363.
4. Ibid, p. 328.
5. *The Australian Financial Review*, March 6, 1995, p. 13.
6. Luen Foo Siang, Rocha J (eds), *Singapore 1995*, Ministry of Information and the Arts, Singapore, 1995, p. 140.

CHAPTER 2

1. *Newsweek*, reprinted in *The Bulletin*, March 14, 1995, p. 55.
2. *Money Matters*: Australian Broadcasting Corporation, October 1994. Producer: Stuart Goodman, Reporter: Paul Barry, Researcher: Ticky Fullerton.
3. Ibid.
4. Ibid.
5. Ibid.

CHAPTER 3

1. *Time magazine*, March 13, 1995, p. 27.
2. Rawnsley J, *Going For Broke: Nick Leeson and The Collapse of Barings Bank*, Harper Collins 1995, London, p. 72.
3. *The Sun*, March 28, 1995, p. 16.

4. Ibid.
5. Ibid.
6. Ibid, p. 25.
7. Ibid.
8. BBC, Panorama, *The Boy Who Broke The Bank.*
9. Rawnsley J, p. 80.
10. Ibid, p. 78.
11. Ibid, p. 81.
12. BoE Report 5.3, p. 78.
13. The Report of Inspectors appointed by the Minister for Finance (Singapore) Appendix 3k, p. 179.

CHAPTER 4

1. BBC, Panorama, *The Boy Who Broke The Bank.*
2. BoE Report 2.59, p. 31.
3. BoE Report 2.14, p. 20.
4. BoE Report 2.18, p. 21.
5. BoE Report 2.45, p. 27.
6. *The Australian Financial Review*, October 16, 1995.
7. BoE Report 11.22, p. 168.
8. BoE Report 11.22, p. 168.
9. BoE Report 2.20, p. 21.
10. *The Sunday Times*, reprinted in *The Australian*, July 24, 1995, p. 21.

CHAPTER 5

1. The Report of Inspectors appointed by the Minister for Finance (Singapore) Appendix 3k, p. 179.
2. Ibid 2.11, p. 9.
3. Time magazine, March 13, 1995, p. 24.
4. The Report of Inspectors appointed by the Minister for Finance (Singapore), 15.42, p. 116.
5. Rawnsley J, Going For Broke: *Nick Leeson and The Collapse of Barings*, Harper Collins 1995, London, p. 156.
6. Ibid.

7. BBC, Panorama, *The Boy Who Broke The Bank*.
8. BoE Report 2.53, p. 29.
9. *The Financial Times*, July 20, 1995, p. 11.
10. The Report of Inspectors appointed by the Minister for Finance (Singapore) Appendix 3k, p. 179.

CHAPTER 6

1. *The Man Who Broke The Bank: Nick Leeson Tells His Story To David Frost*: British Broadcasting Commission, September 1995. Interviewer and Executive Producer: Sir David Frost; Producer: Trevor Poots; Researchers: Elizabeth Dudley and Michelle Fleury.
2. Rawnsley J, *Going For Broke: Nick Leeson and The Collapse of Barings Bank*, Harper Collins 1995, London, p. 152.
3. The Report of Inspectors appointed by the Minister for Finance (Singapore) Appendix 3k, p. 179.
4. Ibid.
5. BoE Report 7.12, p. 121.
6. Ibid.
7. Ibid.
8. Ibid, 2.27, p. 23.
9. *Time* magazine, March 13, 1995, p. 22.
10. BoE Report 2.35 (c), p. 25.
11. Ibid.
12. Ibid, 2.35 (d), p. 25.
13. Ibid, 2.54, p. 30.
14. Ibid, figure 9.1, p. 141.
15. Ibid.
16. The Report of Inspectors appointed by the Minister for Finance (Singapore), 5.16, p. 44.
17. BoE Report 10.28, p. 156.
18. Ibid, 10.29, p. 156.
19. Ibid, 10.30, p. 156.
20. Ibid, 10.33, pp. 156–7.21.
21. The Report of Inspectors appointed by the Minister for Finance (Singapore), 5.18 p. 44.

22. Ibid, p. 45.
23. *The Financial Times*, reprinted in *The Australian*, June 27, 1995, p. 71.
24. Ibid.
25. BoE Report 11.47, p. 172
26. Ibid, figure 11.2, p. 174.
27. Ibid, 11.48, p. 173.
28. *The Sun*, March 29, 1995, p. 21.
29. *Newsweek*, reprinted in *The Bulletin*, March 14, 1995, p. 52.
30. Rawnsley J, *Going For Broke: Nick Leeson and The Collapse of Barings*, Harper Collins 1995, London, p. 157.

CHAPTER 7

1. *The Sun*, March 29, 1995, p. 21.
2. *The Japan Times*, January 28, 1995, p. 1.
3. Ibid, January 20, p. 2.
4. BoE Report 4.86, p. p. 74–5
5. *The Australian Financial Review*, January 19, 1995, p. 10.
6. BoE Report 4.20, p. 61.

CHAPTER 8

1. BBC, Panorama, *The Boy Who Broke The Bank*.
2. BoE Report 4.22, p. 61
3. BoE Report 5.40, p. 86.
4. The Report of Inspectors appointed by the Minister for Finance (Singapore) 16.12, p. 121.
5. Ibid, 16.46, p. 131.
6. Interviews with traders who operated alongside Nick Leeson at Simex at the time of the collapse.
7. BoE Report 7.58, p. 129.
8. BoE Report 11.119, p. 186.
9. *Time magazine*, March 13, 1995, p. 20.
10. Ibid.
11. Ibid.

12. *The Financial Times*, reprinted in *The Australian*, June 27, 1995, p. 71.
13. BoE Report 1.55, p. 10.
14. The Report of the Inspectors appointed by the Minister for Finance (Singapore) 17.6, p. 150.
15. Ibid, 17.10, p. 151.
16. BoE Report 1.60, p. 11.

CHAPTER 9

1. *The Sun*, March 29, 1995, p. 21.
2. BoE Report 1.63, p. 11.
3. BoE Report 1.62, p. 11.
4. Ibid.
5. BoE Report 1.64, p. 11.
6. BoE Report 1.63, p. 11.
7. Ibid.
8. BoE Report 1.64, p. 12.
9. Ibid.
10. BoE Report 1.65, p. 12.

CHAPTER 10

1. *Wall Street*, Twentieth Century Fox Film Corporation, 1988. An Edward R Pressman production. Written by Oliver Stone and Stanley Webster; Directed by Oliver Stone; Starring Michael Douglas as Gordon Gekko.
2. *Newsweek*, reprinted in *The Bulletin*, March 14, 1995, p. 52.
3. Reuters, Febraury 27, 1995.
4. Ibid.
5. *The Australian*, February 28, 1995, p. 4.

CHAPTER 11

1. BBC, Panorama, *The Boy Who Broke The Bank*.
2. Agence France-Presse, February 27, 1995.

3. Australian Associated Press, reprinted in *The Sydney Morning Herald*, March 6, 1995, p. 10.
4. *The Daily Telegraph Mirror*, March 2, 1995, p. 26.
5. *The Associated Press*, reprinted in *The Australian*, February 28, 1995, p. 1.
6. *Reuters*, reprinted in *The Sydney Morning Herald*, March 1, 1995, p. 41.
7. Ibid, p. 45.
8. *The Financial Times*, reprinted in *The Australian*, March 1, 1995, p. 37.
9. *The Sun*, March 29, 1995, p. 21.
10. Ibid.
11. The Report of the Inspectors appointed by the Minister for Finance (Singapore) 3.29, p. 23, footnote 50.
12. *The Sun*, March 29, 1995, p. 21.
13. *The Times*, reprinted in *The Weekend Australian*, March 4–5, 1995, p. 15.
14. *Reuters*, reprinted in *The Australian Financial Review*, March 28, 1995, p. 12.

CHAPTER 12

1. BoE Report 13.80, p. 249.
2. The Associated Press, March 2, 1995.
3. Ibid.
4. *The Sydney Morning Herald*, March 7, 1995, p. 53.
5. *The Sydney Morning Herald*, March 15, 1995, p. 44.
6. *The Australian Financial Review*, March 17, 1995, p. 41.
7. *The Sunday Times*, reprinted in *The Australian*, March 27, 1995, p. 32.
8. Reuters, reprinted in *The Australian*, March 9, 1995, p. 43.
9. *The Sydney Morning Herald*, March 1, 1995, p. 45.
10. *The Australian*, March 9, 1995, p. 17.
11. *The Sun-Herald*, March 5, 1995, p. 32.

12. Rawnsley J, *Going For Broke: Nick Leeson and The Collapse of Barings*, Harper Collins 1995, London, p. 160.
13. Ibid, p. 124.

CHAPTER 13

1. BoE Report 3.57, p. 48.
2. *Vanity Fair*, June 1995, p. 45.
3. Ibid, p. 48.
4. Rawnsley J, *Going For Broke: Nick Leeson and The Collapse of Barings*, Harper Collins 1995, London, p. 185.
5. BBC, Panorama, *The Boy Who Broke The Bank*.
6. Rawnsley J, p. 186.

CHAPTER 14

1. *The Man Who Broke The Bank: Nick Leeson Tells His Story To David Frost.* BBC, September 1995.
2. Reuters, July 12, 1995.
3. Ibid.
4. Ibid.
5. Ibid.
6. Reuters, April 5, 1995.
7. Ibid.
8. Reuters, May 24, 1995.
9. The Associated Press, July 18, 1995.
10. BoE Report 14.1, p. 250.
11. BoE Report 13.37, p. 239.
12. The Associated Press, July 18, 1995.
13. Ibid.
14. Knight Ridder Financial News, July 18, 1995.
15. BoE Report 12.24, p. 197.
16. *The Financial Times*, July 19, 1995, p. 7.
17. The Associated Press, July 18, 1995.
18. *The Financial Times*, July 19, 1995, p. 7.
19. Ibid.
20. *The Financial Times*, July 20, 1995.
21. Ibid.
22. *The Financial Times*, July 19, 1995, p. 7.

23. BoE Report 6.92, p. 110.
24. According to sources who spoke to the authors on the condition of anonymity.
25. *Business Times*, September 14, 1995.
26. Ibid.

CHAPTER 15

1. *The Australian*, December 4, 1995, p. 10.
2. *UK Mail*, October 29, 1995, p. 1.
3. *Publishing News*, October 20, 1995, p. 7.
4. Ibid.
5. *The Sydney Morning Herald*, May 18, 1995, p. 35.
6. *The Times*, reprinted in *The Australian*, December 28, 1995, p. 9.
7. *The Straits Times*, September 28, 1995.
8. *The Business Times*, September 28, 1995.
9. Agence France-Presse, October 18, 1995.
10. Ibid, October 19, 1995.
11. Ibid, January 25, 1996.
12. Ibid.
13. Ibid.
14. The Report of Inspectors appointed by the Minister for Finance (Singapore) 16.87, p. 148.
15. Ibid, executive summary, point 34, p. Bix.
16. Ibid, point 36, p. Bx.
17. Ibid, point 18, p. Bvi.
18. Ibid, point 37, p. Bxi.
19. Ibid, point 27, p. Bviii.
20. Ibid.
21. Ibid, point 28, p. Bviii.
22. Ibid.
23. Ibid, point 31, p. Bix.
24. Ibid, point 32, p. Bix.
25. Ibid, 16.82, p. 146.
26. *Bloomberg Business News*, October 30, 1995.
27. Ibid.

28. Ibid.
29. Ibid.

CHAPTER 16

1. The Associated Press, reprinted in *The Australian*, November 24, 1995, p. 33.
2. *The Straits Times*, November 24, 1995.
3. *The Australian Financial Review*, March 10, 1995, p. 67.
4. *The Business Times*, November 1, 1995, p. 13.
5. *The Sunday Times*, reprinted in *The Australian*, December 1995, p. 21.
6. Ibid.
7. Ibid.
8. Ibid.
9. *The Sunday Telegraph*, December 3, 1995, p. 2.
10. *The Business Times*, December 4, 1995, p. 1.
11. *The Daily Telegraph Mirror*, December 4, 1995, p. 24.
12. *The Sunday Times*, reprinted in *The Australian*, December 4, 1995, p. 21.
13. *The Times*, reprinted in *The Australian*, December 27, 1995.
14. Ibid.
15. *The Financial Times*, reprinted in *The Australian*, December 11, 1995.
16. The Associated Press, reprinted in *The Australian*, December 29, 1995.
17. Ibid.

BIBLIOGRAPHY

Aitchison J, Theseus Chan, *Sarong Party Girl*, Angsana Books, Singapore, 1994.

Aitchison J, Theseaus** Chan, *Revenge of the Sarong Party Girl*, Angsana Books, Singapore, 1995.

Amos J M, Sarchet B R, *Management for Engineers*, Prentice-Hall Inc, New Jersey, 1981.

Bannock G, Baxter R E, Rees R, *The Penguin Dictionary of Economics*, Penguin Books Ltd, Middlesex England, first published 1972.

Barings Annual Report, 1993.

Carew E, *The Language of Money*, Allen & Unwin, Sydney, 1988.

Carew E, *Derivatives Decoded*, Allen & Unwin, Sydney, 1995.

Fairbairn J, *Fairbairn's Crests of the Families of Great Britain & Ireland*, New Orchard Editions, Poole Dorset, 1986.

Internationale Nederlanden Groep** Annual Report, 1993.

Kidd C, Williamson D (eds), *Drebett's Peerage & Baronetage*, Macmillan**, London, 1990.

Lim M, Tan N, Barings Futures (Singapore) Pte Ltd, investigation pursuant to section 231 of the Companies Act (Chapter 50), Singapore Ministry of Finance, 1995.

Luen Foo Siang, Rocha J (eds) *Singapore 1995*, Ministry of Information and the Arts, Singapore, 1995.

Mackay C, *The Extraordinary Popular Delusions and the Madness of Crowds*, Richard Bentley, New Burlington Street London, 1841.

Rawnsley J, *Going For Broke: Nick Leeson and The Collapse of Barings Bank*, Harper Collins, London 1995.

Read D, *The Power of News — The History of Reuters*, Oxford University Press, New York, 1992.

Report of the Board of Banking Supervision Inquiry into the Circumstances of the Collapse of Barings, Ordered by The House of Commons, July 18, 1995, London: HMSO.

Tate C, *Understanding Options Trading in Australia*, Information Australia, Melbourne, 1990.

Who's Who 1995, A&C Black (Publisher)** Ltd London.

Ziegler P, *The Sixth Great Power: Barings 1762–1929*, Collins, London, 1988.

Sources and Acknowledgements

Print media and newsagency sources

Asian Business Review, Asian Wall Street Journal, Asiaweek, AFX, AFX-ASIA, Agence France-Presse, Associated Press, Australian Associated Press, Bloomberg Business News, Business Review Weekly, Far East Economic Review, Fortune Magazine, Harvard Business Review, Jiji Press, Knight-Ridder Financial News, La Segunda, Newsweek, Publishing News, Reuters, Singapore Business Times, The Australian, The Australian Financial Review, The Bulletin, The Business Times, The Daily Telegraph, The Daily Telegraph Mirror, The Economist, The Financial Times, The Guardian, The International Herald Tribune, The Japan Times, The New York Times, The Straits Times, The Sun, The Sunday Times, The Sun-Herald, The Times, The Wall Street Journal, Vanity Fair, *Without Remorse*, Tom Clancy, BCA by arrangement with Harper Collins, Sydney 1993.

Television/ cinema productions

Money Matters: Australian Broadcasting Corporation, October 1994. Producer: Stuart Goodman; Reporter: Paul Barry; Researcher: Ticky Fullerton.

The Boy Who Broke The Bank: British Broadcasting Commission; Panorama; March 1995. Producer: Barbara Want; Reporter: Jane Corbin

The Man Who Broke The Bank: Nick Leeson Tells His Story To David Frost: British Broadcasting Commission, September 1995. Interviewer and Executive Producer: Sir David Frost; Producer: Trevor Poots; Researchers: Elizabeth Dudley and Michelle Fleury

Wall Street: Twentieth Century Fox Film Corporation, 1988. An Edward R. Pressman production. Written by Oliver Stone and Stanley Webster; Directed by Oliver Stone; Starring Michael Douglas as Gordon Gekko